Crazy: A Diary

Linda Waltersdorf Cobourn

Copyright © 2014 Linda Waltersdorf Cobourn

All rights reserved.

ISBN:0692257489
ISBN-13:9780692257487

CRAZY:
A DIARY

LINDA WALTERSDORF COBOURN

Linda Waltersdorf Cobourn

DEDICATION

This book is dedicated to my Children: Dennis Stewart Cobourn, Bonnie Cobourn Widger, and Allen Harvey Cobourn. It is often because of you that I continue

Linda Waltersdorf Cobourn

A NOTE TO THE READER:

This work is not meant to be a scientific or informational article on mental illness. I have tried to present some relevant facts, but I am neither a psychologist nor a medical doctor. I am, however, the wife of a man who has suffered from bipolar disorder and clinical depression, as well as the aftermath of a vehicular accident. What I have written is our experience; it may not be yours.

I also wish to point out that my family has a very warped sense of humor. We have used it to survive the changes in our family brought about by mental illness and co-occurring disorders. In this book, I have at times used the common vernacular "crazy" or "loony" when referring to Ron's illness. I have made no attempt to be politically correct. If you have a problem with these terms, I offer a simple solution:

Do not read this book.

FORWARD

Do you remember the books about Dick and Jane? Created as a series of readers by William Gray, they were used to teach children in the primary grades between 1930 and 1970. Heavily criticized as lacking in cultural awareness, Dick and Jane books are now pop culture items and can fetch as much as $200 on E-Bay. But I learned to read with Dick and Jane. Sitting in the reading circle at Edgewood Elementary School, the over-sized book propped up by my teacher, Mrs. Hottenstein, I laid out my future, a slightly updated version of the text. Two kids, a boy and a girl. A house in the suburbs. A husband that went to work each day carrying a brief case and wearing a hat. The ideal life. A small, safe life. Unknowingly, my plans also placed God is a small, safe place.

We were a Christian family, if not overtly religious. My mother raised my brother and me as Catholics, taking us to mass on Sunday and enrolling us in catechism classes so we could make our First Communions. My father was a Methodist and, as far as I could tell, spent Sundays doing home repairs. My grandmother was also a Methodist and took my brother and me to Sunday School whenever we spent the weekend at her house. In truth, the Methodist Church seemed to be more fun than the Catholic Church, but I wasn't really looking for my spiritual beliefs to be amusing. I was looking for them to protect me, a magic cloak that would hide me from the evils of the world.

I wanted my small, safe life. I worked towards it, the good girl who obeyed the rules. I gave God only a tiny space in my life, with no room to grow.

My life is no longer small. I live an enlarged life, messy and chaotic and full of challenges and decisions that Dick and Jane never had to face. I know far more about hospitals than I want to, including how to talk my way past security guards after visiting hours. I have watched my husband hover at the edge of death on more than one occasion, and I have figured out how to change the oil in the car and throw baseballs to my son. I have been forced to show my children a suicide note left by their father one dark day when he was bent on self-destruction and rejoiced with them when he was found unhurt. I have sat in various waiting rooms for the outcome of 26 surgeries and visited my husband in six different hospitals and one mental institution. I have prayed fervently, on my knees, for my life to be different, to be calmer to be—yes—smaller. I have made bargains, sworn oaths, and lived in fear of ambulance sirens.

And I have survived. I have survived and grown and within my hectic, chaotic, messy world, found what Dick and Jane did not.

I found God.

**BOOK ONE
"CRASH"**

*Yea, though I walk through the Valley of the Shadow of Death,
I will fear no evil, for thou art with me.
Psalm 23*

THROUGH IT ALL

I do not always see Your hand
My way is overcast
I do not always know my feet
Travel on Your path.

Quite oft I feel I've left the road
And wandered far astray.
But You always manage to guide me back
And set me on my way.

The journey's often long and hard
And stress can take its toll.
But You, dear Lord, will guide me through
And save my very soul.

CHAPTER ONE

March 2, 2000. 8PM.

It has been an excruciatingly long day, but then Thursdays always are. I am driving home from my evening class at West Chester University and I have been on the go since 5:30 AM, with no break for supper. The class tonight has been less than exhilarating and my attention has drifted often. I leave at 7:15 with a twenty-page paper on reading strategies due in two weeks and midterms looming ahead. There are times I hate graduate school. As I drive home along Route 322, my stomach growls and my eyes water from the lights of passing cars. Despite two cornea transplants, my night vision is not good and my damaged corneas turn each headlight into my own personal display of Fourth of July fireworks.

I spy Bonnie's car as I pull up to the house. She is the one I worry about most often, picturing her stranded by the side of the road and at the mercy of evil strangers. She is a trusting soul. My peace of mind is the reason she has a cell phone she sometimes forgets to take with her. I breathe a sigh of relief at the sight of her blue Subaru parked outside the house. Supper will have been made, then, and there might be a plate of something for me waiting in the microwave. I am momentarily glad that I did not pull into the *Wendy's* on Chichester Avenue and order a chicken sandwich at the drive through. I park my car behind hers and lug my heavy book-bag out of the back seat. Teachers are the original bag ladies. I have papers to grade tonight and a workshop to prepare for next week's Shakespeare Festival. I lean against the car for a moment, acknowledging that I am feeling weary. One more week to go, and then spring break. I have made plans to escape to my parents' house at the beach. Ron and the children can fend for themselves.

Ron has, of course, strenuously objected. "You're leaving me!" he shouted when I imparted the news several weeks ago.

"Only for a few days," I told him. "Only to get a little rest. You'll survive."

His psychiatrist has assured him that he will, in all likelihood, survive. That this will give him a chance to assume some adult responsibility and rebuild some rickety bridges to his children. All of it means little to him when his mind is clouded by his battles with clinical depression.

It is while I am leaning against my own car that I notice Ron's white Taurus is not parked in its usual spot under the streetlight where the ambient glow makes it look like a pale ghost. He parks it here, across the street, for two reasons. First, more than one driver has miscalculated the curve of the road on the next block and careened dangerously close to the curb. The second reason, though, is more important. He parks it here, across the street, because the short walk gives him a chance to pull himself out of his lethargy long enough to kiss me hello and ask after the children. This short routine takes the toll on his energy burst. The time before supper is generally spent on the couch, the television set tuned to a sporting event he dozes through, while I plod around the kitchen banging pots and pans and grumbling that I, too, have worked all day.

Thursdays, though, are different. On Thursdays Ron needs to pull himself together sufficiently to be able to make supper for himself and the kids—or at least order out for pizza—because on Thursdays I have a graduate class and am not home until late. The rest of the week may be open to phone calls from the nurse at Ron's plant or mad dashes to the emergency room due to an onslaught of anxiety disguised as heart attacks, but on Thursdays Ron is forced to maintain some semblance of sanity. At least until I get home.

Tonight is clear and cloudless and I am tired, the math tests in my book bag and the twenty page analysis due next week adding their weight to my burdens. All I want is a hot shower, a cup of tea, and a chance to put my feet up and nibble whatever has been supper. But Ron's car is not in its usual spot. Four years of dropping everything and rushing off to hospitals because my husband cannot handle the world has trained me well; there will be no rest for the very weary tonight. Disappointment, bordering on anger, begins to brew.

It is just before I reach the front door that a chilling though occurs to me; something has happened to Ron. Something really bad. A cold hand grips my heart, squeezes. There will be no supper for me, that is clear, and I am feeling upset that his ongoing emotional battles have to take a toll on me as well. I think, fleetingly, that I would be better off without him.

I paste a smile onto my face before I enter the house. Whatever has happened will not be easy to deal with, but my children will need to know that, as usual, Mom can handle it.

"Hello!" I say. Even to me, the cheerfulness sounds forced. The house, with two teenagers still in residence and one who lives down the street stomping around in his roller blades, is in its usual state of chaos. The smell of slightly burnt spaghetti assails my nostrils. My resourceful offspring, whatever may be the foibles of their parents, will not let themselves to starve. From the dining room comes the sound of a computer game at high volume; my son is once again out to save the world from evil space aliens. It is a relief to hear Allen's voice as he explodes another space pod and to see my daughter sitting on the couch, the cordless phone in her hand. Whatever has happened to my spouse has happened to him alone.

I shake the cobwebs of tired from my head and drop my book bag on the floor. Bonnie jumps off the couch to hug me, nearly knocking me off my feet with the force of her embrace. Tears stream down her face and her voice quivers.

"Mom," she begins. Gently. She is a gentle child, unwilling to inflict hurt on anyone. Her father, too, when not in the grips of a manic cycle, is gentle. "You need to sit down…"

I stand my ground. The anguish on her face rends my heart and for a moment I am engorged with rage at Ron, who continues to put us through these scenarios again and again. "I don't need to sit down," I tell her, struggling to keep the sharp edge from my voice. "Just tell me where we need to go and we'll go."

It is evident that she has been crying. While our marriage has been seriously strained by Ron's problems, they have nothing to do with her. She is still Daddy's Little Girl. I wait while she struggles with her words. "It was a car accident," she says. "A truck hit him on the way home from work." For a brief moment, I think that he is dead. I am not sure how I feel about it. Sorry? Sad? But she goes on, quickly. "He's at the hospital. At Crozer. The paramedics said that his…diaphragm ruptured. Or something like that. He's in surgery. Pop Pop said…"

I feel terribly, terribly sorry for her that she has to be the one to impart this bad news to me. The tears roll down her cheeks and in bits and pieces I understand that the paramedics have rushed Ron to the hospital and called my in-laws. Reese has come down to the house to tell the children. Bonnie was instructed to bring me to the hospital as soon as I arrived home. My mind reels with a hundred questions. Has Ron finally made good on his threats to end his miserable existence? Leave it to him to botch it, I think, and then am terribly contrite for even thinking it. I tell myself—again—that Ron's cyclic depression is not of his choosing. I take a deep breath, willing my mind to focus.

She is standing by the door, her car keys in her hand, waiting for me. "One minute," I say. I peek into the dining room, where Allen, my youngest child, is playing computer games with his friend Jonathan. He looks calm enough, but his eyes are glazed over. Computer games or tears? It is impossible to tell. "Okay?" I ask him and he nods. He's fourteen and no longer wears his heart on his sleeve. This one has visited his father behind the locked doors of a mental ward. His silence protects him. "Jonathan," I say, "can you stay here for a while? Until we get home?" Jonathan nods, too involved with launching star crafts on the screen to answer me.

I pick up the phone. I know time is important, but if Ron is already in surgery, all I can do is wait. I make a few phone calls: to my best friend Chris, who promises to call others from our church to pray, to my parents, to my school principal. Phyllis is not home so I leave a message, brief and terse. "Phyllis, my husband has been in a serious car accident. I will not be in school tomorrow. I'll call you when I can." I have no time to review my words or soften them. I try to call our pastor, but his line is busy. I write his number down on a pad by the phone, then call our oldest son's house in the city. I know that even now he is on the road, traveling with college friends to New Orleans for the Mardi Gras, but perhaps one of his roommates knows a number where he can be reached. They are staying, I remember, with Alana.

Jeff answers the phone on the first ring. I make my request

brief. Jeff, a sensitive soul, begins to panic. "What can I do?" he says. "How can I help?"

"Just the phone number, Jeff," I say. I am a model of calmness, an example for all wives of accident victims to follow. My hand does not waiver as I add Alana's number to the phone pad.

Bonnie is still standing at the front door, jingling her car keys. Probably wondering why it is taking me so long, why we are not dashing down the highway to her father's side. I dial Alana's number. The answering machine picks up. I leave another blunt message, no time to carefully word it.

I thrust the paper with the phone numbers at Jonathan. "Keep calling these numbers," I tell him, "until you get someone." He nods laconically.

"Man the phones," Bonnie tells him as we depart. Jonathan is practically a member of the family. We have made this request of him before.

It is a clear night, the moon and the stars bright against the black sky. The black road and the black night make it easy to pretend that I am floating, not walking at all, but suspended somewhere in time. *Put one foot in front of the other*, I tell myself. *Keep walking. Keep breathing. This is not real.* I slide into Bonnie's car. *This is not happening.* For one instant—no more—I think how odd it is that I can accept the possibility that my husband has tried to kill himself. A photograph from our wedding album flashes into my mind: Ron, so tall and handsome in his powder blue tuxedo, me leaning against his arm as we leave the church. My white veil billows around us. We are both so young. It is a lifetime ago. I wonder, almost without emotion, if he will die.

Bonnie turns the key in the ignition and her headlights cut the black night. I feel as if we are enveloped in a cocoon. Perhaps we can just drive forever into the black night and never have to arrive at the trauma unit. We head towards I-95, the radio off. It is a moment for silence only. We do not talk. I have no words of comfort to offer to my daughter. In truth, I am beginning to feel a little numb and light-headed. I remember—an after-thought—that I have not eaten in eight hours. I think about showing up at the hospital with a sack of burgers from McDonald's, the concerned wife who had time to stop for fast-food. It is a ridiculous notion but I am living a ridiculous life. I stifle a laugh.

My daughter shoots me a look, mistaking my laugh for a sob. "He'll be okay," she says because she has to believe it. I grip the hand rest of the passenger door tightly.

My cell phone rings. I carry one, too, since last summer when Ron was in Friends' Hospital—originally named The Asylum for Persons Deprived of the Use of Their Reason –and Allen was alone all day. I am tempted not to answer it; only Bonnie and Allen have the number and they use it only for emergencies. Usually, an emergency is anything involving their father. I push the green button, "Hello." My voice echoes in the car, sounding foreign even to me.

It is my best friend, Chris. "I called the house," she says.

"Allen gave me the number. What hospital is he at?"

"Crozer," I tell her. "Fourth floor. Intensive Care." An image of my grandfather flashes before me, his thin body surrounded by a web of wires that used to monitor his every function. I went to the Intensive Care Unit here at Crozer the first time to gather up his personal effects and take them home to Nanny.

"I'm coming," she says. I begin to protest, my usual self-effacing "I'm alright and can handle this routine", but she sees through it. "I'm coming anyway. I'll pick up my mother and we'll meet you there." She clicks off. I fold the phone back up and put it in my purse. I wanted her to come but would not have asked. I know my in-laws are even now waiting at the hospital. Past experience has taught me that they will be able to offer me no comfort tonight.

MARCH 2, 2000. 8:30 pm

It is regrettable that I know so much about this hospital. I have been here far too often. We do not need to ask directions to the trauma waiting room but push the button for the fourth floor like the old pros we are. Bonnie is hugging my arm, but I am not sure who is holding up whom. While we have not spoken of it, we know that what awaits us will just be one of many trials this evening will bring.

We are alone in the elevator. The ride to the fourth floor is short, but long enough for me to compose my features into what I hope is a look of extreme concern. I do not really know what my feelings are at the moment, but I know that my in-laws, already pacing the floors, will expect their son's wife to emanate distress. Despite the difficulties of the last four years, Ron is still their child.

We see them the moment we step off the elevator, sitting in the glass-enclosed cubicle off of the ICU. It seems cruel to allow people in crisis to be exposed to the looks of passers-by. I lift my hand to wave, think better of it, and nod my head instead. Reese's face is set in a grime line. Betty, sweet woman, offers a weak smile. My grip on Bonnie's arm tightens and I try to steal some strength from her. My own has drained away.

There is no preamble or greeting at the door. Reese speaks quickly, brusquely. "A truck hit him. Crossing Paoli Pike. Speeding. His diaphragm is ruptured. And other things inside. The paramedics say all his internal organs have shifted up into his chest. It's a mess." He shakes his head and his voice trails off.

I find my own voice. "When? How long has he been in surgery?"

Betty fills in some details. Her face is soft and pink but it is evident that tears have been falling down her cheeks. She is a gentle woman. She has raised an equally gentle son. In contrast to her husband, whose abruptness serves as a shield against his emotions, she is open with her feelings. "He was on his way home from work, "she says. "Around 4:30. The paramedics got to him right away and the hospital called us around 5:30. He's been in surgery since we got here."

I glance at my watch. It is almost 8:30 now. Three hours.

When Ron was wheeled into surgery, I was in EDR 517, taking notes on reading comprehension. "Why didn't someone call me?" I ask. I am the last to know that my husband's life has hung in the balance for several hours.

"The hospital called us," Reese says flatly, as if that explanation covers it all. It is hardly a secret that Ron's problems with depression have taken a toll on our marriage.

Betty's explanation is softer, kinder. "Ron told the paramedic that you wouldn't be home until 8:00 and he didn't want the kids frightened. So he gave them our number."

Ron was conscious at the scene of the accident? And had the presence of mind to remember that it was my evening at school? This is surprising. In recent weeks, he has barely been able to remember his children's names. "But I have a cell phone," I stammer. "Bonnie knows the number…" I turn to my daughter, whose hand grips mine.

"We didn't want you to drive home knowing. We were worried about you." I realize that the voice saying this belongs to Reese. He has made it clear these past years that he considers me strong, almost too strong. It makes Ron look bad. Although my father-in-law for twenty-four years, he has shown me little approval of late.

I drop into a seat, a green metal-framed chair common to waiting rooms the world over. I've been in enough to offer an opinion. The television set is on. There is a phone on the wall by the door and a rack of hospital literature and magazines nearby. It seems quite odd that I notice these details and that my heart is beating at a normal rate and that my hands are not clammy or cold. We are alone in the waiting room. Other families have been spared similar tragedies tonight.

"Have you spoken to the doctor? To anyone?" I am beginning to acquire more pieces to the puzzle but larger questions still loom ahead. The one I most want to ask will have to wait.

Betty has affirmed that, yes, the surgeon came out and spoke with them about an hour ago. She reported that Ron's injuries are serious, even life-threatening. Most of his internal organs need to be moved back to their original positions. There is a possibility of damage to the liver, the spleen, and the pancreas. I am not even sure what the pancreas does.

"The owner's card on the Taurus is expired," Reese states flatly. "Did you know that?"

I inhale deeply. Now it will begin. The owner's card sat on the dining room table for two weeks awaiting Ron's signature. "Yes, I knew."

The anger needs to be turned onto someone and I am handy. I always am. "You can't trust him to do things like that. You know he can't remember things."

The tears I have been holding back, unable to shed for my own husband, pour from me. This is unfair. These two people have not lived with Ron on a daily basis for these last few years. While they make an attempt to hide the fact that they consider me to blame for Ron's depression, they have fallen into the habit of assigning all responsibilities to me. "It sat on the table for two weeks," I falter. "I reminded him every day."

"I should have taken him to get it," says Reese. "I should have given him the money and taken him myself."

This is part of the ongoing problem with Ron's mental issues. Too many people do too many things for Ron. He is expected, quite literally, to do nothing for himself. "He went to the tag store Tuesday evening," I say. "They were closed."

Reese continues to shake his head. "Probably lose his license. Probably get a fine."

I stifle back a laugh. Ludicrous to think—while Ron is still in surgery—about a fifty dollar fine. "He needs to do some things for himself," I rush on. "It isn't fair that everything falls on me. I work. I go to school. I take care of the house and the kids and the bills. There has to be something Ron is responsible for!" I close my eyes against the hot tears. While I feel my anger is justified, I regret having unleashed my tirade here. In this place. Bonnie pats my arm and we sit in silence for long moments, each of us bound up in our individual grief, wondering if the time has come for us to say good-bye to Ron.

I have been saying good-bye for years. The man I married has been replaced by a silent, gloomy robot whose only emotions are expended on himself. I think of him now, lying on the operating table, his chest exposed to the surgeon's knife. I offer a single prayer. *Change him*, I pray.

MARCH 3, 2000. 1 AM.

The first thing I notice about her is her kind smile, this surgeon who has somehow put the pieces of my husband back together again. She touches my arm when I rise from my seat, urging me to sit back down. She pulls her green plastic chair closer to mine. I introduce my daughter, my friends, Ron's family, and our minister and his wife. She nods at all of us, smiling pleasantly, but it is my eyes she focuses on and her voice is very gentle.

"You've had a long night," she says. "You must be exhausted. Have you eaten?" I shake my head, not really thinking iced tea and crackers count as a meal. "When you leave here," and she glances at her watch, "you are under orders to go home and sleep. Do not set the alarm. Just sleep."

I nod, still not trusting my voice to speak so it is my friend, Chris, who asks, "How is he?"

Dr. Huffman inhales. "He," she says, "is a lucky man. He has a lot of internal injuries. And there are possibilities of complications. But he is alive. That, in itself, is a miracle. A lesser man," she smiles, "could not have survived."

I find my voice. "We were told he had a ruptured diaphragm, but we aren't clear on what else."

She nods. "The ruptured diaphragm was most certainly the most serious injury. His chest was impacted by the steering wheel and cut off his breathing. I don't know how he survived until the paramedics came. He also has several broken ribs, a severe laceration on his left arm all the way to the bone, a torn pancreas, a collapsed left lung, damage to his spleen, and compression of his internal organs. There might be some damage to his aorta, too. We'll watch him through the night. And the pancreas and the spleen are very tricky to handle. We're not at all sure what the outcomes will be. But," she grips my hand tightly, "he's alive. And conscious."

Ron has been in surgery since 5:00 PM. It is now past 1PM.

"Can I…we…see him?"

She nods. "If you'll promise to go straight home afterwards. And get some sleep. You know, I worry about the families of my patients as much as I worry about my patients."

My in-laws rise along with my daughter and I. So does Pastor Tripler. Dr. Huffman smiles again. "Just family now," she says.

"I'm his minister," replies Pastor.

"Then we need you by all means," says Dr. Huffman. She leads us down the corridor to the recovery room.

At the door, Pastor Tripler grips my arm. "Linda," he says, "this won't be pretty. He won't look like himself. Can you do this?"

I think back over the many things I have had to do these last eight years since Ron was diagnosed with clinical depression and bipolar disorders and I nod. "I can do it." So with Pastor on one side of me and my daughter on the other, I walk up to Ron's bed. He is still and gray, a ventilator making his chest rise and fall. My knees buckle, but my supporters are strong. There are tubes everywhere and I hardly know where to touch him, although I want to. There is a bare spot on his right shoulder. Lightly, I put a finger there. "Ron," I whisper. His eyes flicker open. He blinks at me. They close again.

"That's enough for tonight," says Dr. Huffman. "Go home. We'll take good care of him."

Before.....

We are sitting outside under the tree in the front yard, enjoying the coolness that sometimes comes at the end of a hot summer day, stitching together the pieces of a plastic canvas Noah's Ark that will be our gift for a friend's new baby. We work in companionable silence, instinctively picking up each other's stitches. It is my daughter who breaks the silence, asking the question I knew she would one day ask.

"Why did you marry Dad?"

It is not an easy question to answer. With the wisdom of a college freshman, Bonnie has seen the changes wrought in our household the last years since her father began his battle with mental illness. I think a minute and choose my words carefully, speaking to her of the love and faith Ron and I had shared...

> *My daughter asks a question*
>
> *"Why did you marry Dad?"*
>
> *I pause and carefully consider;*
>
> *I don't want to make her sad.*
>
> *"I married him because*
>
> *Of the kindness in his face*

His gentle, loving spirit,

Things time cannot erase.

While dark clouds now

Have weighted him

And given him to grief,

Yesterday's still part of him.

This is my belief.

When he slides,

Unknowing,

Into some gray and long abyss

I remember days of sunshine

And joy

And smiles

And bliss.

My own spirit has grown

As his has slowly ebbed away.

Tomorrows are just echoes

Of what passed

Yesterday.

I have been empowered

By his silent abdication.

I've had my own successes

My joys and my elations.

Now, I wait in silence

For the

Man

That I once met and knew.

It was through his despair and darkness

That my light and my strength grew.

CHAPTER TWO.

MARCH 3, 2000. 3 AM.

The phone next to my bed jangles loudly and I reach for it across the sleeping bodies of my daughter and son who, after trudging off to their respective rooms a scant hour ago, have dragged back blankets and pillows and crawled in next to me. I am grateful for their warm presence and grab the phone quickly, my heart lurching into a staccato pattern that will become commonplace as the months wear on. The voice on the other end of the phone is faint and choked with tears.

"Is he still alive?" I shake my head a moment to clear the cobwebs of sleep deprivation, recognizing the voice of my oldest son. I have half-forgotten the message left a lifetime ago on Alana's answering machine. While I have been cocooned by my family and friends, Dennis has had only the cold comfort of a terse message: "Dennis, Dad's been in an accident. It's bad. Call as soon as you get this message."

"Is he still alive?" my child repeats, fairly screaming now.

I find my voice. "Yes. Yes, Dennis, he's alive. He's in intensive care and he's had several surgeries but he's still alive."

"I'm coming home."

I shake my head, knowing he has been on the road for two straight days already. "No. Don't come. There's nothing you can do but pray and you can do that there. Stay a few days and rest before you come back."

"What happened? Did he do it on purpose?" It was the very question I have been afraid to let myself think about. "No, I don't think so. He was coming home from work and a pick-up truck ran a red light and hit the driver's side of the Taurus. It's totaled. Dad's lucky to be alive."

Dennis gulps. I can imagine his tall, 6 foot 9 inch frame shaking. He is a grown man in most respects, but he is still my child. And it is not the first time he has come close to losing his father, in one sense or another. "What's…what's wrong with him?"

I run through the litany of injuries, one I will repeat often for friends and relatives as the day progresses and more phone calls are made and received. I shudder to myself at the extent of damage a human being can sustain and still live. On the other end of the phone, I sense Dennis doing the same.

"But he'll be alright?" Dennis has always been a bottom-line kind of guy.

"We don't know yet. There's a lot of things that can go wrong. But right now…as of the time I left the hospital…he's stable. I'll call the ICU in the morning. Well, later on in the morning."

"How are you? And the kids?" It is typical of my oldest son to ask. During the year he has lived away from us, several emergency calls have buzzed across the phone wires. After ascertaining that his dad is "okay"—a relative term—it is always his next question.

"We're alright," I say. "Exhausted. Scared. But alright."

"What can I do to help?"

It is becoming a common question. Everyone wants to help. I repeat what I've said to everyone who has asked thus far: pray. But to this oldest child of mine I add another request. "Allen's going to need someone around for a while. Dad's going to be in the hospital a long time. He's going to need a big brother."

Across the miles to New Orleans, I can almost see my tall son smile. Here is something tangible he can do. "Tell Allen that whenever he needs me, and whatever he needs me for, I'm there."

A few moments later, I hang up the phone and snuggle back down under the covers for a few more hours of sleep, holding close to me the images of my wonderful children.

MARCH 3, 2000. 9AM

When Bonnie and I arrive at the hospital, we are still exhausted but propping each other up. The nurse I spoke with at 6AM told me that Ron had a quiet night. My own was punctuated by the sounds of crashing metal and squealing brakes. Later, I called various schools and reported absences. We haven't brought Allen this time; we want to be able to prepare him for what we will find. Last night Ron was still and gray as a waxed image. My daughter and I paste smiles onto our faces and hold each other's hand tightly. We are not unfamiliar with hospitals. In the ICU, the whir of medical machines hum as we walk down the hallway to Ron's blue-curtained cubicle.

We enter on tiptoe, hesitant to disturb the silence. Ron lies on a raised bed, his arms tied down with tubes and straps. The ventilator makes his chest rise and fall and emits the sound of whooshing air. I touch his hand. He stirs. Eyelids flicker. On the other side of the bed, Bonnie rests her hand on her father's shoulder. He shudders—as he does sometimes when he is having a bad dream—and opens his eyes. We hold our breaths, waiting. He blinks several times.

Then we see it, that spark of recognition. He gives us his lopsided smile. Tears fall onto the bed sheets. It doesn't matter whose tears they are. It is enough, for these few moments, to just be near him, touching him, reassuring ourselves that he is still alive. I want to say—so much—but words are not important right now. I can feel Ron's pulse in his hand. The monitors over his bed register his vital signs in an eerie green glow.

Minutes—or hours—pass. Ron dozes. We wait. Nurses walk in and out on quiet crepe soled shoes, offering us smiles and nods. One thoughtfully pushes two chairs into the cubicle, but we do not sit. We do not pace. We wait. Ron's body has been terribly damaged. We do not yet know what the injuries will mean to his mind.

Suddenly, Ron jerks, startled out of his sleep. His eyes fly open. His hands flail. The monitors signal a rise in his blood pressure and a beeper sounds. He groans, grunts. Tries to open his mouth. A nurse enters, all efficiency. She checks his tubes, straightens his covers, touches his brow. She nods toward us.

"He's trying to tell you something," she says and produces a memo pad and pencil from the pocket of her blue uniform.

I position the pencil in Ron's hand and hold the pad at chest height. Laboriously, he prints. Each letter takes an eternity. I do not watch the pad but focus my eyes on his face. I telegraph a question to Bonnie and she nods. She, too, is worried about what Ron's first words will be. We have lived with the effects of bipolar disorder too long to predict.

Finally, the writing is finished. Nine words, printed crookedly on a hospital memo pad. It takes me a moment to decipher the letters. They lean awkwardly against each other. My hand goes to my throat. Tears cloud my vision. I pass the pad to my daughter.

"I am beginning to see how precious my life is." These are words of hope. We have a very long battle ahead of us, but, for now, hope is enough.

MARCH 3, 2000. 2 PM.

Hope. There have been times in the last few years when hope has seemed to be a cruel farce. Much better, I would think sometimes, to be done with hope. To just let go and move on. But hope continues to propel me forward on the day following Ron's accident. I find myself in the hospital again that afternoon; visiting time in the ICU is divided into fifteen minute fragments.

I am walking along the corridor that connects the parking garage to the hospital building when I encounter Ron's aunt and uncle leaving. We stop for a moment and chat; they have been up to see Ron briefly and are happy that he seems alert. Aunt Shirley touches my arm. "You are just the sort of wife Ron needs," she says. We exchange a few more words and I give them both a hug before I move down the corridor and take the elevator up to the ICU. Aunt Shirley's words echo in my ears. *I am just the sort of wife Ron needs.* Am I? In the years since hospitals and psychiatrists and therapists have become a way of life for us, I have often questioned if I *am* what Ron needs. My friends and my minister have assured me that "God never gives you more than you can handle." I question myself, though, and my own strength. Can I really handle all of this?

There is a white-coated man in the cubicle with Ron when I enter. The ventilator is still in place, but Ron is alert and smiles at me. The doctor has set up a chart with shapes and letters on Ron's bedside table. He is, I believe, administering a test to ascertain if there is brain damage. Dr. Huffman mentioned it last night. I pick up Ron's medical chart at the foot of the bed and flip thorough it. No one stops me. I will discover that no one ever will.

I have heard the list of injuries before, but it is startling to come face to face with them in black and white, written in a nurse's neat hand. *Critically ill male adult. Split diaphragm, broken ribs, deep muscle laceration on left arm, torn pancreas and spleen, collapsed lung. Currently breathing on ventilator. Morphine infuser. At risk for pneumonia and pulmonary edema. Contact: Wife.*

I sit down in the chair at the foot of the bed, trying to arrange my face into positive, cheerful lines. The list of injuries is daunting. How can one human being survive so much? Just what the heck do the spleen and the pancreas do? The machines around me hum as Ron is ventilated and infused and monitored. Dr. Huffman had told us last night that it would be a "couple of weeks" before Ron will be well enough to leave. In the cubicle of the ICU, the truth begins to dawn on me. Despite Dr. Huffman's optimism, we have a very long road ahead of us. There is no going back. It will, in reality, be far longer than two weeks when Ron is able to leave the hospital and our lives are forever changed. Today starts the part of our lives I come in time to think of as "after."

But I know none of this as the neurologist leaves the room and I take my place by my husband's side. I know only that somehow, for some reason, we have been brought to this place. I take Ron's hand and begin to pray, not only for his recovery but for my endurance.

MARCH 3, 2000. 4 PM.

The notepad by the phone is full of memos when I return home. The house is quiet. Bonnie and Allen have taken refuge in their beds and are catching up on some missed sleep. I sit for a moment, adding things to do onto the notepad.

Calls from Phyllis, Charlotte, Gus, Debbie, Aunt Meryl. Church is bringing supper. Dottie from work called. Call Dr. K. to let him know about Ron. Cancel knee surgery on 3/14. Leave message for bowling league. Call insurance agent. Was ER notified that it was a car accident? Give insurance cards to admissions office. Gus found our car at Truck Maintenance. Need to get things out of trunk. Cards from secretaries at TCA. E-mails from Ross, Deb, Brittney, Michelle, Harvey. Lawyers say Ron will need to sign medical authorization and power of attorney to me. Police report is favorable; other driver blew red light. Two eye witnesses. Received insurance cards and report from West Goshen police. Call from Chris.

It is overwhelming. For the second time since my arrival at the hospital, less than 24 hours ago, I allow myself to cry.

THE GATES

The gates of madness open wide

Beckoning, please come inside.

Leave your troubles at the door.

Pray, they'll trouble you no more.

Leave your worries,

Leave your strife.

All it will cost you

Is your life.

CHAPTER THREE.

BEFORE...

1992

Things have beginnings. According to Ron, it happened very suddenly. He was coming out of a K-Mart and he remembered watching *Father of the Bride* on television the night before. He started crying, right there in the middle of the parking lot. By the time he made it home, he was a blubbering mess.

But I was standing on the other side of Alice's looking glass. From my perspective, the downward slide began way before that, innocently and slowly. Ron had sleepless nights. I would awaken to find him sitting on the side of the bed, rocking back and forth. If I asked him what was wrong, he would say, "Nothing. Go back to sleep." And often I did. He would toss and turn, occasionally driving me to the couch when the turbulence became too much. I would come home from school to find him sitting on the same couch, his head in his hands. He began to pace, like a lion in a cage. Once in a while, when the demons that now dwelled inside his brain became too much for him, he would pound his fist against whatever was handy. Our furniture began to suffer.

My own life was clouded with issues. After putting it off for years, I had returned to college in the winter to get my teaching degree. But my vision was giving me problems and the degenerative disease I had been coping with for years, kerataconus, made itself apparent. The condition affects about 1 in 2,000 people in the general population. Usually, a diagnosis is made in the late teens. I was 19 when Dr. Scheie of the Scheie Eye Institute at the University of Pennsylvania confirmed mine.

My optometrist, Dr. Neil Schwartz, told me that it was time to consider a transplant. Generally, it takes six months to a year for the eye to recover from this type of surgery. Everyone I spoke with—my family, my friends, my co-workers at the library—thought I was nuts to risk my vision and take on a college program. I know, because I took a poll. Each one suggested I put off school for another semester and have the transplant.

I remember calling my pastor one night. The pressure I was getting to return to the halls of academia was great. And the pain in my right eye caused by the degeneration of the cornea greater still. "Well," said Dr. Hopson when he answered my call, "anytime anyone asks my advice I always pray that my words will be godly. And I think, Linda, that you need to consider your physical needs first. Your body is, after all, the temple of God." I chalked up another dissenting vote. That made it twenty-five to one.

They were not good odds. Even to my eye doctor, who had shepherded me through the progression of my disease since I was nineteen, advised me to sit out school a little longer. "You don't really see, " Neil told me, "but you're so good at pretending you can that you fool everyone, even yourself."

I decided to fool myself just a little longer. The changes in Ron scared me, but I did not know what I could do about them. Here, though, was a tangible problem I could solve. Three weeks into my first semester, I had a cornea transplant to replace the damaged cornea in my right eye and began my first semester back at college with an eye patch and a tape recorder. My friend Chris typed and proofed my papers. I tried to act as if everything was fine. I became good at it.

But, again, I was fooling myself. Ron's problems became difficult to ignore, more than just little quirks. He had an accident at work involving a forklift and was demoted. The financial setback caused us to take on some piecework as a family, delivering circulars on the weekend. We tried to make a game of it with the kids, tossing flyers onto lawns from Ron's moving van, aiming for mailboxes and flowerbeds.

In April of 1992, my beloved grandmother became seriously ill. I added hospital visits to my already over-crowded schedule. Nanny died on July 4 of 1992. The summer dragged along, hot and muggy and laden with textbooks I needed to read with a magnifying glass. I took Ron to his first therapist that summer, looking for answers. They were as elusive as my ability to read with my right eye. I began to think of our lives as a carefully constructed house of cards. If the kids and I didn't breathe too loudly or move too quickly, we could make it through the day without an outburst or a crying jag.

The house began to topple over in August. Ron's uncle was killed in a motorcycle accident. A few days later, a casual stroll past a tennis court and an ill-placed lobe sent a ball speeding towards my right eye, destroying the nearly healed cornea. My surgeon told me there was nothing he could do immediately; it would take the eye months to heal from the trauma. My father had driven me to the appointment, and I gave Ron the bad news over dinner.

"Just my luck," he said, pounding on the kitchen table for emphasis, "to have a blind wife." Although I knew his mental state had provoked those words, they hurt nonetheless. In a very short space of time, our lives had suffered major upheavals: financial, employment, death, illnesses. Something had to give. Ron simply stopped trying to hold it all together.

But I was still gluing the pieces back, doing my best to make it right again. The same events that had sent him over the edge had also affected me. Why, I wondered, was I still standing on my feet while he dissolved into a quivering mass? I was simply too busy to let go of the hope that I could, somehow, reclaim our lives. I had two teenagers and an adolescent at home. I had classes and a job. I had household chores and bills to pay. I had one eye that still functioned. And I had a husband who was now consumed by invisible and uncontrollable enemies.

Someone had to be in charge. I elected myself.

I finished my teaching degree in two and a half years, propelled by the notion that someday Ron would be unable to work. My dear friend Dr. Schwartz wanted me to have a second cornea transplant to replace the one destroyed by the tennis ball, but I wanted to student teach. I won. I wore dark glasses to my graduation, hiding my eyes from the sun. My father-in-law took me aside that day and whispered into my ear: "Don't go rubbing it into Ron now that you have a damn degree." Thanks, Dad.

Ron's problems at work continued and he was laid off for the summer. Although exhausted and in need of a break as well as a second cornea transplant, I took a job at a daycare for the summer, gambling my vision for a few more months. In September, my new degree in hand, I got myself onto every substitute list in the county and went to work almost every day. I took two weeks off in February for my second cornea transplant. The summer of 1996 saw me working at another daycare center, but I managed to find a fulltime teaching position for the fall. Ron was seeing a psychiatrist weekly now, a rather dour man who insisted I come to the appointments but seldom wanted to speak to me. He diagnosed Ron with bipolar disorder. We were trying medication now, and Ron was sleeping a bit better and no longer abused the furniture.

I wondered if I could breathe yet.

Bipolar disorder became the ruler of our lives. Some days Ron could function fairly well. Some days found him depressed and withdrawn. And there were a few days—always wildly scattered throughout the weeks—that plunged Ron into a frantic, manic state. He would be consumed with activity and plans, taking Allen to the basketball courts back at the B's Field to play HORSE, tacking new projects—which would never be finished—around the house, full of exuberance and hope. I began to think of the cycle we lived in as a roller coaster ride.

The ascent is thrilling as the cars speed upward and the rules of gravity are suspended. The wind whips your hair back and the world below you blurs as the car picks up speed and you come closer and closer to the top of the world. From the summit, you can see the earth below, small and insignificant. Why should anything down there really bother you? You feel, for an instant, as if you could fly!

But the laws of our world cannot long be defied. Once the hill of the rollercoaster is crested, there is no way to go but down. Suddenly, your stomach lurches and flips over, the gorge threatening to rise in your throat. Your hands clench tightly onto the restraining bar and your back stiffens. You have lost control over your body and there is no way to stop the break-neck speed at which the car descends. You hear screaming in your ears and are surprised to hear that it is coming from you. It takes only a few seconds and then you are back on level ground again, darting towards the next mountain. There is no way to get off.

Often, we hoped that something—anything—would break the cycle for Ron. We left no stone unturned to seek a cure, or at least a compromise. I became acutely in tune with the ups and down, the twists and turns of living with bipolar disorder. The only thing that I could ever really be sure of was that the frenzied race up the mountain would always be followed by the downward plunge, as heart-stopping and mind-numbing as an rollercoaster ride in its velocity, intensity, and depth. The higher the climb, the further the fall. I came to hate roller coasters.

I exchanged words with the nurse at Ron's plant on an almost daily basis. It was clear that in the spring of 1999 he was in a downward slide, but there seemed to be nothing we could do about it. At the close of the school year, Ron and I chaperoned a group of high school seniors on their class trip to Niagara Falls. He was withdrawn and uncommunicative, not even showing interest in the massive forces of nature displayed. I kept up a running stream of conversation to make up for his silence. It became a habit; I would always find a way to fill in the gaps left by Ron's emotional or physical absence. Two days before the seniors graduated, Ron's fragile hold on reality snapped. He, as the kids put it, "freaked out" at work. His father went to pick him up and take him to the crisis center at Crozer Chester Medical Center where I would meet them.

The man I had married was broken. The only thing that I knew for sure was that I had not been the one to break him. Perhaps he came that way? The last seven years had been, on my part, one long attempt to fix him, heal him, bring him back. We tried counseling, medication, religion, and meditation. Now, as Reese and I sat with Ron waiting for the ambulance that would transport him to Friends' Hospital in Philadelphia, we talked about electric shock treatments. It was a last resort and it seemed a drastic solution. Somehow, despite our best efforts, he remained a man whose inside mechanisms were unable to function.

I had once told a counselor that Ron was like a hollow man. The counselor jumped to the conclusion that I was talking about the Tin Man from *The Wizard of Oz*. What I really referred to was T.S. Eliot's poem about the straw men who live without hope, somewhere between heaven and hell, unable to make a decision in either direction. It is, Eliot says, the way the world ends, "not with a bang, but a whimper." It was the way Ron seemed to be ending it. By choice or design, he would sit alone in a mental hospital, powerless to heal himself, powerless to end it all. It was a permanent kind of limbo, far removed from the world the children and I inhabited.

Some part of me believed that, on some level, Ron made the choice to leave us in favor of his illness. I was left holding the bag. I fought resentment. He was locked away behind metal doors, and I needed to continue on with my life. We talked on the phone every evening. He would tell me that he loved me. I could not respond. It would have been a lie. What was there left to love? He had become an object of pity. I felt for his pain, but I could not heal it. The kind and gentle man I loved was now buried under an avalanche of self-contempt and remorse. He was so sorry for what he had done; he was trying so hard, he said. But I had heard it all before. He made promises he would not or could not keep.

I was amazed at my own calmness, the resolute way in which I made the trip up to visit him in a mental ward, then returned home to pick up the burdens he had thrown off. I learned to start lawnmowers, change fuses, install air-conditioning units. I learned to balance work and home and school and family, paying the bills on time and cooking meals in the crock-pot, helping Allen with his homework while I studied Education Theory 589. I locked the doors at night and checked the mileage on the car. I slept in the middle of our bed, the pillows heaped around me.

I scarcely missed him.

I had already spent seven years saying good-bye. I had cried oceans of tears. But, in the end, the tears had done nothing to save Ron. He alone could save himself. He might be too weak to do it. I, on the other hand, had become a woman of daunting courage. Each piece Ron lost was a strength I was forced to gain.

I did not need Ron, in that summer of 1999. I could take care of myself.

The question then, was not of need, but of want. I had no answer. My needs had only intermittedly been a part of our marriage since bipolar disorder became the ruler of our lives. Most things the last seven years had been about Ron. Ron could not remain forever in the rubber room at Friends' Hospital. Where would Ron go when he was released? I am sure my in-laws assumed that he would come home. But I did not. The children did not. Ron had become a stranger to us, someone we must be wary of. Could I trust him again? Did I want to? Without him in the house, life was peaceful. We could not go back. Ever.

So, I was forced to ask myself, it this how it ends? Not with a bang, but a whimper?

BETWEEN

Between is

        Beige waiting rooms

            With molded

Plastic chairs

        Long corridors

            Connecting

Here to there.

CHAPTER FOUR.

March 6, 2000. 2PM.

I feel like Alice in a distorted version of Wonderland, watching the corridor that connects the parking garage to the hospital grow each day to immense proportions. It takes one minute and twenty seconds walking at a normal pace to complete the trek. I time it, but it seems longer most days. My shoes make only muffled sounds on the carpet, my tired smile meets the faces of other weary travelers: doctors, nurses, visitors. We all look shell-shocked, like victims of a national disaster, thrown into this corridor. It is the last place on earth we want to be, but for the time being it is the only place we can be. Our real lives have been suspended; this corridor, stretching from here to there, is all we have.

I am bone-tired. It is an expression my grandmother would use when I would try to cajole her into playing a game of jump-rope. "I am bone-tired," she would say, dropping into an old wooden rocking chair that creaked no less than her joints. I would laugh and run off to my games, leaving Nanny to rock in the sunshine, each squeak of the rocker's gliders sing-songing her weariness.

I am bone-tired now, so tired that I can feel the ache from the tips of my toes to the roots of my hair. I wonder every day if I will be able to traverse the corridor or stop somewhere along the way, sinking into a liquid puddle of weariness, no bones or cartilage or organs, just a large wet spot as my flagging energy seeps out onto the gray carpet.

Yesterday, someone stopped me on my corridor journey and said, "I don't think I would have been as well-prepared for this as you have been." Prepared? You can be prepared for such a tragic accident? Who plans or expects that in one blinding instant of crashing metal that a loved one will be so grievously injured? That lives will be forever altered?

I did not plan. Even now, I do not plan. It is only dogged determination on my part, German stubbornness coupled with Native American tenacity that keeps me putting one foot in front of the other and marching on.

Ron is dozing when I enter his cubicle in the ICU. I check the chart at the end of his bed. *Critically ill adult male. Catheter taken out, drainage tube may come out tomorrow. Patient was up and walked around bed. Still on O2 tank. Psych consult reports patient is handling things well. Scheduled to leave ICU tomorrow.*

I plop down onto the visitor's chair and check the list I carry in my pocket. I have dropped the insurance cards off at the admissions desk. Ron signed the power of attorney to me yesterday. Reese had gotten Ron's things out of the trunk of the wrecked Taurus. The book bag in my car is filled with sixth grade essays to read. Someone from church—Ann?Joan?—is bringing supper tonight. For the moment, no one needs me and I close my eyes briefly, trying to ease the headache that settled in three days ago. I have been the one that demanded the psychiatric consult. Perhaps someone could come and talk to me to see how I am handling it.

I watch Ron sleep, the monitors and wires connected to him beeping and whirring. In the last week, I have become all too familiar with their functions. This one monitors his heart, this one his respiration and blood pressure. This tube from his chest is draining fluid off his damaged lung. The IV in his arm feeds Ron nutrients since his damaged pancreas cannot digest food. The kids call it "banana pudding." The morphine infuser doses out his pain medication.

From all accounts and reports, Ron is doing well, or at least as well as anyone can who has been hit by a truck. The kids and I tease him about it, our black sense of family humor rising to the occasion. "Stop being so stubborn," we teased Ron last night when he balked at his breathing treatment. "What, do you need a truck to hit you?" He laughed along with us, although the movement compressed his chest and set off an alarm, bringing a nurse.

It will be, says Dr. Huffman, two weeks until Ron can come home. She is optimistic that we are over the hump. Watching Ron now, seeing all the machines and monitors and tubes, it is hard to believe that he will ever walk out of here. We will need to arrange for home care during the day while we are all out of the house and at night I will take over. My depleted strength makes me wonder if

I will have the energy to teach all day and tend to Ron at night, but I do not express my fears. Pastor Tripler has assured me that God will not give me more than I can handle.

Ron groans in his sleep. I wonder if the scenes of the accident flash before his eyes. He says that he remembers only a little; there was the sound of screeching brakes and an impact. After that, he says, it was a blur. He does not remember kicking open the passenger side door, or crawling out of the car. He does not remember talking to the paramedics, although they report that he was standing on his feet when they reached the scene. I am grateful for his lack of memory. The image of the accident haunts my own dreams.

Ron's body will, Dr. Huffman says, heal. He is strong. But it is not his body I am worried about as I watch him sleep. I cannot help but wonder what this will do to his mind. We are not yet a year away from Friends' Hospital and the breakdown that sent him there. Despite the psychologist's very brief examination, there is something I cannot quite put my finger on yet, something different about Ron.

"He seems good," Reese said last night. "Don't you think?"

And I responded that, yes, Ron seems to be healing nicely.

Reese tapped his head. "I mean here," he said. "He seems better here."

I nod reluctantly, because who can really tell at this juncture? Up until twenty-four hours ago, Ron was unable to speak because of the ventilator. Yes, he seems to be in a more positive frame of mind than I would have thought, but is that just relief that he is still alive? And, yes, his first words, written on the nurse's pads, spoke of hope, but we still have a long road ahead of us and hope can wear thin. I know that my husband likes instant solutions. Despite what the psychologist has said, I have lived with Ron's mood swings for eight years. I know that he can sometimes seem—well, normal—for a few days, then quickly he will hit another skid and begin the downward slide.

At the moment, watching him sleep, eyeing the monitors that surround him, I want to be hopeful, I want to share Reese's perspective. But still, there is that seed of doubt.

Something is just not right.

MARCH 6, 2000. 6PM.

The list the kids keep by the phone has grown again by the time I arrive back home. A "church lady"—Allen can't remember who—has dropped off supper and Bonnie is ladling out chicken and rice. I check the phone pad while she puts it on the table. *Gus called insurance agent. Spoke to Sergeant at West Goshen. Power of attorney letter arrived. Ron needs to sign. Don't let Ron talk to insurance agent!!!! Cards came from students at Westtown. Heinz sent a basket of fruit. Calls from Jim, Celeste, Kelvin, James.*

Bonnie, Allen, and I say grace before digging into the casserole dinner, making Ron's recovery the focus of our prayers. I chatter on, talking about how well their father looked today, the fact that he is leaving the ICU tomorrow and that the drain in his lungs might soon come out. They add little to the conversation, although Bonnie offers to return to the hospital with me that evening.

"Are you coming?" I ask Allen. He shrugs. He has seen Ron once in the last two days, a visit that made him grab my hand tightly and avert his eyes away from his father's damaged body. He refuses to talk about the accident. I have made an appointment for him tomorrow with Steve, the therapist Ron was seeing. During the years we have been dealing with Ron's mental illness, Allen has sometimes retreated into himself.

I often think of Allen as my neglected child. His older siblings assure me that it is not really true, that Allen has always had any time and attention he needed from me, but it still feels as if he is often pushed to the bottom of my list. I carry guilt that he and I did not share picnics in the park as I did with Bonnie and Dennis, that his early years had been spent in the care of a babysitter since I was a working mother, that school and classes have disabled me from serving as his homeroom mother at school. Allen asks very little of me, but my heart is often burdened for him.

When he was four, Allen was diagnosed by school officials as being educable mentally retarded. The news was handed to me over a conference table with little explanation, dropped like the proverbial ton of bricks. I was crying in the parking lot when the school psychologist came up behind me and put her arm around me. In the years that I have managed my own classroom and sometimes needed to impart difficult news to parents, I have remembered the feeling of having my insides torn out. I would never want another mother or father to go through it.

Ron's reaction to Allen's diagnosis was typical, given the mental state he was in at the moment. "It's your fault," he said, "because you've always worked." He did not really mean it, of course, and later on said he did not even recall saying it. Nonetheless, the words tore at me and some part of me has wondered if it can be true.

I watch Allen as he heads out of the kitchen. We have come a long way from that initial, devastating diagnosis. Allen has learned to do things once thought impossible. While he still requires an adapted curriculum and special services, it is clear that he will one day be able to maintain an independent life. I have fought hard for him, my youngest child, calling state representatives and school administrators for services, advocating that he have the least restrictive environment and be mainstreamed when possible, and refusing to treat him with medication. The reason for Allen's various learning disabilities was a rare condition involving elevated blood ammonia. We discovered it, almost by accident, when he was four. Since then, we have carefully controlled his intake of protein, a major cause of the elevation.

Kids like Allen need practice before performance, Dr. Purcell told me. We do everything we can to make sure he is thrown into unfamiliar circumstances as seldom as possible. When he went to a new school, we took several tours ahead of time and made sure he knew how to find the gym and the cafeterias. We talked to his teachers and walked him through a typical school day. One time when he wanted to buy a snack at school and did not know how to negotiate the snack line, Bonnie set up a practice line at home. After a week, he felt confident enough to do the real thing. When he entered middle school last year, it was helpful that I had been a long-term substitute there three years before and knew the routines and the art rotations and what the heck a "mini" was.

But how do you practice this? How do you prepare a child for the grievous injury and possible loss of his father? Then again, Ron has spent most of Allen's childhood as a broken man. It is Bonnie and Dennis who show Allen photos of long-ago family vacations and help him to remember a father he never really knew. "Is that Dad laughing?" Allen will ask when he sees a picture of us at the beach, burying Ron in the sand. His older siblings will nod. Yes, Dad used to laugh.

The phone rings. It is my friend Debbie, calling for the latest report. It seems the line is always busy. Her son Seth, who is four, interrupts her. "Say hello to Miss Linda," Debbie says to him. "Say something comforting because Mr. Ron was hurt and is in the hospital."

Seth's lisping voice comes over the phone. "How did Mr. Ron get hurt?" he asks brightly.

I smile to myself, imagining Seth's chubby hands holding the phone. "Well," I say, "a truck hit him as he was coming home from work."

There is a sharp intake of breath. "Oh, my gosh," Seth exclaims, "You could get killed like that!" Debbie grabs the phone away from him. "That wasn't comforting!" she admonishes. Yes it was, the sort of black sense of humor we have all used to survive. It reminds me that while Ron's road may be long and difficult, I can still laugh. It is a gift.

MARCH 6, 2000. 9PM.

Once I return from the hospital, I spend the evening returning the phone calls that have been added to the pad, believing that anyone who has called to ask us about Ron deserves a personal update on the situation. I try to keep the calls brief, but often I am drawn into conversations. Do we need anything? *Yes, I need my husband back as a whole man.* Is there anything they can do? *Yes, they can pray and remember to always wear their seatbelts.* Most people concentrate on Ron: his vital signs, his spirit, his prognosis. Once in a while a dear friend will ask how I am doing and I will always give the same reply: I'm hanging in there. I'm okay. It has, for years, been my standard response.

The kids have gone to bed long before I finish my phone calls and my paperwork for school. The last call has been from my oldest son. He will be home tomorrow, he says. I protest that he not cut his vacation short, but he stops me. He needs to see his father, he says. He will be home around 3 and go to the hospital with me for the afternoon shift.

I hang up the phone and check all the locks on the door. I know that Dennis, like Allen, is wondering if Dad will ever laugh again.

I check on my two sleeping offspring before falling into my own bed. Bonnie is snuggled next to the ancient stuffed pig that has inhabited her bed for years. Her room is strewn with discarded clothing and movie posters. She looks, for all outward appearances, to be a normal teenager. She has been places few teenagers had to go.

Allen's lanky form barely fits beneath his Star Wars quilt. One leg has fallen out of his double bed. I push it back onto the mattress, cover him over gently, and kiss his forehead. His skin tastes slightly of salt, an indication that his blood ammonia may be on the rise. I feel something hard and sharp as I tuck the covers around him. Pulling back Han and Chewie, I discover that Allen has secreted a hammer from Ron's toolbox between his sheets. I cannot fathom a reason for its presence, but I do not remove it.

ON THE BREEZE

The soft breeze whispers

Through the leaves

Murmuring in the world

"There is hope and light

In the

following of God's Word."

Dark clouds may sometimes shroud

The rays of the shining sun

But the promise always glimmers

In the hearts of His chosen ones.

CHAPTER FIVE.

APRIL 7, 2000. 5PM

I pause tonight in my supper preparations, watching Allen in the backyard. It has gone by many names, the piece of wood he deftly wields. He twirls it, crouches low, then brings the stick around, ready to attack. The monsters in the backyard have been gone for years, chased off by Allen's older brother and this same formidable weapon. Dennis called it "Ooga-Booga", but in Allen's possession it has become a light saber, a limbo stick, and a submachine gun. The one-eighth of me that is Irish recognizes it as a shillelagh. It does not matter what name it goes by. What matters is what it has come to mean to my youngest child.

He has grown this winter, I think as I turn away from the window. At fourteen, he tops me by two inches. The hands that hold the stick are larger than mine, but they are still the hands of an adolescent, hands that will need more years of guidance and training before their owner can, like his older brother, leave the nest and find his own way in the world. They are hands that still need a father.

I lay the plates for supper on the table. There are only three.

It has been six weeks since the accident and in some respects our lives have returned to normal. The church ladies no longer bring us meals. I go to work. The kids go to school. We eat and do laundry in the evenings after hospital visits and play long games of Monopoly when we cannot sleep. In the early days, Allen dragged his sleeping bag into my bedroom most nights, settling himself down at the foot of my bed without a word, the threadbare Clifford dog that has accompanied him through childhood clutched in his arms. Bonnie usually joined us, carrying her pillow and the afghan stitched by a great grandmother long passed on. We huddled together in the hours before dawn, listening to the tick of Ron's alarm clock and waiting for the phone to jangle its ominous ring.

Lung collapse. Blood clots. An unidentified bacteria. Kidney problems. Bowel obstruction. I became an expert at deciphering the medical codes on our insurance forms.

Nightmares punctuated Allen's sleep. The hammer between his sheets was replaced by a succession of other tools that found their way into his room. "Protection," he told me when I finally asked. "In case someone breaks in during the night, so I can take care of you and Bonnie." What an immense pressure to put on an adolescent!

The boy in the backyard, wielding the stick, no longer sleeps with the stuffed red dog or the hammers and wrenches. Since the reappearance of the shillelagh at our house, Allen has taken on a new strength, trying hard to be the man of the house. It is no accident that this gnarled piece of wood re-entered our lives just when he desperately needed the support. The shillelagh and Dennis arrived on the doorstep at the same time.

Dennis came home six days after the accident, staying for a week to pace the floors of the ICU with us. He visited his dad, played games with his brother, and went to school with his sister. He let me talk about the tests and the doctors and the surgeries and while he had little understanding of them, he listened and patted my shoulder. Dennis and Allen walked to the river together one afternoon, punching each other in the shoulders. And when he left the next day to return to his own life in the city, the shillelagh stayed in Allen's care, propped up next to him at the dinner table and slid discreetly under the couch as he watched *Small Soldiers* in the evening. It, instead of a tool, was tucked between his covers at night.

"Did Dennis say you could have that?" I asked casually at breakfast the next morning. Life cannot forever stay on hold in intensive care wards and Allen was bolting his cereal in order to catch the school bus. The shillelagh sat on the floor.

Allen nodded and took a gulp of juice. "He said I could borrow it. For as long as I wanted."

"Well," I said slowly, "you can't take it to school."

"I know."

After Allen flew out the door, book bag trailing behind him, I examined the stick more closely. Dennis had always carried it so easily, his tall frame dwarfing its length, his straight back and shoulders a contrast to the twisted handle and gnarled wood. To Dennis is was merely a prop, purloined from a school play. He did not require its support.

Allen does. Ron's therapist said that Allen was handling this latest tragedy "as well as anyone could" and that he needed lots of family support and routine right now. Supper is almost ready and I open the back door to call out to my youngest child, the one who has felt the absence of his father most keenly. I pause, watching him for another moment. The wooden shillelagh has become a cane. He leans his weight upon it and its strength holds. He is lucky, I realize, to have a wise older brother who knew that words alone were not enough to help this fourteen-year-old cope with the enormous changes in his life. The shillelagh is more than just a stick of wood or a tool for the imagination. It is a bond between brothers. In the endurance of that bond, as in the endurance of the wood, there is strength.

Allen gives a final Ninja yell before catching sight of me. He runs towards me and throws an arm around my shoulders. As we walk into the house, the shillelagh dragging along, I notice the daffodils by the fence are pushing their heads up above the ground.

They are not the only things that have bloomed this spring, things Ron has missed.

APRIL 10, 2000. 12 AM.

I carry my cell phone in my pocket during the day, its weight always a tug on my heart. The principal and I have an agreement. If the hospital calls, I will leave no matter what I am doing. Each morning I arrange my lesson plans in scrupulous detail, in the event a colleague needs to pinch-hit in my sixth grade classroom. The faculty here at Westtown Quaker School have been more kind and supportive than I could have imagined. When I lean my head against the wall in the hallway for a few moments, trying to siphon some energy from the middle school population, it is almost inevitable that a colleague will come and offer a shoulder or the chance to grab a cup of tea while he or she covers my study hall. Ron's various hospital rooms—four, so far—have been decorated with handmade cards and posters from the students here at Westtown. My class sent a crookedly sewn teddy bear sporting white bandages. Bonnie named it Patches.

I am crossing from the main building in the dining hall when the phone rings. I freeze, knowing it is bad news. If I ignore it, will it just go away? Just last week Ron underwent a thoroscopy to re-inflate his left lung. Two incisions needed to be made into his back so his ribs could be separated. A tube now drains off the excess fluid that collected. I take a deep breath—my own lungs still seem to work—and pick up the phone.

"Yes." There is no need for a greeting. This is the Bat Phone, used only for emergencies.

"Linda." It is Dr. Huffman's gentle, soothing voice. Unlike other surgeons we have had recourse with the last few weeks, Joanne always makes the calls to me herself. "It's his pancreas," she says. We had talked about his last night. Despite the time and some healing, Ron's pancreas has been unable to digest whole food. He has been receiving most of his nutrients through the "banana pudding" bag and central line that were put in the first night. This time last year I had no idea what a pancreas did, although the high school students would joke about "having a pain in the pancreas." Now I know the pancreas is a gland that breaks down and processes food. Ron's was virtually crushed out of shape by the steering wheel in the Taurus and has since been invaded by pernicious bacteria.

We had prayed for healing. Ron's supper last night consisted of some chicken broth and lemon-lime gelatin—a hospital favorite—and we had hoped his system would be able to handle it.

"His fever's spiked to 104," says Joanne. "He's a bit out of it and in a lot of pain. I think we're going to have to go ahead with the surgery, but I need you to come and sign the release." Since Ron had given power of attorney over to me, I needed to okay all medical procedures. "I don't think we'll need to remove it all," she hastens to say, "just the tail end that was virtually dead anyway."

A person can live without the whole pancreas, Joanne assured me yesterday. But Ron's body needs more nutrition that the central line can currently give him. He's losing weight and the lack of nutrients makes him prone to bacteria and leaves him in a weakened state. I head towards the middle school building, grab my purse from the desk drawer, and stop by the secretary before I exit. I'm leaving. I do not know what tomorrow may bring. Marie pats my hand and murmurs sympathetically. It will be okay.

But will it? I check my watch, knowing I will not be able to reach any of the children at 12:30 and loathe to leave a message on the home phone. Let them have a few more hours of peace, I decide. They will know soon enough.

APRIL 10, 2000. 6PM.

It seems as if I have been sitting in this same waiting room outside the operating suite for days, not hours. Ron was heavily sedated when I saw him at 1:45, just before they wheeled him up to surgery. He will not be returning to One North after the procedure is over, so I busied myself for a while with packing up his meager belongings: cards, socks, shaving gear, underwear, his Bible, a few sports magazines. I take down the cards from the Westtown students, a colorful array of cheerful drawings and hopeful messages. He will be assigned a room on the surgical floor when he is out of recovery, so I place his personal effects in a plastic carryall bag supplied by the hospital. It is generally for carrying a patient's belongings home, not to the trunk of my car where it will stay for a day or so.

I have grabbed my book bag from the car while I was there and I am trying to study Ladson-Billings *Dreamkeepers* for a paper that is due next week. I reread the same words for the third or fourth time, slam the book down, and walk to the pay phone. Time to give the kids a call. We have come to refer to these as "life checks." Earlier, I had called them on my cell from outside the main lobby doors, visitors around me puffing cigarette smoke into the crisp air. I thought of Ron's damaged lung, struggling to inflate. In deference to the sign on the waiting room wall, I have turned off my cell phone. I drop coins in the slot of the pay phone in the hallway.

"Hello," Bonnie answers, her voice just a tad shy of its usual cheerfulness.

"It's me," I say. "No word yet. Just checking in. The nurse said it might be another hour or so."

"I should come," my daughter says. "You shouldn't be alone."

I hesitate, wanting her warm presence with me. But it is Wednesday, Bible study night. "More important that you and Allen should go to prayer meeting and let everyone know what's going on," I tell her. "Have you called MomMom and PopPop?"

There is a pause. "No." Then, "Do you want me to?"

Yes, I want her to. I have already waited too long to tell them. They will wonder why I waited and while they will try not to show it, they will question my decision. I will need to reassure them that all will be well when what I need is someone to reassure me. But I cannot let my teenage daughter carry this burden. "No," I say, "I'll call them later on. When I know more."

There is a sigh on the other side of the phone; I know it to be relief. "I love you," says Bonnie. "Wait a sec. Allen wants to talk to you."

"Hi!" pipes my son, owner of the magical shillelagh. "Do you want us to save you supper?

"I don't know," I say. "What was supper?"

"Bonnie made burnt macaroni and hotdogs," he informs me, though I hear his sister protesting in the background.

"Ummm. Pass," I tell him. "I'll get something here if I'm hungry."

"Eat something," he urges me. "You need to keep up your strength." Just when did he become the parent?

"Yes sir," I say. "Go to youth group and ask them to pray for Dad. Maybe I'll be home when you get back."

"Love you," says Allen. He hangs up.

I should call my in-laws. They will want to know. They will want to be here. They will offer as much support as they can muster, but in the end I will end up feeding my limited energy to them. There will be questions to which I have no answers.

I return to my molded plastic chair and pick up the book I am not reading, exchange a few words with a mother and daughter waiting on word about a valve replacement, and flip a few pages. Waiting rooms. We do so much more in them than wait. They are places set apart from the rest of the world where we relive the past, hope for the future, laugh a little, cry a little, and commiserate with total strangers, joined against the common enemy of time. Those of us within these beige walls are on hold. Waiting.

Waiting for someone to come and comfort us. Waiting on a green-gowned figure to alarm or reassure us. Waiting, as the second hand of the wall clock continues its cycle, for a release. For an end.

I have met them in waiting rooms, these worried parents and

bereaved children and concerned friends and relatives. I am one of them. We wring our hands. We question God. We rail against our fates. We wait.

I tap my fingers on the arm of the chair, debating. I am sorting out my thoughts as I wait, not concerned with my laundry or the cleanliness of my kitchen floor. Just Ron on the others side of those double doors. I think about things I've said and wished I hadn't and things I didn't say but wished I had. I pray for one more chance.

Waiting rooms give us a taste of our own mortality, the knowledge that our lives are finite. Some day it will be too late to make amends. There will be no second change. Waiting rooms stop us dead in our tracks and force us into molded vinyl chairs next to other human beings who have been rudely torn from their lives.

We wait. We pray. We catch our breath. We move on again. Maybe we recognize that this chance might be our very last.

I rise from my seat again and stride to the pay phone to call Ron's parents. They need to be here.

APRIL 10, 2000. 11:30 PM.

It is after eleven when I arrive at home. Bonnie and Allen are still up, playing Monopoly and munching on frozen pizza. The burnt macaroni and hotdogs were apparently not sustenance enough. We sit and talk. Ron is out of surgery, out of recovery, safely ensconced in a room on the third floor, away from our familiar One North. He lost part of his pancreas and had a great deal of difficulty coming out from under the anesthesia. He is back on oxygen since his damaged lung still refuses to function. He is barely coherent but the infection seems to be abating. There is some continued concern about his aorta, so he is hooked up to telemetry machines. I fear power outages but am assured by the staff that there are backup systems.

I however, have no backup system at the moment. Allen jumps up to bring me a paper plate of pizza and a glass of iced tea. We sit and move the Monopoly pieces around the board, not really playing, not really talking, until the streaks of sunrise peek though the dining room windows. We are just being together right now, treasuring one another's company like the survivors of a shipwreck. I think that, in a few more hours, we will all call in absent to our schools, allowing ourselves the luxury of sleep and visiting Ron when we have filled up on pancakes at Denny's.

More than pizza or pancakes or burnt hotdogs right now, we need time.

THINGS THAT BREAK

It was beautifully wrapped in silver paper and topped with a purple bow
But when it slipped from her hands and hit the pavement
One shake was enough to know
That this crystal pitcher, so carefully chosen
Would not be part of the bride's trousseau.

Crystal pitchers are not the only things that break.

Zippers break and will not slide
Carousels break and you cannot ride
Bones break and snap in two
Chalk can break, computers too
Thread, so fragile, can easily give way
Leaving the mending for another day
My grandmother's china, so dainty and rare
Will shatter to pieces if I do not take care.

Lots of things can break.

Friendships can fracture with one thoughtless word
Silence be broken by sounds best unheard
Families torn apart with strife
And marriages destroyed, souls damaged for life.
Dreams can be shattered like delicate, spun glass
And lives ripped apart and withered like grass.
Promises made and easily broken
Relationships torn by words left unspoken.

But sometimes the outside still looks good.
The wrapping is not torn. The bow is still in place.
We smile. We nod. We can save face.

It is easy to hide behind the pretty wrappings.

Like hearts that beat on in spite of the break
And spirits that falter beneath the deep ache
And churches that wander away from God
And feet that are bruised but continue to trod.
God is not fooled by our outward wrappings
He sees into our hearts, despite our trappings.

Are we so deaf
We cannot hear,
The sounds of broken glass so clear?
Wrapped up in silver and tied with a bow
These things are not fit for the Bride's trousseau.

CHAPTER SIX.

**BEFORE...
1999**

Electric shock therapy. Or it's better known term, ECT. It conjures up images of Frankenstein's monster being attached to electrodes that are ignited by a lightning bolt. But ECT, Dr. Malachi has told us, is a very safe and often effective way to treat patients who suffer from severe depression. After four weeks at Friends Hospital—four weeks of trekking up Roosevelt Boulevard on the weekends and holding the world together alone the other five days—Ron seems to be only a little better. He has graduated from a red band—which meant he needed constant supervision—to a yellow band. The yellow band allows him to accompany us to the cafeteria for ice-cream or for walks around the pond and through the quiet paths that border this mental institution. Despite the pastoral scenes, it is hard to forget that we are behind high and guarded walls.

Reese and I are in the waiting room—a different waiting room—while Dr. Malachi administers the first of Ron's ECT's. There will be eleven in all. We think we are prepared. Mild electric shocks would be sent through electrodes attached to various parts of Ron's body, stimulating nerve sensors that were now, in common jargon, all jangled up. There might be a temporary state of amnesia for a short while after the procedure. Ron will feel only mild sensations during the ECT, rather like static electricity shocks. It still seemed to me the stuff of science fiction novels and late night black and white movies, but Dr. Malachi has said the treatment was so safe and effective he would recommend if for his own mother.

I did not ask him if he had a mother.

Reese holds out high hopes for these treatments. He envisions Ron walking out of the treatment room a totally new man, all mental problems left behind. I busy myself with filling out insurance forms, wishing one of my own parents had come today as well. If this does not work, would will it do to Reese? Can I handle two depressed men?

Friends Hospital of Philadelphia was found in 1813 by the Religious Society of Friends, the Quakers. The institution was originally named, "The Asylum for Persons Deprived of the Use of Their Reason." It seems to aptly apply to Ron, no longer sure what socks to put on or how to tuck in the corners of the bedspread in the small room he now occupies alone. Historic photographs grace the hallways, pictures of the original Friends' Asylum, with its patient rooms along one corridor, patients playing croquet on the lawns, the miniature train that provided amusement to the residents, people working in vegetable gardens, and others strolling along wooded paths. There are also paintings of the founding

Quaker fathers: Thomas Scattergood, Isaac Bonsall, William Turke. At a time when many viewed the insane as less than human, Quakers saw "the true light that lighteth every person that cometh into the world (I John 1:9)". Somewhere inside Ron, I have to believe, there is still a light and a sense of reason.

In the four weeks that Ron has been behind these walls, Allen has been here only four times. He comes on Sundays after church, usually tucking a game of Stratego or chess under one arm, determined that his father will remember the intricate moves involved. The game box always sits on the table in the common room unopened and after a few minutes of trying to engage Ron in conversation, Allen takes out his Game Boy and entertains himself until it is time to accompany his father to the dining hall for ice cream bars. Dennis has not been here yet. It is doubtful he will ever come. With a personality similar to Ron's, he sees himself reflected in his dad's face; it is too close for comfort. He prefers not to confront the abyss. And Bonnie? She, as usual, will never let me come alone because, "It's a pretty scary place." While not really the creepy stuff of B movies, Ron is still housed behind locked doors.

Reese generally drives us up on Sundays. Allen counts the cars abandoned and stripped of their tires along the way. Bonnie keeps up a cheerful line of conversation with me while Reese sits stoically behind the wheel.

"He seems better," my father-in-law will say on the way back. "Don't you think he seems better?" And I will acquiesce that perhaps he seems a little better but still has to be at Friends for a while longer. I am determined that my husband stay as long as his needs and the insurance allows.

Despite the air conditioning, it is warm in the room where we wait for Ron's first ECT to end. I am finished with the insurance forms. Since I had left the employ of The Christian Academy at the end of June, we are now funneling everything through Ron's insurance company and Medicare. When I begin my new job as a sixth grade teacher at Westtown in September, my new insurance will also kick in.

The decision to leave The Christian Academy has been a difficult one. I had taught high school English there for the last three years. I had come to love the staff and the students. The salary I earned was not large, but it was enough for a second income.

That changed the night Ron was taken to the crisis center and stripped of his shoelaces and his belt. Now into July, it looked doubtful that Ron would be able to resume his job anytime soon.

In the meantime, I had an offer from Westtown on the table, a phone call suggested to a dean by a graduate school professor. I had no idea where or what Westtown was, but I had visited the campus the very day before Ron's breakdown. I called the principal at the middle school the day Ron was carted off to Friends and told her that, due to our current status, I would have to decline her offer. Phyllis, principal, called back a week later and urged me to reconsider.

I went to Pastor Tripler for advice, my usual list of pros and cons in my hand. The salary I made at The Christian Academy would not pay the mortgage and feed my family. The salary Westtown offered would.

"Your choice seems simple," said Pastor Lou. "Your first obligation is to your family."

"But what about teaching in a Christian school?"

He smiled. "Quakers are Christians. Professing Christians, anyway. I can imagine you shaking them up a bit. But, Linda," he put his hand over mine, "you were called to teach. It seems to me that this offer is from God's hands so that you can care for your family."

I nodded, tears streaming down from my eyes. I knew then that I would tender my resignation to the principal and headmaster at TCA. I folded up my pro and con list and put it away, rising to leave.

"And how are you in all this?" asked Pastor Lou.

I shrugged. "Okay."

"That's what you always say."

"I'm handling it," I said. "Do I have a choice?"

He thought a minute, his eyes fixed on mine and his hand still over mine. "Yes," he said finally. "You do have other choices. But none that you would choose. Still," and he hesitated, "if this all becomes too much for you, if Ron cannot recover, if at some point you feel you just cannot continue to carry his burdens as well as your own, I want you to know that I would not rebuke you. I would understand. And so would God."

Bonnie accompanied me to TCA the next day where I spent hours packing up my room into cardboard boxes and orange milk crates. As head of the English Department, I had started a systematic cataloguing of the novels assigned in each grade. The principal, Anita, came down to my room to tell me I did not have to finish it. With tears in my eyes, I told her that I would indeed finish it and leave it as my legacy. She hugged me and whispered, "You leave more than this."

It is now almost an hour after Ron has been ushered into the treatment room; the door opens to release him. He shuffles out, his head hanging low, his mouth slack, reminding me of models I have seen of the evolutionists' idea of prehistoric man. Half-ape, half-man. Not really human. His arms dangle at his side loosely. My heart jumps into my throat and I gasp.

I have destroyed him, I think. *Now he really is a hollow man.*

But Reese is on his feet in an instant, clapping a hearty hand onto Ron's back. "Wow! You look better! Do you feel better? You're walking just like a man!"

When I get home from the hospital that day, I place my wedding band in the box it came in over twenty years ago. The plain gold band winks at me from the velvet lining. In the first year of our marriage, I glanced at it often, winding it around my finger with my thumb and enjoying the smooth, cool feel of it. It was, the minister had pointed out, a perfect and unbroken circle. The intervening years had worn the band thin in spots and left the engraving on the inside hard to discern. *To LKW Forever RAC.* The ring comes off my finger with a slight rug, not the wrenching pain I had expected. Perhaps I was now beyond pain. I close the lid on the box and tuck it into my lingerie drawer, not certain that I will ever wear it again.

OUTWARD CHANGES

(Inspired by Fiona during Meeting for Worship)

Six weeks ago, he was like a thousand other men—
Maybe taller—
Going to work every day at a job he didn't really like
And coming home to his family each night.
A good man.
Not a rich man.
Not famous.
But good.

Now he is fed through a tube
Has a drain in his pancreas
Walks with a limp
And does not always remember what you say to him.

But on the inside, where it counts,
He is still the same good man.
Not rich.
Not famous.
But good.

And I hate to think that sometime, somewhere
Someone will look at him and only see
That he is fed through a tube
Has a drain in his pancreas
Walks with a limp and doesn't always remember what you say to him
And not see that, inside, where it counts
He is still the same good man.

CHAPTER SEVEN.

APRIL 12, 2000. 4PM.

Wild violets have grown up in the backyard. I discovered them—tiny stars of purple against green crabgrass—as Allen and I raked and trimmed. I wonder how they have survived the harsh winter, the ice and frost of neglect. Yet they have grown, struggling to push themselves out of the hard earth towards the pale spring sunshine. Despite last summer's drought and the sub-zero temperatures of winter, they have survived and now grace my backyard with their beauty.

They remind me of the past seven weeks, spent on hold in waiting rooms and hospital lounges. Just this morning on our way to visit their father, I said to the two offspring that were with me, "We're a tough family. It takes a lot to knock us down."

"We take a lickin' and keep on tickin'", my youngest quipped and we laughed.

But there is a lot of truth in Allen's words. We have taken a beating. No one could argue that. Ron's ongoing hospitalization has thrown obstacles and burdens our way that we could never have imagined. Long and complicated surgeries. Mounting medical bills. A leaky water heater. Car repairs. Yet, we have not been beaten. We have struggled to survive, pushing our heads above our circumstances and seeking out the sun.

I pause in my raking, marveling at the beauty of these wildflowers. The Book of Matthew tells us to "Behold the fields in all their glory; even King Solomon was not arrayed as one of these." The purple majesty of these small flowers is a gift from God, a miracle of the cycle of the seasons and a reminder of Christ's resurrection. That these violets have survived against all odds in a testimony to God's grace.

Our family has survived. Allen is bagging up brown, winter-torn leaves at the end of the yard. His back is straight, his form tall. The shillelagh remains inside most days, propped beside his bed. The backyard no longer holds monsters and there are no more terrors of the evening. In the dark, dankness of tragedy and despair, the children and I have continued to feel the warm love of God.

We are peeking our own heads out now, allowing our bruised spirits to be warmed by the sun. We are secure. We are safe. We do not know what tomorrow may bring. We do not know when Ron may come home. We are not yet sure if he will recover from his wounds. The predicted two weeks have lengthened into time not measured by human calendars.

The medical chart at the end of Ron's bed read like this on our morning visit: *Patient moved to step-down unit. Morphine infuser out. Dressing off arm and chest. Ultra sound on lung and chest X-*

ray. PT walked patient down the hall. Still on O2 but seems to be breathing better.

The phone rings constantly and people leave messages. I send e-mails in the evenings, saving myself hours of phone calls and spending time with my kids. We are in a calm period now, a few days with no emergency phone calls and no surgeries.

But we have no guarantees that this will last. Our battle is far from over.

Allen and I have finished our chores now. I point out the wild violets to him. He bends his lanky form down, touching them with his hand. Like these violets, he is starting to turn his head towards the sun.

Maybe, just maybe, we will yet come into the light of summer.

APRIL 14, 2000. 1PM

Her nametag identifies her as Karen and she is an RN. But she is not dressed in scrubs or wearing a white uniform. Instead, she has on a black skirt and a stylish pink jacket. I rub at the sleeve of my own green sweater, aware of the chalk board I brushed up against before I left my classroom an hour ago.

"What we need to do," she says, "is to figure out what will be the best course for Ronald now that he is ready to be released from the hospital." It is still incredible to me that Ron is leaving, being booted out of One North—our home away from home—and sent out into the world with his central line and his feeding tube and his pancreatic and lung drains. Maneuvering him down the hallway to therapy requires two orderlies. Yet they expect that I will be able to manage him at home? "Of course," says Karen brightly, "there will be a hospice nurse coming in three times a day. So," she continues, "what hours are you home during the day?"

I shake my head. We have had this conversation on the phone already, but perky Karen has refused to believe that I am "never home" and has insisted that I review my schedule before meeting her at the hospital today. I take my calendar out of my ever-present book bag. Never know when an extra-long surgery might give me time to grade a few papers or read a few chapters. "Well," I say, "I am out of the house by 6:30. I drop Allen off at school around 6:45 and then drive to my school."

"Every day?" she asks, as if this daily routine is somehow abnormal.

I nod. "Yes. Then I am at school until 3:30. But on Tuesdays and Thursdays I tutor students after school, so it's more like 4:30. And on Monday there is a faculty meeting until 5:00. On Wednesday I have class at West Chester until 7:00. So the earliest I am ever home from school is 4:30, but most evenings it's more like 6:00. And on Wednesdays it's 8:00."

"So that leaves Fridays and the weekends," she says brightly. "You're home then, aren't you?

"Sort of," I answer. I know I am disappointing her. "I usually spend time at the library doing research on my master's thesis. So I'm not really home a great deal of the time."

"Ummm," she says. How can the sound be accusatory? What kind of wife am I, it seems to imply, not to rearrange my schedule to bring my invalid husband home? "What about your children?" she asks. "Who takes care of them when you're at work?"

"They take care of them," I say. "They don't need someone all the time. But apparently Ron will." The kids and I have had this discussion last night. Yes, we want Ron home, but only if there is fulltime nursing care. To think of me adding his daily care to my already over-packed schedule is ludicrous.

"Ummmm." That sound again. "Suppose you cut out the graduate class this semester? That would work, wouldn't it?"

I shake my head. "No, that would not work. I'm already halfway into the semester. Too late to bail out." Not that I would anyway. Too much depends on my getting my master's degree. There are several more moments of silence. She taps her pencil against Ron's medical chart, looks over the information she has written down, and sighs. Disappointed.

"Well," she drawls, "perhaps Ronald coming home just now isn't the best idea. Let me see. Your insurance"—and she refers to the chart—"would provide for a rehabilitation center. Maybe that would be best until he's a bit more stable."

I heave a sigh of relief. Yes. Much better. The thought of being responsible for Ron's various gadgets and wires has terrified me for twenty-four hours. I would rather tell Reese Ron is not coming home and let him heap the blame on me than risk doing something wrong or misreading some vital monitor.

"Alright," says Karen. "Let me see where there are beds available and get back to you." She names several possibilities. Two of them are relatively close to our house and might make my life marginally easier.

I drop in at Ron's room briefly to tell him what we've decided. He is disappointed he is not coming home, but I breezily reassure him that it won't be long now. I take a peek at the medical chart Karen has handed to me to hang at the end of his bed.

Speech pathologist will contact wife regarding short term memory loss. Some blood may be collecting in left lung. Patient walked three hundred feet with assistance. Running slight fever, spikes at night. Will be released home when home care can be set up.

Karen has crossed out the last line and written, *to rehab center when an available bed is found. Wife feels incapable of handling the demands.*

Darn right, I think. Wife is incapable of handling anything else at the moment. Let Wife figure it all out first.

Karen calls Westtown that afternoon and leaves a message. She has found a bed at Harlee Manor, a rehabilitation center in Springfield. It is further from our house than the hospital by about twenty miles. An ambulance will transport Ron there tomorrow. Will I please come and pack up his things and sign the necessary papers? It is Friday, so luckily I can leave at 3:30 and make my way to the hospital. For the last time.

The nurses on One North are sorry to lose Ron. He has been a good patient and our family has been a frequent and cheerful presence on the floor. In fact, the nurses early on allowed me to assume some of Ron's care, helping him to wash and shave, and changing his hospital gown. I know where the clean sheets and towels are kept. Still, his possessions are meager and there is not much to pack. He will need to wear street clothes at Harlee, Karen has told me. I have brought several outfits for Ron, but I will pack a suitcase and bring more to the rehab center tomorrow. We will need to do his laundry while he is there. My mother-in-law, sweet woman, has volunteered for this duty.

APRIL 15, 2000. 9AM.

Saturday. All of the nurses on One North come to say goodbye and wish us luck. Dr. Huffman arrives to sign the release papers. She hugs me and asks if perhaps we can meet for coffee sometime. "You are an extraordinary woman," she says, but I don't feel extraordinary, just depleted. Harlee Manor is a good half-hour drive from our house on the oft-congested Blue Route. I have not yet figured out a direct route there from Westtown. Bonnie and Allen are both with me today and we carry Ron's things out to my ancient 1985 Celebrity. It, too, has taken a lickin' and keeps on tickin'. We wait with Ron for the ambulance to arrive. Once he is safely strapped into the back, his tubes and lines now the responsibility of a new team, the kids and I head to Harlee Manor.

It is not hard to find. On the outside, there is a large porch that winds around the front of the building. Parking is difficult but we find a spot near the entrance. Luckily, Ron's possessions are still few. Inside, it is dark and overcast. The halls are filled with elderly people shuffling in their walkers. Ron, at forty-eight, will be the youngest person in the building. His roommate is a gentleman approaching eighty who does not talk. We find out later that he does rifle through Ron's drawers during the night and one morning is found wearing one of my husband's shirts. There is the usual raft of paperwork to be filled out. Television and phone are, of course, extra. I write the check and hand it over.

And then we wait. The ambulance is taking its time getting here. We explore the recreation hall; it consists of several large round tables and a TV set. "There were more things to do at Friends'", says Allen. We are all so savvy about various hospitals now. We end up on the portico, playing a game with the cards Allen has in his pocket. The nutritionist comes to speak to me. She is concerned that Ron is not getting enough nutrition through his "banana pudding" bag. Duh. She has no solution.

It is close to four O'clock when the ambulance finally arrives. Ron's central line has pulled out somewhere on the Blue Route and they had to return to the hospital to have it reinserted. Wouldn't that have been a good thing for his waiting family to know? We get Ron settled and take him on a slow tour of the facilities. There isn't a lot to see. The staff seems kind and caring but I cannot really imagine Ron in this place for long. His feeding machine needs to be switched to one owned by the rehab. There is some difficulty finding the right size tubing. The first machine brought in does not pump and needs to be taken away. The second one works but makes a loud noise. The staff will find a new one on Monday, I am told.

We stay until eight O'clock. There is no cafeteria where we can grab a salad or a burger so the kids and I are starving by the time we leave. We will be back after church tomorrow, we promise Ron. We would call him tonight but the phone line will not be hooked up until Monday.

And so we leave him here, among the octogenerarians and well-meaning but harried nurses, cut off from communications with us for the time being. We go home and try to sleep, although guilt weighs me down.

APRIL 23, 2000. 7AM.

Palm Sunday. Rainy. There is a faint rumble of thunder. Raindrops tap on the roof and splatter across the windowpane and my own teardrops add to the melancholy of the day. It has been forty-five days that Ron has lain in one hospital bed or another, waiting for his damaged body to heal. Forty-five days that I have spent facing the world alone and struggling to hold our lives together.

I am far beyond exhaustion and yet my mind cannot sleep. I awake at odd hours for no apparent reason and watch the luminescent numbers of the digital clock tick away. Tears, so carefully controlled for most of these six weeks, are never far from the surface.

Palm Sunday. Certainly we expected him home by now, if not totally healed at least on the road to recovery, free from tubes and machines and back with us again. Instead, a high fever yesterday sent him from the rehab center back to the hospital where the doctors are still searching for the source of infection. Pancreas? Lungs? My limited knowledge of the human anatomy has grown by leaps and bounds and I can now easily talk with medical personnel of enzyme levels and pancreatic fluids. We are back on One North again. It almost seems like we have come home.

Guilt burdens me and I ask myself why I did not rearrange my life and let him come home. Would I have noticed the signs of pneumonia sooner? Perhaps not, but I would have made sure his slippers were not stolen, forcing him to walk the tiled halls barefoot. I would have talked to him and spent time holding his hand so he did not become discouraged. If he had been home, if would have been different. Or so I tell myself.

My friends tell me it is not my fault. My father-in-law tells me that it is. Who am I to believe? For now, I can only pace the halls of the hospital again, praying for him with every ounce of energy I possess.

But I cannot heal him. Only God can do that.

Palm Sunday. Despite the rain, the birds still chirp and sing. Perhaps they know something we do not. Or is their faith in the

Father so great that they do not question that the sunshine will eventually follow the rain? When I was a kid, Palm Sunday meant getting the palm branches at morning mass, hearing the homily of Jesus' ride into Jerusalem, and anticipating a week off from school. Today it is a reminder to me of our Savior's deliberate actions in going to Jerusalem, in full knowledge of what awaited Him there. But He did it anyway. For us. For me. For Ron.

It does not heal Ron's body or bring him home. But it does redeem his soul. Whatever battering his physical being and his mental state have taken, his soul remains intact. It is a cause for rejoicing.

The birds know what they are doing.

APRIL 24, 2000. 10 PM.

I sleep on Ron's side of the bed most nights. It sags a bit from his greater weight and I curl myself into the hollow, seeking the familiar. It has been a slow trek across the expanse of my queen-sized mattress.

I began, in those first days after the accident, on my accustomed side of the bed, struggling to block out the sounds of crashing metal from my ears and the image of my husband's battered body from my eyes. After Bonnie and Allen returned to their own rooms at night, I would toss and turn, clutching the pillows for comfort. The silence hung heavily; no sounds of sonorous breathing punctuated the night, no leg flung over mine pressed me to the mattress. No warm presence wrestled with the sheets or snatched the covers from my shoulders. My nights were quiet. Empty. Lonely. Slowly, I inched my way to the middle, gradually leaning towards Ron's side and the pillow that still smelled faintly of his aftershave.

The middle of the bed was awful. I felt like the spine of a book with two wide, wide margins on either side of me, great expanses of unfilled space where once, or so it seemed, there had hardly been enough room for two. I continued my progression towards the other side, creeping across the cold sheets, seeking comfort and warmth.

And so I sleep on Ron's side now, sniffing the male fragrance that still clings to his pillows, wrapping my own arms around my waist and waiting out the long hours until morning. There are times when I sleep soundly, then awaken suddenly, startled to find myself facing the room from a different angle, closer to the closet, further from the door.

Perhaps this change is good for my point of view. Perhaps I was too secure, too boxed in. I awaken now, seeing what Ron used to see each morning. And praying that he will again.

PEOPLE SAY

*People say that
They know how I feel
And they compare this last season
That Ron has been hospitalized to
"the time my mother had pneumonia"
Or
"the two weeks I was on bed rest before the baby was born."
Trust me.
It is not the same.
Just as I don't know what those times were like for you
You cannot possibly know what this has been like for me.
I have been, for all this time,
Without my partner, my soul mate, my sounding board.
I have coped with the world
Alone.
I feel as if an arm has been severed from my body
As if my heart has stopped beating
And I have been holding my breath for
A long, long, time.
I kept putting one foot in front of the other because
The world has not stopped
But kept its turning. And I have faced it
Alone.
So, to those of you who offer comfort,
I give you my thanks, but know that
Despite your compassion*

You don't really understand.
Only God does.
Lord, help me to remember this lesson,
To offer compassion
Not comparisons.
To have the courage to say,
"I don't really know what this has been like for you,
But God does."
In Him
I am never
Alone.

CHAPTER EIGHT

APRIL 30, 2000. 1 AM.

Early on Easter Sunday, I sit at my laptop and write a letter I will never send:

Dear Other Driver,

I've thought about you a lot this week as we approached the holiest of Christian holidays and Ron underwent yet another operation to repair the damage your truck did to his body. This was a second thoroscopy. Do you know what that is? Neither did I until recently. Surgeons needed to make an incision in Ron's back between his third and fourth ribs, spread the ribs apart, and insert a tube to drain the fluid that has collected around his left lung. They made another incision into his chest to re-inflate the lung. This Easter Sunday, while his family attended church services, Ron remained in the hospital, a pleuravac pumping out the fluid, a tube still draining his pancreas, an IV still giving him antibiotics and morphine, another tube feeding him.

And I thought about you and wondered what you, the other driver, would do this Easter Sunday. Attend the church of your choosing? Sleep late? Enjoy dinner with family and friends? It's nice to have options, isn't it? We wish Ron had them.

I could, if I wanted, get your name from the police report. It is in my files. And, in this day of the world-wide web, it would be easy to find you. But I prefer to think of you as nameless and faceless. It's easier that way. Allowing you to have an identity would make you too real. There is a chance—however slim—that I could feel sympathy for you. Or hate. I am not a vindictive person, but the longer Ron remains in intensive care, the more surgeries and complications that arise, the more time our children miss with their father, the angrier I get.

In the fifty-one days since the accident, have you ever thought of Ron? Does the blur of the accident plague your dreams? Do you still speed down Paoli Pike and run red lights? Or does the memory of March 1 cause you to slow down—maybe a little—as you pass Five Points Road?

Ron's accident has changed our lives. There is no going back. I hope it has changed yours as well. It is the only way I can find any reconciliation with this whole, awful event. It is the only way I can sleep.

Easter Sunday. The day Jesus rose from the ground, the penalty for our sins fully paid. It is a day of rejoicing and hope for those who believe in Him. Despite the fact that Ron remains hospitalized, and the children and I will attend church without him and dine without him, it is a blessed day for us. Christ lives. Ron lives. We have hope. We have peace.

Do you?

May 2, 2000. 7AM

This morning we awakened to a light coating of snow! This crystal surprise—so late in the spring—reminded me of the enchantment of childhood, when a snowstorm on Sunday was guarantee of a Monday free from school, frolicking in the soft, white powder.

Ah, snow! Despite the damage and the hazards a snowstorm can cause, who does not delight in watching the gently falling flakes, pressing our noses against the windowpane? Snow brings magic.

It is magic reminiscent of Frosty and his enchanted hat, reindeer that can fly, and ice queens whose hearts can be melted by love. Snow makes us children once again, inspiring us with wonder. It makes us believe, if only briefly, in magic.

It demonstrates to us once again God's power and control over the world.

Ron is still in the hospital.

My water heater still leaks.

My bank account holds a negative balance.

There are a thousand questions to which I have no answers.

But tiny crystalline structures, no two alike, each a unique and beautiful creation, fall from the sky and astound me once again with their beauty.

God is still in control. It's all I really need to know.

MAY 8, 2000. 4PM.

Life on One North is predictable. Now settled in a room near the nursing station, free from the pancreatic drain, Ron is starting to look more like a human being. Slowly, his pancreas is digesting food and while the central line will remain in for a while longer, lime gelatin and chicken broth now work their way into his system. He is pale. Like legendary vampires, he has not seen the sun. We make his room as cheerful as we can. A poster saying, "Get Well Soon!" and signed by every student at Westtown Middle School decorates an entire wall. Each day, I tack up new cards sent by my students, oblivious to the marks I am making on the wall. Doctors and nurses come in daily to read the new arrivals.

There are flowers and books and treats he cannot yet eat but shares with frequent visitors. Balloons are tied to his bed rail. The infection is gone, his lungs are clear, and the pleuravac has been moved to the aid of someone else. Dr. Huffman talks about him going back to rehab.

But I cannot let that happen. The guilt that surrounded me from the pneumonia incident still grips me. Despite the care he will need, I will bring him home when he is ready. I will rearrange my life. I will give up sleeping. But I will not send him back to Harlee Manor.

Dr. Huffman comes in for her daily chat, admiring the cards

on the wall and the fresh bouquet of flowers from the church. Kelvin from Ron's plant has just been here and given me an envelope of money collected from the guys on Ron's floor. It will pay the mortgage this month. I make a mental note to send an e-mail thanking them all. At least twenty people from Heinz have asked me to add them to my weekly updates. Most will e-mail me back.

I continue to pray for you and your family.
I admire your strength and faith.
Please let me know if there is anything I can do.
You should be a writer; I love reading your reports on Ron!

Joanne smiles at me. "Yes, I think…I really think…we can talk about releasing Ron. I want to keep an eye on his lungs, do another X-ray tomorrow to make sure we won't have a relapse of pneumonia. But everything else looks good." She looks over the chart. "Is Friday afternoon good for you?" It is like Joanne to always be concerned with my schedule and not expect me to bend to hers.

I nod. "I can be here by 4. Will the visiting nurse be able to come on Saturday? Or will we will be on our own until Monday?"

Joanne pauses to think. "I'll talk to them myself, tell them that someone needs to come Friday night and Saturday. Can you get someone to be with Ron while you are at work? His parents, maybe?"

I nod with more optimism than I feel. "We'll work it out."

"I have a few suggestions," she says. "Get a little refrigerator in his bedroom or at least an ice chest. Keep water and juice in it so he doesn't get dehydrated. And put some extra cushions on your chairs. Ron's going to have trouble getting up and down. You have steps?" I nod. "He shouldn't use them alone. And I don't think you're the candidate to help him up and down. His dad, maybe?"

"Maybe," I say. "We'll work it out." My mind has gone into overdrive. This is Wednesday and I have a conference with Allen's teacher tonight. Tomorrow is graduate school. When, exactly, will I pull all of this together? I remind myself that this is about Ron, not me. He's coming home. He needs to be home.

MAY 8, 2000. 8PM.

Cris has been Allen's caseworker for two years now. As the mother of a special education student, I assist with the writing of Allen's Individualized Educational Program (IEP) each year. Cris has been sympathetic to Allen's feelings these last few months. She is jubilant that Ron is coming home.

"Allen worries, you know," she confides to me. "At first, after Mr. Cobourn's accident, he seemed really withdrawn and scared. I thought about referring him to Dr. Purcell." I nod, knowing Cris would have called me had it remained a concern. "But then it seemed as if he grew up. It was kind of amazing to see." I smile and tell her the story of the shillelagh. She presses a hand to her pregnant belly. "I can't wait to be a mom," she says. "So many wonderful things happen!"

Allen will be mainstreamed into a regular science class next year and I am concerned about the textbook he will be expected to use. Cris says she will give me a copy of the book and put me in touch with the science teacher he'll have. I make some notes on ways to adapt the book to Allen's needs: go over the vocabulary with him ahead of time, make outlines, read ahead. Cris and I talk about the adjustments Allen will need to make with his dad back him again. "Good ones," she says. "But we'll all be understanding if his attention in class wanders. There are bound to be challenges."

It is 9:00 when I leave the middle school and I thank Cris exuberantly for her time. She has been a mainstay to Allen this year. "Good luck," she says and gives me a hug. She has sent me several notes during this interim, assuring me that she is praying for our family. I tell her I will pray for her and the new baby.

I remember this clearly: looking up at the stars as I come out of the school and cross the parking lot to my car. I remember marveling at the distance to the stars, the miracle of light reaching us millions of years after it has left its own planet. I remember breathing deeply and holding the air in my lungs, letting it out slowly. I remember thanking God that Ron was on his way home and praying for the strength to handle it. I remember thinking, "We made it."

When I arrive home there is a message, carefully written out and left by the phone. *Call Dr. Azer at the hospital. Very important.* There is a beeper number beside the message.

My heart sinks.

MAY 8, 2000. 10 PM.

"I tried to reach Dr. Huffman," says the very young Dr. Azer. She is blonde and pretty, dressed in green scrubs and the same type of surgical clogs Joanne wears. "And when I couldn't, I called Dr. Thumble. He said to do a CT scan and reinsert the pic line. We've also got him hooked up to the telemetry machine because of the heart arrhythmia." She pauses at the door to the cardiac unit. "I don't want you to be alarmed by the machines," she says.

I want to laugh. I have seen more machines on my husband than she can possibly imagine. "I'll be okay," I assure her.

"I was doing rounds and I knew Mr. Cobourn was scheduled to be released on Friday. So when I noticed the fever and chest sounds, I was a little worried."

"So it's his lungs?" I ask.

She shakes her head. "I'm not sure. There are decreased breath sounds, but I really think it's an infection."

"We've been through several."

She nods sympathetically. "I've read over his chart. It's pretty thick. You guys have been through a lot."

"We thought it was over. Hoped it was over." I almost laugh.

Her blue eyes fasten on mine. "I wasn't really sure what to do, you know. It could have just been an elevation of temperature. Sometimes that happens at night." She is preaching to the choir. "But I wanted to be cautious. I know he's lost a lot of weight. We don't want him going home and coming right back."

I thank her for her thoroughness. I am relieved that the infection was caught before he came home. She leaves me at the door to Ron's room. "Just for a few minutes," she says. "Visiting hours are over, but the nurses will ignore you for a while." She promises to run some more tests in the morning and call me at school.

Ron is still awake when I enter his room, staring out the window. "Hey," I say. "I know you're disappointed. So are we."

He shrugs. "I thought I was ready to come home. I guess the time's not right yet." I hold his hand and we talk for a few minutes, trying to accept that we need to wait a while longer. We are both disappointed.

But I am lying to both Ron and myself. I am not so much disappointed as relieved. For a while longer, my critically ill husband will remain in someone else's charge.

COUNTING THE COST

The medical bills are insurmountable! No sense worrying about them!
There are far more important things that the careless act of a thoughtless driver has cost Ron, such as
Bonnie's B+ on a math test, a subject she struggles with
Allen's new moves on his skateboard
The way our new kitten presses his nose against mine in the morning
Family Monopoly Night
Our daughter in her new Easter hat
The daffodils blooming in the backyard
Lighting candles the night the power goes out
Sunday comics spread over the living room rug
Dennis's new hair cut
Watching the sunset from the back deck
Allen standing up to Mike—finally!
Pizza on Tuesdays and Buffy the Vampire Slayer
Doing the dishes and blowing soap bubbles

Life is made up of countless insignificant moments that will never come again.

For countless days, in countless ways, Ron has missed them.
They are gone forever.

CHAPTER NINE

MAY 12, 2000. 3 PM.

My friend's husband is going on a pilgrimage to Chakra, where he intends to walk the labyrinth. Before he leaves, he asks people to write down the burdens they are carrying onto slips of paper. He collects them all solemnly, puts them in his backpack, and promises he will stop at each turn of the labyrinth to pray for those whose burdens he now carries with him.

A lot of the burdens he carries are mine.

Ron is still in the hospital, back in intensive care as be fights off the latest infection. Each day brings new tubes and new problems. Seeing him is painful and I am beginning to wonder how one human being can ever recover from so much physical damage. I am worn out and tired, dragging myself through each day. It has occurred to me that these burdens may be mine to carry for a long, long time. Bonnie is having a difficult semester at school, her mind always on her father. Some of Allen's old fears have returned and he sees "bad guys and monsters" in the shadows.

So I wrote all of these things down and put them in Denis' back pack.

Denis will be at Chakra for six days. And during those six

days, whenever I am tempted to fret about the course of events that have overtaken our lives, I will remind myself that Denis now carries my burdens around the labyrinth. Someone else is doing the fretting and the praying and the worrying. I can cast my cares upon Denis for these six days and in the maelstrom that has become my existence, I can find a place of calm.

I think of the symbolism here. Just as Denis carries my burdens to Chakra, Jesus bore my sins to the cross. But His promise goes far beyond that. Jesus wants to carry our burdens every day. Even now, when my weariness is overwhelming, Jesus wants my burdens. So why do I fret and worry?

Because I am human. God knows this about me. Jesus warned his disciples in Luke 21:34 that they "take heed to yourselves, lest at anytime you be overcharged with…the cares of this life." Just as I so easily added my slips of paper to Denis' pack, so I should easily give them over to the Savior.

Yet I seem to hold onto them, unable to let go.

MAY 25, 2000. 1 PM.

I can hear the sounds of my students on the playground, shouting in the clear spring sunshine. Winter has finally given way to some crisp, clear days. I lean my head against the cool metal frame of the stall in the Ladies' Room, seeking some comfort for my aching right eye. Two days ago I was forced to admit that the pain—manageable with ibuprofen for the last week—was out of control. My ophthalmologist berated me for waiting so long to come in and I did not explain that I have been living inside the walls of a hospital for three months. Three of the remaining ten sutures in my eye had come lose and needed to be removed. What a blessed, twenty-four hour release from the throbbing pain when Dr. Morris anesthetized the eye to remove the stitches! But the ache was back now, complicated by the infection I had inadvertently caused by waiting too long. I avoid light whenever I can and keep my classroom in semi-darkness.

I am reluctant to leave the peaceful quiet of the restroom, but the bell will ring soon to signal the end of recess. A stack of books sits on my desk and taunts me; I have a final next week. My professor has offered me the opportunity to take an incomplete for this semester and finish over the summer, but I cannot even imagine what challenges the next season may hold. So I plow ahead, determined to finish what I began before the world collapsed around me. I have opted out of the summer term. I simply have no energy left.

Talk in class last night turned to stress. Are teachers more prone to stress than other professionals? And I sat behind my dark glasses, my right eye throbbing, wondering if anyone in the room could possibly comprehend the amount of stress in my life. Yet I try to remain calm, putting one foot in front of the other and moving on.

We are all moving on. Bonnie has finished her first year at Delaware County Community College and while it has been an exceedingly difficult year, she has scraped by. About a month ago it looked as if she would not make it so—against her wishes—I called her professors and told them what had been going on in her life. They were all sympathetic and gave her chances to make up work she had missed during long night hospital vigils. She was seeing a young man from work for a while, but that fizzled out in April. She seems none the worse for it. I admit I hardly noticed the changes in her social status, so erratic are my own hours these days.

And Allen is once again the man of the house. In church on Sunday, the pastor asked us to join hands in prayer and when mine was gripped by a firm, strong grasp to my right, I almost gasped. Was this the hand of my youngest son? It felt like a man's hand, certain and sure. I found my own hand enveloped in that of a fourteen year old. I was not totally unaware of the changes that time has wrought upon this child. He is eye-level with me now and certain mannerisms reflect his father and his brother. The way he reaches for his wallet, squares his shoulders, answers the phone with a masculine, "Hello." These are reminders to me that my youngest child is striving towards adulthood. As the long, strong fingers closed over mine and applied pressure to my palm, I recalled the small hand that held mine on his first day of school. Then, he was the one to cling to me.

Mommy, don't let go.

Sometimes, now, I find myself clinging onto him and I remind myself that my children completely fill the void left by their father. My children have their own lives to lead. But the longer Ron remains hospitalized, the more accustomed I become to our family unit numbering three. When I think of the future, making sketchy plans as to where we might be in a year or so, I see Bonnie and Allen and me. Ron is added as a hasty afterthought.

I hear the recess bell ring. Time to leave my sanctuary. I check myself in the mirror to see if I can in any way resemble a sane person for the rest of the afternoon. I am emerging from the Ladies', on my way back to my own classroom, when I see the principal walking down the hall towards me, carrying a pink phone message slip. There are tears in Phyllis' eyes.

A cold hand grips my heart. I collapse against the wall. Can I pretend not to see her? If I just go on into English class, won't it all just go away?

But Phyllis grabs my arm before I can reach my own classroom. "I'll cover for you," she says. "You need to go."

I wonder what organ has broken now, what complication has set in that the doctors had not foreseen. I wonder, nonsensically, if there will be any supper tonight. Then I notice that, despite the tears, Phyllis is smiling.

She offers me the pink message slip and I glance at Dr. Huffman's name scrawled across the bottom. Phyllis puts her arms around me. "He's coming home," she says. "They're releasing him now. He's finally coming home."

FRAGMENTS

Pressed between the pages
Of the pandemonium
Bits of dried posies
Shattered and scattered
Still retain a sweet
Fragrance.
Clutched by the clutter of
The chaos
Pieces of color
Broken and blended
Still gleam a clear
Clarity.
I am not yet obscured by
The obligations of
My family
Just pared into pilfered pieces
And dispersed among
The tumult.

CHAPTER TEN.

MAY 30, 2000. 3 PM.

Ron's birthday. Today we gather to celebrate his 49th year, and all of us present think about how close he came to not reaching this milestone. Just weeks ago, he hovered closer to the other side than to us. But, by God's grace, he is home again and if not yet completely well, at least on the road back. It will be, we are painfully aware, a long and difficult road.

His homecoming has made changes both large and small in our home. We have rearranged the furniture to accommodate his physical needs and arranged for care while I finish out the school year. I jump out of bed at all hours of the night if he needs something, if he is in pain or cannot breathe. My exhaustion continues, but at least I am no longer spending time in hospital rooms. The kids and I all hover closer to home these days, reluctant to put distance between ourselves and Ron. Even our grown son Dennis contrives errands that bring him home.

Our celebration today is simple: just burgers on the grill and ice cream cake. Ron's parents and our children are the only guests, but many cards continue to arrive in the mail and I write almost daily e-mail updates to an extended list of well-wishers. While Ron napped one afternoon, I sent out the following:

Dear Friends,

The lives of our family were forever altered on March 1, 2000. Even as we gathered in the ICU family room at Crozer Hospital, praying for Ron and waiting out the long hours while he underwent emergency surgery on his diaphragm, pancreas, and spleen, we knew God's arms were around us and we were at peace, trusting the life of our loved one to our Heavenly Father. We could not have known then that the long hours of evening would stretch into months spent pacing the floors and bowing our heads. Nor did we know that Ron's accident would come to affect so many outside our family circle.

God works all things together for good to them that love the Lord. We clung to that promise as complication after complication arose. Phone call to phone call, heads bowed and knees bent as God's people offered their prayers for Ron. Dr. Joanne Huffman continually worked to restore Ron's body, guided—we believe—by the Great Physician.

The faithful prayers of so many have uplifted Ron's family as well. Many, many times I received a phone call or a simple note reassuring me of prayers and support. Often, it was the encouragement I needed to keep on going. Every card, every visit, every phone call, every prayer, every meal given to us demonstrated God's abiding love through the obedient hands of His servants.

This has been what has guided us. The children and I have learned to lean heavily on God. Even when Ron's fever climbed and the poison of septic shock coursed through his veins, we knew our loved one was safe. Some tears flowed as we were, time and again, forced to acknowledge the possibility that Ron might be called Home.

God has chosen, instead, to being a new work, in Ron, in me, and in our children. We treasure each moment on earth as a gift from God and an opportunity to give glory to our Creator. These last three months we have had the opportunity to share our faith with many who crossed our path at Crozer Hospital: doctors, nurses, patients, visitors, and personnel. One dear man said to me one night as I sat praying outside the ICU, "Your God must be very big."

Our God IS big, but He is also the God of details. As Ron's body continues to heal, the ducts and the tubes and the organs that make up our earthly beings must begin to work together again. We trust that in God's own time Ron's healing will be complete.

We covet your continued prayers. We know that we still have many battles ahead. But we also know that God is in control. To say "thank you" to all of you is not enough. Our hearts are filled to overflowing with gratitude to all of you. We pray, in turn, for each of you. Rejoice in the part that you have played in our own miracle. Treasure, as we do, each moment as a precious gift.

In His Name,

Ron, Linda, Dennis, Bonnie, and Allen

Our party is soon ended. Ron's stamina fades quickly. He insists that he will go to church with us tomorrow, so I shoo everyone home at an early hour and settle Ron into bed. Dishes are piled in the sink, but I stand on the back deck, breathing deeply for the first time in months. Hours spent in too many waiting rooms have wrought changes in all of us. We need to focus now on what is really important.

It is not our bank accounts or job titles or clean kitchen floors. It is each other.

And yet, despite my upbeat attitude, despite the smile that is continually on my face, despite my belief that God really *is* in control, I do not really feel what I wrote in my cheerful letter. I do not feel elated or grateful or excited that Ron is home. I do not feel hopeful, although I will continue to spout the words I believe others want to hear from me. As I turn into the kitchen to attack the pile of dishes, I acknowledge to myself what I really feel.

I feel empty.

MAY 31, 2000. 10 AM.

Ron is carefully dressed in gray sweat pants and a blue Phillies jacket when we herd into the elevator at church the next morning. We arrived purposely during Sunday School so Ron will not be jostled in the hallway. His three-footed cane has inadvertently been left at the hospital. I will retrieve in on Monday. For now, Ron leans on Allen's shillelagh. It is ironic that it now lends support to another member of our family.

Ron's progression up the aisle is painfully slow, but we are in no hurry. Bonnie, Allen, and I stand ready to assist him if needed, but he manages to maneuver himself to a seat without our help. He is very thin now and his skin has a waxy pallor to it. His hair needs trimming. He does not look around until he is seated in a pew about halfway up the aisle.

"So here we are," he says and grins. "I missed this place." He comments on the flowers on the altar and I go the vestibule to get a bulletin for him. When I return, several deacons have spotted him and are busy pumping his hand and patting him—gently—on the back.

"It is a miracle," they are all saying. "To see you here, in one piece! God is good!" And I nod my head in agreement. God is good. My water heater still leaks and I have a final on Tuesday and I cannot sleep at night because Ron always needs something but God is good.

Other people are entering the sanctuary and most want to speak to Ron. But the organist begins and we take up our hymnals, rising for the first song. Ron sits, too wobbly to risk standing up.

Pastor Lou has spotted Ron and smiled in our direction. "Before we begin today," he says from the pulpit, "I would like us to give special thanks for God's graciousness in bringing our brother Ron home to us." Lou beams. "When I saw you, Ron, I knew that here was our own miracle. To see you here, in God's house, surrounded by your family, is proof once again of God's faithfulness."

I barely hear the rest of the service. After the final chorus, Ron is once again surrounded by well-wishers. Two deacons volunteer to see Ron down on the elevator while I pull the car around to the handicap entrance. I am hurrying down the hallway when a hand taps me lightly on the arm.

"Linda," says Pastor Lou, " as wonderful as it is that Ron is home, I worry about you. Is this all too much for you?"

I am frightened for a moment that Lou has read my thoughts and seen into my soul. Then I realize he has simply seen the dark circles under my eyes and noticed my fatigue. Nothing more. He cannot know that I do not really feel thankful right now, that my water heater still leaks and I have a final on Tuesday and I cannot sleep at night because Ron always needs something.

"I'm a little tired," I admit." But I'll be fine. Soon, school will be out and I will have a chance to catch up on some rest." I give him a bright smile. "The important thing is that Ron is home."

I can do this, I think as I pull the car up and Ron is helped in. I can keep on saying the words until I can feel them.

JUNE 7, 2000. 7:15 AM.

I drop Allen off at school at 7:15, but just as I am pulling out of the parking lot, my engine light glows amber. Generally, I ignore this sort of thing. I am usually in too big a hurry to stop and check and this morning is no exception. The last week of school is a hectic run through the chaotic gauntlet of middle school madness. But I am trying to let Ron's accident teach me something about slowing down. I drive a mile out of my way and pull into a service station. There is no attendant there, of course. Mechanics do not keep teacher hours. But there are a few truck drivers refueling their rigs. I unlatch the hood of my car and peer into the engine, trying to look like I know what I am doing. I must be pulling it off, because I am offered no assistance. Story of my life.

No smoke billows from the engine. I check my oil. Seems okay. I puzzle for a moment and sit with my engine turned off. The morning is clear and bright and despite the fumes from the diesel fuel I breathe deeply. Being late for school on the second to the last day might not be the worst thing in the world.

Slowly, I turn the key in the ignition again. The light does not go on. I wait. Still, no warning glow. I pull away from the service station, marginally less harried than I was when I left the house and determined to keep an eye glued to the dashboard. I leave the radio off and turn my thoughts to people I know who are in need of prayer. Kim, dying of leukemia with two small sons to raise. Angel, about to give birth to her first child far away from the comfort of her mother. Before I realize it, I am at school and there are still a few minutes before homeroom begins.

I walk from the parking lot to my classroom, thinking about

engine lights. I have been hurrying these last months, little realizing how fast I am moving. With teaching, graduate school, Ron's hospitalization, and a family to care for there has been little time for self-reflection. Since Ron's first bouts with depression, burdens he once shared are mine alone.

I have been guilty of rushing on, my own timetable paramount in my mind. Seldom have I taken the time to smell the proverbial roses. My own body's engine lights have been flickering for weeks now and I have been ignoring headaches and dizziness and the syndrome my grandmother called "bone-tiredness."

The macadam pathway curves before me. In just a few more steps I will be at the end of my road. I have canceled my usual flurry of summer activity this year, determined to spend my time helping Ron in his recovery. I will not be teaching classes at the Pennsylvania Writing Project. I will not be going to graduate school, postponing my Master's by a semester.

I have not come to this conclusion easily. I have been the irresistible force, determinedly plowing my way through all obstacles in quest of my goal. Neither rain, nor snow, nor dark of night…My purposes have been noble, I remind myself. Trying to provide for the well-being of my family is not a fault.

I descend the few short steps into my classroom, unlocking the door and flicking on the lights. I wonder why I have tried to continue on my impossible path. I love my classroom and my students. I love teaching. But I need the freedom of summer. I need time for my body and spirit to recover.

In three minutes my sixth graders will descend upon me, their high energy propelling me into this day. I will smile and nod, listening to their bright voices and cheerful summer plans. I will miss their chatter, but their voices will echo over the summer months.

For the last time this year I lay my lesson plans on my desk. The next three months are not laid out nearly as neatly. I have no idea what Ron's therapy and recovery will be like, nor what my role will be. The lack of a definitive plan scares me, but life has no carefully arranged outcome.

I can no longer ignore my own glowing amber lights, flashing at me incessantly. Somehow, I need to find a place of rest.

Yet even as the door to my room slams open and my students fill the void, I wonder. *Will my life ever be calm again?*

RUNNING

Into the morning light I run

Searching for the rising sun

Looking for a place of peace

Waiting for the pain to cease.

However far and fast I speed

I cannot quench my fearful need.

I run until the sun is high;

If I stop, I fear I'll die.

CHAPTER ELEVEN.

JUNE 25, 2000. 9 AM.

Despite the fact that I have been out of school for two weeks now, I am still dreaming of my classroom and waking up tense and tired. Last night alone I taught Geometry to a group of eight-graders, English to my sixth-grade home room, and Science to a bunch of toads who had hopped into my room from the lake down the road. Despite their jumpiness, the toads were by far the most attentive audience, having a true interest in biology and a vested state in animal rights.

What would a dream interpreter make of my nighttime pedagogy? A fear of eighth-graders? A secret desire to become a zoologist? Or a teacher who has found herself completely fried by a long year at a new school compounded by her husband's car accident and long hospitalization?

I have determined this summer to relax, but I attach it with the same ferocity I attack everything, laying up books I want to read and sketching out stories I want to write. Ron is doing well now. Probably better than I am since he has had four months of sitting still. I, on the other hand, am a whirlwind of motion. I have a list posted on the refrigerator of summer projects and another written in my journal of all the new things I have tackled this year. They both exhaust me. In the last ten months I have learned to:

1. Teach four different subjects to four different sections of students
2. Work through the atmosphere and pace of Westtown
3. Head up student council
4. Drive in the dark
5. Install light fixtures
6. Fix leaky pipes and water heaters
7. Learn to speak "Quaker"
8. Change the oil in my car
9. Stretch my paycheck
10. Use paper plates for meals
11. Take care of a cat
12. Start the lawn mower (that one was tricky!)
13. Pace hospital waiting rooms
14. Come to a working knowledge of the spleen and the pancreas
15. Deal with lawyers
16. Fill out medical forms

The list goes on and on. What I have not learned is that the world can probably manage to limp along without me. At the moment, it seems that I am still needed everywhere. I do not know how to just lay it all down and walk away.

JUNE 30, 2000. 7PM.

Today, Ron drove for the first time in over twenty weeks, maneuvering my ancient Celebrity down Naaman's Creek Road and into a parking lot at Target where we purchased a 26 inch tube for Allen's bike tire. A momentous journey. I sat in the unaccustomed passenger seat, an almost unwilling accomplice to my husband's maiden voyage.

I sat with my hands in my lap, my feet firmly planted on the floor, my stomach in knots, and my eyes darting everywhere. Front window. Rear window. Side window. Ron's face. Dr. Huffman had said to be prepared for a panic attack during the first drive. I was prepared, ready to offer reassurance, ready to grab the wheel, ready to dial 911 on my cell phone. I willed the trucks to stop at all the red lights, focused all my energy on keeping the car centered in the middle of the lane by my amazing kinesthetic powers. Due to my superior concentration alone, we made it to Target in one piece. Ron got out of the car—he still moves slowly—tossed me the keys, and sauntered into the store. I took a moment to breathe a prayer of thanks for journey's mercies and followed him, grateful for the cold blast of air-conditioning the struck me at the door, cooling my fevered brow.

Our errand took only a few short minutes but my erratic heartbeat returned to normal. We made our purchase, exited the store, and approached my car. I was breathing normally again.

Two steps to go. I approached the driver's side.

"I'll drive," said Ron, sidling neatly in front of me.

Dr. Huffman had warned us about panic attacks. She hadn't said they would be mine.

JULY 4, 2000. 9 PM.

June has too quickly given way to July and now we find it to be Independence Day. Or, as my grandmother called it, Declaration Day. In my carefree childhood, these holidays were always spent on the sands of Rehoboth Beach, cavorting with my cousins and my brother in the ocean's surf, cooking hot dogs and hamburger's on Nanny's back porch and playing horseshoes in front of Uncle Fred's cabin. Homemade ice-cream was the highlight, using Nanny's ancient wood freezer. We would take turns during the hot July day sitting on its lid to hold it down while someone else cranked.

Most of my memories of the Fourth of July are happy ones. Some are not. Nanny died one sad Fourth. Last year, Ron was at Friends' and the kids and I went to Marsh Creek for the day rather than face an empty house and a hollow celebration. Still, July Fourth makes me think of the beach and ocean breezes and silver sparklers.

Today, we are barbequing chicken and packing to go away to Rehoboth tomorrow, avoiding the worst part of the holiday rush. I expect to do most of the driving. We will spend five days laying on the beaches of my childhood and visiting with my parents. It will be good to get away and feel the soft, warm sand between my toes, to let the summer sun wash some of the winter pallor from my face.

Winter has been exceedingly long. Just when the last snows had melted away and spring seemed a certain promise, our lives were changed by the driver of a pick-up truck on Paoli Pike. Spring became a long marathon of endurance through the valley of shadows. Most days there was little light.

But now the brilliant colors of summer have replaced the beige tones of the hospital corridors. Blue skies, turquoise oceans, and the soaring majesty of fireworks are causes for rejoicing.

I tell myself this as I sit on the back deck with Ron, watching the display shot off at Hewes Avenue Park. The kids have ventured up into the crowds with friends, but I have preferred to sit here with my husband, exclaiming over the high ones. We hear the faint sounds of the explosions, then see a burst of color, silver and blue and gold lighting up the night. Slowly, the flickers of light fall back to earth like tired fireflies. Ron takes my hand in his and gives it a squeeze. His grip is not yet very strong. I squeeze back, just a little.

It is true that summer is here and, from all appearances, things seem to be going well. But in my heart I am truthful: I have not yet shaken the winter from my soul.

JULY 11, 2000. 7 AM.

It is Bonnie's second day at her new job and I get out of bed when she does, wanting to share this golden morning with my daughter. We have shared many that began with far less hope. I have coffee and fresh bagels ready when she comes downstairs. She is so beautiful, this chubby baby who struggled to breathe when she was born six weeks early. Her unscheduled arrival surprised me then, but in the last two years she has surprised me in other ways as well. Her hair is red—this week, anyway—her eyes a sky blue, and her face dotted with freckles she pretends to hate. We are similar in many ways. We share a face, a walk, a voice. Like me, she wants to be a teacher and loves to write stories and thinks in terms of metaphors and similes. She laughs a lot, in my timber, and my dimples play around the corners of her mouth.

Unlike me, she is messy, forgetful, and doesn't always apply herself to her schoolwork and can carry a tune without the prerequisite bucket I would need. Her voice—my voice—trills over high notes and octaves I can only dream of. She sings the way I would if I could.

But I cannot.

"It's just about the only thing you don't do well," she will often say to me. She has been my champion for years, her belief in me unshakable. She and her younger brother firmly believe that I can save the world. It is sometimes exhausting to live up to.

She is twenty-one—just—but looks seventeen, a gift from my gene pool. It is a gift she does not really appreciate right now but will when she reaches her forties. In many ways, she seems younger than her age. I have always attributed it to her early and difficult birth, but this young woman before me bears no scars from it. She is 5'7" and tops me by an inch. She sings and dances through life seemingly without a care in the world.

But I have spent countless hours with this dream child. Despite her fragile appearance, she is tough. We clung to each other the night of Ron's accident, waiting out the long hours together. We have clung to each other since then, propping one another up. She has filled in the gaps when my own strength has badly sagged. Last year, when Ron's issues with bi-polar disorder brought him to Friends' Hospital, it was she who helped me make the decision to leave The Christian Academy for Westown, she who helped me pack up my classroom and install light fixtures in the bathroom and take the car to have the oil changed.

Allen sometimes complains that he has two mothers. It is almost true. It has not, as far as I can see, hurt either of them.

So we sit this morning, sharing coffee and bagels and conversation. She loves her small charges at the daycare center and plans for the time when she will have her own classroom. It is good to be looking forward with her. She is, like me, a survivor.

Our minister's wife told me last week that I have been an excellent example to my daughter of what a Christian wife should be. I pray that it is true. Between Ron's accident and mental issues, there has been a lot to endure. I have not always known if I have made the right decisions. Despite it all, we have survived.

Looking at her bright face this morning, listening to her happy chatter, I realize that we have done more than survive. We have, as the Bible says, come through the fire. That which is gold and silver has become brighter for the refining, as bright as her cheery face.

I watch her leave this morning, my daughter, my right arm, my confidante, knowing that whatever else may transpire in her life, she is silver.

She will shine.

July 12, 2000. 2PM.

There should be scars here. Or the markings of skidding tires across the road. Or, at the very least, a remnant of twisted, distorted metal, something to mark the intersection of Five Points Road and Paoli Pike where the truck crashed into Ron's Taurus. The Taurus, poor thing, did not survive. Ron did, albeit with injuries that would have felled a lesser man and which will haunt him for years to come. Today, miracle of miracles, he is driving his new Caravan past the very spot where, four months ago, he became the non-person referred to in accident reports and court litigations as "the victim." It has been a long road. We have almost recovered. This dry run up to Ron's plant today is in preparation for his return to work next week, where he will once again become a man who earns a paycheck, carries a wallet, and jingles car keys in his pocket. Ron's scars are numerous. They will, in time, heal. But it seems impossible to me that the road where our lives took such a drastic turn is unchanged.

It must be, then, the only thing that has remained exactly the same, bearing no imprint of March 1. Paoli Pike, I note, has learned no lessons. Trucks still speed as if all humanity depended upon their prompt arrival. It is hard for me to pass this spot. My stomach twists into knots. My husband's blood was spilled here, but people are passing by as if nothing untoward ever took place at this intersection, going on with their lives unaware. Maybe that is the greatest tragedy.

We all bear scars. Ron's are visible. The accident left none of us unscathed. I am glad. Those of us who lived this nightmare, who lurked in the corners of hospitals, who prayed and wept and questioned God's wisdom, have learned from this. We treasure each day. We treasure each other. We walk a little slower. We breathe more deeply. We live each day with more compassion and faith, never knowing what the next turn in the road may bring.

And I wonder, as we drive past this spot where Ron's body was so badly damaged, at the people who pass by here blithely. Perhaps they are the same ones who pass the Cross of Calvary, unaware of the blood shed there and the eternal life its shedding offers. They move past it daily. Maybe they acknowledge it as history, nothing more. Their lack of understanding does not change the lesson or the gift.

So Paoli Pike remains as it was before the accident.

But we do not.

A SHORT LIST OF REASONS I DON'T WRITE MORE OFTEN

I'd write all the time

--and we know that I would—

But things don't just happen that way.

The bills are still due

On the first of the month

And so far my writing doesn't pay.

If I wrote in the morning

While the sun is on the rise

I could get a few pages done.

But sooner or later

They'd disturb my peace

My husband, my daughter, my son.

I could write in the day

(while they're all away)

Oh, the words that would be wrought!

But the sixth grade students

Who clutter my room

Have come to expect they'll be taught.

If I wrote in the evening

I am ever so sure

A novel would easily be writ.

But the people at my house

Need to be fed

And the cook has just up and quit.

There's homework to do

And papers to grade

And the kitchen's in need of a scrub

I could be Will Shakespeare

If I just had the time

But, ah! There's the rub!

Did people expect Papa Hemingway

To don an apron and cook?

Did Emily Bronte scrub pots and pans

While crafting the pages of books?

The time I do find

To scribble my lines

Is stolen in snatches and snips.

Somehow the writing

All intertwines

With my life as I'm living it.

The truth is if I

Were to hermit away

And shut out these things in my life

My pages would be

All pristine and blank

For I'd have absolutely nothing to say.

CHAPTER TWELVE.

JULY 21, 2000. 12 PM.

God is trying to pull my fingers away. Since Ron's accident, my fists have been tightly balled. Probably I clenched them tightly before that, when bi-polar disorder became the ruler of our lives. The children—especially Allen!—were so young! Like any mother tiger, I wanted to protect my offspring and spare them heartache and harm. There was so much to be lost. I stood as the shield between my three babies and the rest of the evil world.

After the accident, my grasp became even tighter. The rules I was familiar with and had carefully followed no longer applied. I used to tell my children that if you followed the rules and played on the side of right, you wouldn't get hurt. When the truck ran the red light and crashed into Ron, the rules changed. In fact, there were no longer any rules. Suddenly, every evil lurked outside my door, eager to grab my darlings. Dennis—smart one!—had already escaped to the city, proclaiming his independence quite vocally when he was nineteen. He gave me no recourse but to let him go.

Bonnie and Allen were not so lucky. I wonder now that they did not choke and suffocate but—bless them!—they seemed to understand my need to reassure myself several times a day that they were still safe. Bonnie expected me to call Genuardi's if she was half an hour late coming home from work. She carried her cell phone with nary an "Ah, Mom!" and didn't make faces when I reminded her—again—to keep her car doors locked. I know I rained on a parade or two when she'd made plans with friends and I nixed them, pulling the "you live in my house" routine. She never complained. She told me she understood.

Allen learned early that it was easier to leave me notes and messages then have me stomp around the neighborhood looking for him, conjuring up kidnapping plots in my mind. He never failed to tack a note onto the front door if he went out before I came home. If he was cruising the neighborhood on his bike and alighted at a friend's house, he'd call. "Mom, I'm at Greg's. Just wanted you to know."

I have been trying hard these last few weeks, with Ron's return to the work force and the world of driving, to relax a little. I no longer cringe when my family is out of my sight and I hear the sound of an ambulance. I still like to know their whereabouts and estimated time of arrival—I'm cooking dinner here, you know—but I have begun to trust them and their good judgment.

"Oh, my God, I trust in thee," says Psalm 25:2. How can I say this if I do not trust God with my children?

JULY 24, 2000. 3PM.

Ron is planning a garden for next spring. While he is not necessarily gifted with a green thumb, he's decided that the front hill should bloom with bright colors next year to elicit feelings of warmth in passers-by. It may be just a ploy to get out of cutting the grass on the front slope, but the garden Ron is planning will require much more care and concern than a simple swipe of the mower blades. A new garden, with its tender shoots and fragile buds, needs watering and nurturing, snipping and weeding. It is a large investment of time and energy, not to mention trips to the Home Depot, that may not pay off if there is a late frost or a mid-summer drought. It is a risk. But, if all the elements come together in the proper measurements, what a wonder it can be! I can close my eyes and see it now, the way Ron envisions it, a profusion of anemones and petunias, marigolds to keep the rabbits at bay, nasturtiums and blue irises, a rainbow of hues and colors lining our hill.

I am not much of a gardener myself. In fact, I had to open up the "F" volume of my encyclopedia to come up with that many flower names. The fault lies not in my soul—which craves both beauty and poetry—but in my hay-fever and severe reactions at the mere mention of poison ivy. I grow things in pots that do not have to be weeded. I have not been above using silk flowers in an outdoor planter. (In fact, my friend Ginny has a wishing well in her front yard with a gorgeous array of artificial blooms. The little girl next door waters them every day.) Any gardening done around here will be done by Ron.

I realize that a lot of people begin planning their garden at this time of year, sending for seed catalogs and samples from Burpees. It's not something that can be left until the last minute. There is soil to be turned and layouts to plan. That's the whole point: Ron is *planning* a garden. Ron doesn't—or at least, hasn't for the last eight years—planned anything. It has been enough of a burden for him to get through each day. He has lived by the words of Matthew 6:24, "Sufficient unto the day is the evil therof." But he has missed the hope of verse 35, which says," Seek ye first the Kingdom of God." Many were the days he wearily arrived home from work and went to bed, too overwhelmed with shadows to be a part of our family. Or the alternative, even worse: complaining all evening, at every turn of the conversation, about his miserable life. The kids and I became adept at ignoring him, choosing instead to remember the "pre-depression era" Ron. This was hard for Allen to do, since his memories of Ron have been built more recently. He depended upon his older siblings to fill in moments that went with the family photographs.

But now Ron is planning a garden and the key word is "planning." Webster's defines "planning" as "deciding upon a future action." In envisioning next year's garden growing on our hill, Ron relies upon a future. For him. For us. For our family. For those carefully chosen, carefully tended flowers he hopes to grow. It is risky business, given not only the vagaries of nature but of life. It may not turn out as he had planned. He is willing to take the risk.

So am I. For eight years, I have waited and prayed that the demons which poked and prodded him would one day be vanquished. Sometimes it seems as if the darkness would never end.

There may still be a promise of spring.

AUGUST 18, 2000. 11AM.

I DID IT! With two weeks left to spare before I face the world of blackboards again, I have conquered all ninety levels of Skobahn this summer! The mad Japanese transport game came on my laptop and I staunchly ignored it for a year, too busy learning the programs I actually needed for teaching at Westtown to involve myself in anything quite so frivolous. But this summer, I became entranced by the little breathing Skobahn ball that so intently pushed locked boxes through the mazes, lining them up in perfect order. To my disappointment, there was no fanfare when I completed level 90, but it only momentarily depleted from my sense of fulfillment. Along with working on my novel and getting a second hole in my ears, beating this game has been right up there with my summer goals.

I haven't finished my novel yet and I'm still sorting out all of my journals from the accident. The material for my new kitchen curtains is lying on my sewing machine. The basement is only half-cleaned out. But I have had victory over that controlling, heavily breathing blue Skobahan creature and its locked boxes! My daughter watched me complete the last two levels with something akin to amusement. Mom? Computer games? She commented that I had developed "fast fingers" and ran through each course much more quickly than I had in June. I've made fewer mistakes in the last twenty levels. In fact, not to brag, I completed levels 88 and 89 on only one try.

"Must be getting easier," I told Bonnie.

"No," she replied. "You're getting better."

Getting better. Ear piercings aside, it was what we all needed and wanted this summer. There was an ad a few years back—I forget for what—that decried, "You're not getting older, you're getting better!" It has become my battle cry this summer as we all drifted away from the hospital zone and learned to treat Ron as a "normal" person again. I say it with fervor. We are all getting better. Ron's gentle rise from the gripes of bipolar depression has raised our own spirits. The last eight years have been shrouded in gray clouds. The sky seems a bit clearer.

I wonder sometimes at the stress I was able to bear and still keep on going, mostly smiling. The "better" me marvels at the woman who held it all together.

True, I still bear a lot of responsibilities. While improving, Ron needs a lot of encouragement and help. Slowly, I am trying to transfer back to him some of the responsibilities given over to me. He is now handling his own credit card bill. I needed to walk him through the process, step by step, just as I did the older children when they began to handle their own finances. Ron is once again responsible for car maintenance and repairs. The bulk of our home-life and finances is still mine, but I have a little breathing room.

I am getting better. In those final levels of Skobahn, I realized I was carefully scrutinizing the board for possible problems before I began to move. Most of the time, it enabled me to avoid the pitfalls altogether. I sailed through the final stages, planning each step beforehand. It is just one more lesson learned from the Japanese game: look for the potential problems and avoid them before they occur.

I return to the real world in just ten days. There is a classroom to be readied, lesson plans to finish, new students to meet. But I will return better than I left, renewed, refreshed, and rested. Ready. The respite of the summer and the lessons learned from a computer game will carry me across the long stretch of blackboard jungle.

I'm getting better. As a woman, as a wife, as a writer, as a teacher. Better because—for the first time in a long time—I gave myself a break and spent some time doing something that wasn't going to make a hill of beans difference to the world. And as I moved my little Skobahn creature, huffing and puffing its way around the board, the world went on without me.

It's probably better for that, too.

AUGUST 20, 2000. 8PM.

Our twenty-fifth wedding anniversary looms ahead. The kids like to look at our wedding album and point out how young their dad and I were. They laugh at the powder blue tuxedos—it was the seventies, after all—and Uncle Tom with an Afro. And they are planning an anniversary service for us, complete with music and ushers and a reception and a chance to renew our vows. Invitations have gone out to sixty people. Most are coming. Even Pastor Lou, who will be leaving our church for a position in New Jersey next week, is coming back to do our service.

Ron has already written the words he will recite to me. I heard this from Bonnie, who helped him print them out on the computer. I have thought carefully about what I will say but have not yet put pen to paper. I admit I was a little nervous about asking Ron to write his own. He's not what you call a poetic soul, particularly since the clouds of depression have obscured much of what is good in his life. When we talked to Pastor Lou about our plans, he gave some pointers to Ron to help him: look through some books and ask for suggestions from friends. The most important thing will be, Lou pointed out, that Ron speak from the heart.

Ron wrote them without help. Yesterday afternoon when the house was deserted of all life except one cat, Ron composed them on a piece of lined paper that is now printed out and folded into his wallet. He reviewed them again and again, making the words familiar to his mind. Since the accident, we have found that things sometimes slip through the cracks of his brain. Language that was once familiar to him looks foreign. He is determined that the words he speaks on October 7 be familiar and said without hesitation.

It doesn't matter what he has written. The simple—difficult

for him—act of writing them, of looking at them several times a day and practicing the words until they can roll off his tongue, are my true gift. It is another indication that Ron is healing. I cannot imagine the pre-accident Ron, who lived in a world composed of dark thoughts, committing himself to such a loving task.

But the words are there, on that piece of folded paper, tucked into his wallet along with the list of names we planned on giving our children the night we got engaged. There have been more than twenty-five years between those two slips of paper. They are both tangible reminders not only of our love and commitment to each other, but of God's love for us.

Promises made. Promises kept.

MEMORY CHAIN

"Just remember," says the quote, "we're all in this alone."
All alone.
Lonely.
Lone Ranger. Hi, Ho, Silver! Saturday afternoons with my brother and candy from Joe's corner store.
Silver bullet.
Silver lining.
Does every cloud really have one?
Clouds have shapes. Sometimes they look like spilt milk.
A gallon of milk. A half-gallon of milk.
An empty milk carton. Dennis must be home.
Home alone.
Home sweet home.
Home, home on the range.
Range of motion. Range of freedom. Range in my kitchen. My new kitchen!
Kitchen cabinets.
Cabinet doors.
Front door.
Back door.
In and out.
Out to dinner. Out to lunch. Out for the count.
Out of luck.
Lucky day. Happy day.
Daybreak. Daylight.
Light of my life.
Life long. Long life.
Life preserver.
Life saver.
Save! Save! Save!
Sale! Sale! Sale!
Sail away, blown away, gone away. In and out the doors.
Revolving doors.
Way out. Way in. which way to go?
Going my way. Going your way. Go away. Far away.

Way down upon the Swannee River. River of hope.
River of dreams.
Dream at night.
Nighttime.
Time to go. Out the door. Front or back.
Go alone.
All alone.

CHAPTER THIRTEEN.

AUGUST 24, 2000. 9AM.

We spent some time in the emergency room yesterday. A hernia has popped up on one of Ron's many incisions, so today we are on our way to see Dr. Huffman again and schedule more surgery. Poor Ron must feel like a pincushion by now! But this surgery, we've been told, can be done as an out-patient. No big deal. Funny how my perspective about surgery has changed this year; it used to be that any procedure would be a big deal

The doctor who saw us at the ER (Dr Brauvard? Who can read a physician's handwriting?) was impressed with the thickness of Ron's chart. She asked him to explain what happened during the accident, but Ron's memory became disjointed and his words began to stumble. She turned to me. It has become a new role of mine, being Ron's translator to the world. "You've been through quite a lot," she said, " but the good thing is you're able to talk about it. You're up and walking around and with your family."

All things in perspective, we have been blessed. *Lord, help me to remember that as the medical bills roll in from yet another hospital visit.*

Dr. Huffman is happy to see us and greets both Ron and me with a hug. "You look well," she says to Ron. "You look tired," she says to me. We are ushered into the examining room immediately because, "you people really need to move on with your lives." Joanne is pleased with Ron's improvement and asks about work and memory problems. Carefully, she probes his abdomen. "This happens a lot when someone's had abdominal surgery," she says, "and Ron's had many. The muscles just aren't as tight as they were before." She would prefer, she says, to wait until January when Ron has had more time to heal and recover. "The body," she says, " is amazing at regenerating itself. I'd like to give it more time to recover." Ron becomes insistent. He wants it done now. He wants to get it over with and put it all behind him. I see the sense of this. But I also know that Ron out of work for several more weeks will put a severe crimp in Christmas. I sigh to myself. Our shoestrings are used to being tightened. Dr. Huffman writes some notes on Ron's chart and checks her schedules. She has rather reluctantly agreed to expedite the surgery. "We can get this done before Labor Day." she says. I take out my pocket calendar and we agree upon a date.

Ron is given a sheet of instructions to follow. No eating after midnight the day before surgery. No medications. Arrive at the hospital at 10:00 AM. Ron is chatting with Joanne's assistant when the surgeon pulls me aside.

"Are you alright?" she asks me.

I am startled. I have convinced myself and everyone else that I have spent the summer resting and recharging. I nod. "I'm fine," I say. "School starts next week, so I've been busy getting things together."

"Is that all it is?"

"Sure. Ron's better. Things are good."

She gives me a long, hard look. "Linda, you've been carrying a lot. Have you talked to anyone about all this?"

I shrug. "Some. A little. But I'm okay. Really. It's Ron who needs your concern. Not me."

"Remember what I told you that first night, Linda? I worry about the families of my patients as much as I do my patients."

"You don't need to worry about me, "I assure her. "I'm fine. I can handle it." I offer her my brightest smile.

She nods, unconvinced. "Talk to someone," she says. "Now. Before you need to."

"Alright, " I agree reluctantly. I am already wondering whom I could talk to. My pastor, who has already left for his new job across the river? Ron, who is not yet a whole man? My friends, who extol my virtues as a wonderful, strong Christian wife? Or my children, who need to know that they still have one parent left that can count on?

I can handle this, I tell myself as we leave Joanne's office. This is a minor bump in the road. We've been through much worse than this.

AUGUST 24, 2000. 5 PM.

In a way, the car accident has made it easier to explain Ron to the world. Bi-polar disorder is a complicated and little understood malady, as hard to define as it is to live with. When Ron's first episode landed him in the hospital, an acquaintance asked me if I had known Ron had mental problems when we married. It was a startling question. Had I? How could I? I was twenty years old with stars in my eyes. Ron was tall and good-looking and had the same beliefs I did. He loved me and if I sometimes worried me that he loved me more than I loved him, it was all the love I had to give. I panicked a week before our wedding, wondering if I was indeed doing the right thing. I knew Ron would never have an important job or be rich. Those things meant little to me. What mattered was the way he made me feel: safe and loved. His mother had told me that she felt he probably had some learning problems that had never been diagnosed, that he was a "little slow" at learning new things. And in the year we dated before our marriage, I was aware that his tongue often stumbled over difficult words.

And so we wed. For better or worse. When mental problems first began to rear their ugly heads, I repeated the vows to myself. I wouldn't leave Ron if he had diabetes or cancer or heart problems. Why would I leave him now?

The way I answered that acquaintance became the way I answered all others. "No," I said. "None of us knew." A counselor tried to convince me later that of course I had known and on some level had chosen Ron because of the mental problems. He would always be someone I could control. I have never been able to accept that theory. What do twenty-somethings know of mental disorders or miscarriages or mortgages or trauma units? And anyone who thinks you can control someone with bi-polar disorder is just, well, crazy.

After March 1, my explanation for Ron became a lot simpler. Doctors, like the one in the ER with the indecipherable nametag, would turn to me. "He was in a serious car accident," I would say and they would nod their heads knowingly. If he became frustrated making himself understood to store clerks, I would intervene. "A car accident," I would explain and receive a sympathetic nod. Dennis became adept at playing what he called "the Dad card." "If I need a day off from work," he explained, " I just make my face look all sad and say to my boss, 'There's been a problem with my dad.'"

If I sometimes feel like C3PO, cyborg interpreter from *Star Wars*, I just shrug and add it up to my duties as a Christian wife. The list is growing long.

AUGUST 27, 2000. 10 AM.

Before He left His disciples to return to Heaven, Jesus said that He would bring them peace, "but not as the world brings peace." I wonder what those simple, uneducated fishermen thought of Jesus' conditional promise. There were those among them who thought their Rabbi had come to free them from Roman rule and establish an earthly peace. But in those final words, Jesus made it clear that His brand of peace was not something the world could give. Or even understand.

I know this peace. I cling to it. It is the reason I sit here on the 4th floor of Crozer Hospital, pushed once again into a turquoise plastic chair, waiting for the surgeon to come and tell me that Ron's operation is over. I do not pace or tap my foot. I do not bite my fingernails. I know that Ron is in God's hands.

As far as waiting rooms go, this one is not bad at all. It is open and airy, a few green plants and pastel paintings breaking the beige tedium of the walls. There is coffee in one corner and a television set suspended from the ceiling in another. No one is watching it—I have yet to be in a waiting room where anyone really does—but its noise lends a level of reality to this suspension of life. Some people are reading or pacing or conversing with others in hushed tones. I am the only one writing.

It seems important to me that I am able to write and concentrate on ink and words. Since Ron's first surgery six months ago, I have learned a lot about trust, about peace, about letting go. I hope that I have learned enough. Through the long, traumatic months—despite the outward chaos in which I lived—the peace that Jesus promised to His disciples took root in me. While I was often unable to verbalize to others why I could remain so calm, that peace carried me to many hospital waiting rooms. I thought it had carried me past them altogether. I had hoped.

Peace. We think of it as being the lack of disruption or anxiety in our lives. But that is not what Jesus promised. The disruptions will still exist. Before I left the house this morning to bring Ron in for surgery, I had to pick up Dennis' check, run to the bank, pick up fruits at Produce Junction and cold cuts at Dons' Deli, finish the laundry I began last night, write and mail a couple of checks, and start supper in the crock-pot. Life just keeps on happening. But I hummed as I did it all, taking pleasure in my ability to use my arms and legs and brain, knowing that even then God had Ron's surgery and its outcome firmly in His hands.

A hospital is a busy place, full of interruptions and anxieties. My life is also a busy, hectic one, crammed with teaching and home and family and graduate school. To the outward eye, it is far from peaceful. Yet in my hectic home and this bustling hospital, I have found the peace of Jesus. Whatever is happening on the outside cannot disturb it.

Inside, I dwell in peace. It is sometimes uneasy.

August 29, 2000. 7AM.

When I get out of the shower the next morning, there is a handprint on the mirror in the bathroom. No, I do not think that *Hollow Man* has invaded my privacy. As children, my brother and I would often draw in the fog in the car windows, then wipe the windows off with a coat sleeve and wait for our drawings—mostly panda bears wearing big bow ties—to reappear when the windows fogged up again. We didn't know anything about scientific principles. We thought of it as magic.

The handprint in the mirror is too big to me mine or Bonnie's, too small to be Ron's. That leaves Allen as the possible culprit who planted his palm in the middle of the mirror, probably with the same pleasure Harvey and I gained from our panda bears. I choose not to reach for the Windex under the sink and obliterate this eerie image. It is a reminder to me of the unseen handprints in my life, handprints that belong to God.

It is often difficult to see these prints. While Ron has struggled for years with bi-polar disorder and I have attempted to educate myself to support my family, I have not always recognized God's hands. But lately I have tried to me more aware of His intervention in my life. It was He who led me away from The Christian Academy and to a job whose salary has supported us through Ron's recovery.

The handprint will stay, for the time being, on my mirror. I like getting out of the shower each morning and being reminded that God's hand is on my life, even if I do not always see it.

OPEN WOUNDS

Open wounds
    heal slowly
    and need
    c a r e

They need to be kept
    clean and
    dry and
    free from
    i n f e c t i o n

They are not
    pleasant to see
    or
    t o u c h

And while they are mending
and knitting together the
layers of skin and tissue
and muscles and blood

Other things can
    also
    heal.
Not all open wounds
    can be
    s e e n

CHAPTER FOURTEEN.

SEPTEMBER 13, 2000. 7AM.

My daughter's car is out of gas this morning. We are hurrying out the door carrying assorted book bags and trying to get back in sync with the school routine. Allen and I jump in my car for our journey to two separate institutions of learning and Bonnie gets into hers to drive to a third. She puts the car in gear, turns the key. The engine goes "wrr" and tries to turn over. She rolls down her window and shouts across the street to me, "Mom, I'm out of gas."

Perfect. Monday morning school bus traffic to deal with and now this. I sigh, get out of my car, and send Allen flying to the back deck where we keep the can of gasoline for the lawnmower. By the time we dump its contents into Bonnie's gas tank, we all smell like mechanics. Still, the car won't start.

"Not enough gas," I say. "How much gas does it take to start a car?" But both my offspring shrug, clearly their knowledge of car engines and their fuel supplies being no greater than mine.

The clock is ticking loudly now. Leaving the house at 6:45 and dropping Allen off at the high school gets me to school around 7:30 and gives me time to catch my breath and organize before my students arrive. A few minutes later and I am caught behind buses and construction along route 352 where traffic creeps inch my inch. But what's a mother to do?

We grab the gas can, hop into my faithful old ugly duckling of a car that would run on fumes if it needed to and chug off to the gas station. We fill the can—still debating how much it will take to make the engine turn over—and go back to Bonnie's Tempo. While she and her brother pour gas into the tank, I scribble a hasty late note for Allen.

Procedure finished. The car starts amid our cheers. Allen runs the gas can to the back deck and we convoy up to the gas station once again so Bonnie can fill her car for the ride to school. She still has a few minutes to spare. I drive off into the waning morning.

There's a lesson here, I think. There always is, but I have a hard time putting my finger on it right now. Was it about priorities? Cooperation? Planning ahead? Gasoline engine combustion?

As I drop Allen off, it occurs to me. It's simple, really. From time to time we all run out of gas. Our energy supply is low. We're tired. Monday mornings are hard. Panic does not help. Instead it is best to pause a moment, catch your breath, and properly refuel.

How much gas does an engine—car or human—need? The answer is really simple.

Whatever it takes.

SEPTEMBER 14, 2000. 7 PM.

I am in EDR 517 doing a presentation on Native American literature when my cell phone rings. It startles me; I have almost forgotten its sound. The professor frowns. "It has to be an emergency," I say quickly. "Only my kids have the number." Dr. Beeghly nods. She had remembered my husband's accident in the spring semester. "Take it," she says quietly and I step into the hall, my heart beating rapidly, my palms beginning to sweat.

It is Bonnie's voice that answers when I say, "Hello." I am at once relieved that my daughter is not the victim this time. Her voice is calm. "It's Dad," she says. "His incision split open. We're on our way to the emergency room. He's bleeding pretty badly."

I gulp, wondering how my slender daughter will manage to get her husky father into her car. It seems we are all learning to do things we once thought impossible. "He's kind of dizzy," she reports. "I already called Dr. Huffman." Smart girl, I think, grateful for the lessons my children are learning if not for the reason.

"I'll meet you at the hospital," I say.

"No hurry," she assures me. "We'll be okay for while. Dr. Huffman is meeting us."

"Is Allen with you?" I ask.

"Yeah," she says. "He's getting Dad's medications together."

And again I wonder at the resourcefulness of these two who have learned well the rules of the emergency room: call ahead, bring snacks, take medications, carry change for the phone.

I push "end" on my cell phone and return to the classroom. "I have to go," I announce to my waiting classmates. "My daughter is taking my husband to the hospital." I pick up my presentation materials. "I'll finish first," I say to Dr. Beeghly.

"You will not," she answers. "Just go."

I nod and thank her. "I'll finish it next week," I offer.

"You're done," she says. "You've got your A. Now go take care of your husband."

I am not really nervous as I drive down 202. I have done this before and survived. But I cannot help questioning God as I turn my car towards the hospital that has become our second home. "Why, God? Hasn't this poor man been through enough? How much can he take? How much can we all take?" I flip off the radio, preferring my own thoughts to music or talk, waiting for God to answer me.

Dr. Huffman has already seen Ron when I arrive at the ER. I greet several nurses like the familiar acquaintances they are. A room is being readied for Ron on the third floor. "I was afraid of this," Joanne says. "The walls of his abdomen are just too weak right now." The bleeding has been staunched for the time being and Ron is receiving transfusions. Tomorrow, repairs will be made to the operative site. "We'll probably put in a mesh wall," says Joan, " to make it stronger."

When the kids and I leave the hospital, it is once again the wee hours of the morning. We are becoming Night Stalkers, living a vampire existence. I will need to come back tomorrow with some things for Ron. I will need to get a substitute for my classes while I wait out yet another surgery.

God has not answered my questions asked in the car. I want to believe that God is in control, and I look for assurances that He has not forgotten us. It is not easy.

SEPTEMBER 15, 2000. 8 AM.

The next day, I list in my journal the assurances that God has sent to me while I wait in an all too-familiar waiting room.

1. Bonnie was able to take care of this emergency even though I was not home. She knew just what to do and what to grab on her way out the door.
2. When I logged onto my e-mail early this morning, intending to send out some Ron alerts and start a prayer chain going, I found that two on-line buddies had sent me stories that clearly illustrated God's hand at work even when we do not see it. Like the mysterious handprint in my mirror, it may be invisible for a while.
3. Ron is in good spirits. Despite this setback and the anticipation of more weeks of recovery, he is smiling and fairly cheerful. He'll need to learn to give himself injections to stave off infections but he seems comfortable with it.

I continue to try and focus on what is positive. It is what I want other people to see when I send out information about our current challenge. It is, though, getting harder and harder for me to find.

SEPTEMBER 17, 2000. 6 PM.

In my house, duct tape is a necessity. We use it to repair pipes, wires, and the gaskets on my ancient car. Every time the taps on the washer leaks, I add a little more duct tape. We buy it in huge, economy size rolls because our family saying is, "If it can't be fixed with duct tape, it can't be fixed." We cheered when the crew of Apollo 13 used the famous silver tape to make repairs to their ailing spaceship. We could not live without duct tape and its enduring qualities.

What's this got to do with anything in my life right now? Why and I enthusing about duct tape when Ron is still in the hospital, an infection invading his wound and sending him into isolation? Perhaps it is sheer exhaustion on my part, but there does seem to be a connection. I am looking for it.

It is Saturday morning and Bonnie and I have joined other ladies from our congregation in a time of prayer. The original purpose of this group was to pray for our church and our current lack of a pastor, but the eight or ten of us who attend have found ourselves drawn together, bound by a mutual love of our Lord and our church, tender towards one another's cares and concerns. It is sometimes hard to get up early on a Saturday morning and join the ladies, but I am always happy that I did. In the several weeks since we have begun our little group, we have discovered just how strong our bonds are.

The focus of our prayer time today is Ron and his return to the hospital. For 45 minutes, every lady in this group bows her head and speaks to God concerning Ron, our family, and me. Tears flow, but no one tries to stop them. No one is ashamed of them. The 45 minutes these ladies pray today is only a fraction of the time they have spent praying for Ron.

Duct tape, however useful it may be, is noticeable. My household repairs are visible. The bonds that hold this group of ladies together is not. We are bound by love and hope, for each other as well as God. And I know that the love in this small group is growing. Perhaps Ron's ongoing physical problems will be the duct tape of our church—which has many problems and broken places—that brings us all together and wraps us tightly into one unit. After all, Matthew 16:19 promises us "that which is found on earth shall be bound in Heaven."

I have tried for months, along with these dear ladies, to make sense of a senseless accident. I have found many occasions to praise God as we walked through the valley. We have rejoiced as Ron improved both physically and emotionally. When Ron returned to the hospital this past week, I asked, again and again, why.

I still ask why. But so much love and concern has been

extended to our family in these last few days and so much prayer has gone forth on Ron's behalf that I have begun, again, to see our fractured church pull together. Whatever our differences, whatever our problems, we are united as one in prayer for Ron.

Ephesians 9:3 says that we should endeavor to keep "the unity of the Spirit in the bond of peace." Our church, as well as my husband, has been in need of healing. Perhaps this ongoing concern for Ron will be the duct tape it needs.

SEPTEMBER 18, 2000. 7AM.

My daughter walks into my room late at night and asks, in a voice loud enough to wake me from my sound sleep, "Where's Rose?"

I am still groggy, so I mumble into my pillow, "Rose? Who's Rose?"

Bonnie is standing at the door, shaking her head. "I don't know who she is. But she's missing. We've got to find her." There is urgency in her voice.

By now I realize that Bonnie is probably under the influence of sleep and another late night sitting in a hospital waiting room while Ron's fever spiked and brought concerns about his heart to the attention of a team of cardiologists. Perhaps the mythical Rose was a player in her dreams.

"Go back to bed", I say. "I don't know who Rose is and I don't want to get out of bed to find someone I don't know."

At this my daughter takes a belligerent stance adopted as a toddler: hands on her hips, elbows sticking out, feet wide apart. "Well," she says loudly, annoyed at my unwilling attitude, "I don't know her either, and I'm looking for her!" At that she turns on her heel and flounces back to her room, climbing beneath the covers and seeking Rose in her sleep.

The next morning she remembers nothing of our nocturnal conversation. We laugh for a moment about looking for the lost Rose.

But later on I think, is this really a laughing matter? Just because we don't personally know Rose—or other lost souls—does that mean we should not be looking for her? Hasn't Jesus commanded us to be out hunting for the lost and the sorrowful?

Perhaps "Rose" lives next door to me. Perhaps I'll meet her today. I'll remember that she's lost. Or frightened. Or lonely. She could be the next person I meet, someone desperately in need of comfort and a smile.

She could be me.

THE MASK

I have worn the mask too long

Of the strong and capable woman

Allowing others to see

A me

Built of faith and strength

Never did I let them know that

Behind the mask

I cringed in fear, afraid

That one day,

The mask would slip and reveal the real me,

The frightened me,

The me who carried too much for too long

And never asked for help

Until the day

The mask

Slipped.

CHAPTER FIFTEEN.

OCTOBER 1, 2000. 9:30 PM.

My grandmother taught me to knit when I was nine. My first effort was a disaster. It was a scarf, intended for my father, in a soft, camel brown. I dropped stitches constantly, it seemed, and always got the purl mixed up with the knit. It took an eternity to finish the scarf but my grandmother assured me that if I kept on kitting, eventually it would be done. And it was. By then, I was sick of looking at it and thought it was the ugliest thing I had ever seen. It was lumpy and lopsided and full of the mistakes of a beginning knitter. I was ashamed to give it to my dad. But my grandmother had already told me I was knitting him a scarf for his birthday, so I had no choice but to present my imperfect creation to my father.

I thought he would laugh. Or point out the many flaws and errors I had made. The best I could hope for was that he would peep into the box and put it aside before anyone else could see it.

My dad did none of those things. He opened the box, pulled out the much maligned scarf, and wrapped it around his neck. He began to exclaim over its good points: the softness of the wool, the warmth of the weight, the tones of the color. He failed entirely to mention the holes and the dropped stitches and the uneven edges. And as he talked about the good points of my first effort at knitting, I began, to see it for what it was, the loving attempt of an inexperienced girl who had put care into every stitch she'd made because it was for her dad. It didn't need to be perfect.

It didn't seem so ugly anymore.

I'm not sure where the scarf is now, but I can assume it is tucked away somewhere in Dad's many boxes of memories. I went onto knit many other things for Dad and other members of my family; each item was an improvement over the scarf. But I will never forget the way Dad wore the first of my creations. He wore it with pride.

I've been thinking about knitting for two reasons. One is the way that Ron's open wound is beginning to heal. The skin is knitting together, slowly pulling the edges of the wound towards one another. The new skin is soft and pink and shiny. Baby skin. Brand new. The first time I saw the wound—and was required to change the dressing and clean it out—I grabbed onto the dresser next to the bed where Ron lay to steady myself. It was a huge, gaping hole in his abdomen. It was raw and red and oozing. The sight of it frightened me.

I took a deep breath. "Give me a minute," I said to my waiting husband. "I'll do it, but I need a minute to get used to it." The immensity of the wound terrified me. The responsibility of cleaning and dressing it three times a day was overwhelming. How could I do this? Yet in the course of the last two weeks I have not only learned to do it without become queasy, I have perfected it into a two-minute process. Ready the bandages and the saline solution ahead of time. Lay out the gauze strips and pads and the surgical tape. Pull on the rubber gloves and peel off the used bandage with one hand, using the other hand to liberally wipe the area down with saline solution. One hand dries the area off while the other holds the gauze pad at the ready. Once that is in pace, four pieces of surgical tape are snipped and fitted into place. The horror of the wound began, gradually, to take a back seat to the wonder of our bodies and the way they have been designed to heal. Surely only a loving and kind Father could have made us with such detail and perfection! Even from such a large and gaping wound. I feel privileged---if not quite grateful—to witness the power of God within a human body.

The second reason I am thinking about knitting is that I have seen the way my family has knit together these last months while Ron has been recovering. Yes, the kids still have their squabbles and fights but they are unfailingly kind to their father and sensitive to my needs. They seem to know when I am feeling overwhelmed and worried and they gather around me, supporting me with their arms and their love. Bonnie willingly contributes part of her paycheck to what she calls " family importance." Allen ignores the ignominy—for a teenager—of accepting reduced lunches at school and occasionally uses his allowance to treat us all to pizza. While he has his eye on a new $300 bike for his upcoming birthday, he knows it will have to wait. These last eight months have been decidedly difficult on all of them, yet they are stronger for it. It has been hardest on Dennis, who lives in the city and only sees our miracles second-hand.

This week, Ron and I will celebrate our silver wedding anniversary. We are planning a service on Saturday to renew our vows and our commitment to one another. And to God. We, too, have been knitted together. Despite the trials, the bonds between us are strong. Knitting always does that; it takes a single, fine strand and wraps it around others. It is the wrapping that gives it the strength.

Ron's skin is knitting. Our lives are knitting. Slowly, we are beginning to heal from this latest of uphill battles. And while our early attempts may have been laughable, God has been patient with us. He has shown us the good things in our lives and has not pointed out our mistakes. While we may drop a stitch now and then, God never does.

In His sight, we are beautiful. We are whole. God looks on us with eyes of love.

OCTOBER 7, 2000.

"What I have learned from my parents is the meaning of the word, 'courage'." This tribute comes to Ron and me from the lips of our fourteen year old son as we celebrate our anniversary. Bonnie and Dennis have already made similar comments. But Allen's words—simple and heartfelt—burn into my mind.

"What really matters," he continues to explain to the congregation, " isn't money or where you live or what you have. It's love. Thanks, Mom and Dad, for showing me that. For letting me be me. For letting me grow. For teaching me that you just need to trust God. You don't have to understand it all.:"

Courage. Is there a greater gift we could have given this child who so often lacked a father? Is there a greater legacy we could have offered to these three young people that God placed within my care?

I was a starry-eyed bride twenty-five years ago, wanting to give my future children everything; a beautiful home, a good education, a solid grounding, and opportunities to travel. But we still live in the same three bedroom "starter" home. The kids all went to public school. They had limited college choices. We've traveled more in books and movies than in physical miles. But as much as I might lament the lack of material wealth, my children taught me years ago that their home is extremely important to them.

When the world gets tough, they head home. "Home," as Bonnie says, " is the place where they have to take you in."

Time and time again, I have seen it with Dennis, who left home at nineteen to live away at college. When a high school friend committed suicide, Dennis came home. When there were decisions to be made over class choices, Dennis came home. And he continues to come home when his cupboard is bare or he needs to talk or the world just gets tough. It's a rough world out there.

You need faith. You need strength. You need courage.

My children were not born with a silver spoon in their mouths. They will never receive the Grand Tour of Europe as a graduation present. They'll be lucky to get a new watch. But I hope that I have given them what they need to survive.

The circumstances Ron and I have faced in the last twenty-five years have required courage. I would not have chosen these trials, but I do value the impact they have had on my offspring. Their strength, their faith, their perseverance are treasures. Left to choose among worldly wealth or the gifts that Allen speaks of, I'd have to side with the Cowardly Lion.

I'd choose courage.

I, too, have something to say on this occasion of our wedding anniversary, to relate to our gathered friends and family.

"Usually, I find it easy to string words together into an arrangement that is somewhat articulate, but how do you encapsulate 25 years into a few phrases? A quarter of a century is too long to be boiled down into sentences and too short a time to sum up with a tidy ending. We haven't reached the last page of the book yet. We have a lot of pages left to fill.

"I was very young when we married. I went very quickly from being someone's daughter to being someone's wife without ever really know who the 'me' in 'us' was. If I could only thank you for one thing, Ron, it would be for giving me room in our marriage to grow. Even when it was inconvenient for you, you've encouraged me to expand my horizons and my education and you've allowed me to become the woman God wanted me to be. In being your wife, I found out who I really was. Buried beneath Ron's wife, and Dennis and Bonnie and Allen's mother, I found someone I could be proud to be. There is a song from the musical, 'Rent" that asks, 'How do you measure a year? Do you measure it in minutes or in miles? Tears or smiles?' 525,600 minutes are in a year. For us, then , it has been 13,140,000 minutes. And they way that we have measured them is with love."

NOVEMBER 7, 2000.

I watch him walk down the alley to his house, balancing the queen-sized mattress on his head, his strong arms raised to support the weight, his back straight under its burden. I call after him, "You'll be safe if a piece of Skylab hits you!"

"Yeah," he agrees, "I'm totally safe under here."

If only that could be true. One of my main jobs in my early years as this one's mother was to protect him against the wickedness of the world. But a mother's love can offer only limited sanctuary, especially as adulthood encroaches on her offspring.

This one—this tall, handsome man who so easily lifts the mattress from the roof of his dad's van—officially left our home twenty months ago. Yes, he'd lived away from us during college years but still considered our home his. So did we. Summer vacations and holidays would find Dennis back again, vying for space and control of the remote with his siblings. His mail still came to our address and, when he graduated from the University of the Arts in 1998 wearing a pair of size 18 dress shoes I'd searched up and down the tri-state area to find, so did he and his possessions.

"Six weeks," he said as we unloaded his things from the U-Haul. "Just until I find a place of my one."

Six weeks stretched into six months and Dennis reclaimed his half of the front bedroom, scattering his assorted art supplies around the house wherever there was a spare nook or cranny. We ran short on hot water and milk on a daily basis and Tom Waits' CDs wailed into the nights. But I slept peacefully, knowing that all my chicks were safe under the same roof.

Dennis returned to the city in March of 1999 with impeccable timing—just before the pie hit the fan—to a rented house with two roommates, a job in scenic design to pay the bills, and dreams of becoming a painter. His new ID now bears an address different from mine. It always will.

This shift in our lives has, of course, necessitated a shift in roles. I am no longer in charge of his clean socks or feeding his stomach. I do not know what time he gets in at night or who all of his friends are. I no longer have the power to keep him safe. I never really did.

I laid for this child—and the others God entrusted to me—a foundation of love, but that offered no more physical protection than the mattress he so easily hoists up the steps of his house.

Somehow, by God's grace, he has survived harm. His is tall and strong in body, mind, and spirit.

But while his address may be different, he still ventures to that place called home often, pours himself a cup of coffee, and settles at the kitchen table."Mom," he'll say, "can we talk?" And he will spin out his dreams of being a painter, of having his work in glossy New York magazines, his paintings hanging in the Metropolitan Museum of Art. My part is easy. I smile. I nod. I offer counsel only when he asks and bite my tongue when he does not.

Sooner or later, these precious visits end and he returns to the city with a carton of groceries and household appliances we'll never see again. I could not keep him from going. I would not try.

But my role in Dennis' life is no less important than it was when I washed his clothes and walked him to school. He washes his own clothes these days and navigates the city with a grace that astounds me. I no longer guard him against the evils of the world.

Now, I guard his dreams.

NOVEMBER 20. 6:30PM

Once again, the hospital has become our stomping grounds. Ron is showing signs of a urinary tract infection and a culture taken from his wound indicates three different types of bacteria. He will need three types of antibiotics to combat it. Along with changing the dressing three times a day, I am now charged with treating it with Bernadine, a brownish liquid that stains the sheets.

While my routine with the open wound has become a model of economic motions, the Bernadine often slips from my hands and splatters over the dresser top. I am tired of late and my hand often shakes.

Joanne Huffman, surgeon extraordinaire, has laid out careful plans for further surgery while expressing sorrow that there has to *be* more surgery. She can be no sorrier than we are. Once the infection to the wound has been cleared up, she will remove the mesh. This seems to be where the bacteria is growing. This, she says optimistically, will keep him in the hospital for ten days. I listen to this without similar optimism, quite confident that the ten days will stretch to twenty. Once the infection is clear, Joanne continues, an as yet unknown plastic surgeon will take a piece of skin from Ron's inner thigh and graft it to the open wound. While Ron can come home to recover, he will need to stay on his back for five days. Joy. I can only imagine how we will deal with that. This comprises the first stage of Joanne's grand plan.

Once the graft is healing—sometime after the first of the year but the time line is fuzzy—we will go back to the hospital to insert a shield and perform plastic surgery over the muscle. The recovery time on this is unclear; Joanne hedges when I ask her. I know she is reluctant to impart the news to me. But, really, can it be any worse than what we have already been through?

So here I am once again, forced to count my blessings to keep myself from becoming discouraged. The old hymn says, "Count your blessings, name them one by one, count your many blessings see what God has done." Sure, the words are true. But it is becoming much easier to count the trials. On a tally sheet, we seem a little heavy on the negative side. In the wake of Thanksgiving, with three more surgeries and several more months of recovery looming ahead, with a final to study for at graduate school and holiday shopping to do on a taut shoestring, I have my fair share of trials. The upbeat nature my friends refer to as Susie Sunshine has taken a beating lately.

I think about the word, "discouragement." The word itself is depressing: a soft "s" sound followed by a hard "c". A guttural "r" begins the inner word "rage." It ends with a sharp "t". It is a word I try to avoid. There are just too many letters to cope with, too many sounds to say. It is just too hard to handle.

And yet, lately, I am the poster child for discouragement. I admit that I am tired, but it really is so much more than just a physical state. My head swims the very moment I blink my eyes open and I swirl in looping circles behind my eyelids, my body teetering ever so slightly as I struggle to an upright position and keep my eyes open.

I have so little time to contemplate this state! My day begins before the dawn cracks and I heave myself reluctantly into the early morning. A hot shower. Dressing. Blow-drying hair that has lost what vitality it had with the doldrums of winter. There is the inevitable laundry to gather and drag down the stops. Descending into the dark and dank basement on feet wary of a cat in search of his breakfast. The cat is a reminder of our last year. He was to have been Ron's cat, but with Ron in the hospital, little Jimi bonded to Allen. Then I fix Allen's breakfast and make Bonnie's coffee, her necessary jumpstart to the day. I start dinner in the Crockpot and write a brief and cheery note for Ron with a short list of easy tasks for him to accomplish, something to give him a sense of purpose.

I melt into the morning fog, tugging open the frozen doors on my ancient Celebrity and inching my way through the gloom, my damaged corneas blinking back painful tears at the onslaught of approaching headlights. I drop Allen off at school. Pencil? Pen? Lunch money? Homework? He is not a morning person, but I feel obligated to keep up a cheerful line of prattle until he exits the car. Life is hard. Dad is ill. The least I can give him is a mother's smile, the one I carefully paste on most mornings.

After the car door slams, my mind shifts into neutral. I arrive at my destination with little recall of how I got there. At some time in my journey the sun will have begun its rise but I will have missed the pinks and purples while I slumbered somewhere behind my eyelids and my car independently navigated the twists and turns into Chester County.

The click of my classroom keys brings me temporarily to life. I turn the lock swing open the door, and enter my classroom. I turn on the lights and drop my book bag behind my desk. It is a routine that requires no concentration. I check my voicemail. Turn on the hall light. Open the computer lab. I lose myself in the day.

My students bring animation to the room, their voices and energy arriving long before they do. They are the ghosts of my innocence. I smile. I laugh. I teach. For seven hours, they occupy my every molecule. Even my infrequent trips to the ladies' room are done in a rush. Once in a while, though, I will lean against the door of the stall before exiting, allowing my eyes to flutter shut, feeling the coolness of the metal frame beneath my blazer. I could stay here, I think in the quiet and the coolness. But, as always, there are bodies in my classroom and questions to be answered. The day is over before I have begun to taste it and my sixth graders leave the room with far more haste than they entered it. This is not their real life. Teaching is bitter-sweet. I pick up forgotten pencils and papers from the floor. My back hurts as I bend, too many laundry baskets of burdens carried for too long.

Then I pack my book bag with things I meant to get to in the course of the day but didn't. I will cart it home again, an invader to my evening. It may or may not get my attention. It depends on what awaits me.

The sunlight hurts my eyes. I live an indoor life, forays to the dining hall and the science building my only outings. It is bitterly cold today and it bites at me, stealing my breath in sharp, quick pangs. I shield my right eye from the sun, driving home with one hand and squinting. It is the way I see the world, through a vague sort of blur.

My book bag weighs me down like a load of guilt. Spelling tests to grade. Lesson plans. Teacherly articles on non-verbal learning disorder. These things will eat at me this evening, stealing my time. Or they will sit ignored on the window seat, taunting me.

All teachers are bag ladies, carrying in our hand luggage the things that define us. Red pens. Composition books.

I square my shoulders where our front steps meet the sidewalk and whisper a prayer. *Dear God, let it have been a good day.* Even as I utter it, I know what an ineffectual prayer it is, its time lapse evident. I should have prayed this when I stood with my weary head against the stall in the ladies' room.

I do not call home during the day. In the early days of Ron's recovery, I did, offering him tidbits of my day, but I no longer have the energy to give. No news is good news. I have been startled enough by my ringing desk phone or the secretary's soft tap at my door. More than enough trips to the ER or the OR and a parade of green and beige waiting rooms has been the result.

I am tired.

Tired of the worry and the wait. Tired of stretching my paycheck to cover what used to take two. Tired of being needed so very, very much.

Their moods hinge on mine. I slap a cheery look onto my face, force a spring into my step I do not feel. It is a poem by William Carlos Williams that I read to my sixth grade students. *So much depends upon a red wheel barrow.* So much depends upon me.

If it has been an okay day, Ron will be seated on the couch watching ESPN and folding laundry. It is as if he waits for my car to pull up to the house before engaging in this bit of activity, having filled the ten hours I have been gone with other pressing demands on his attention. In reality there are no other demands except for doctors' appointments and the cheery little notes I leave behind. If it has been a down day, he is asleep or feigning sleep and will likely pounce on me like a lion on its unsuspecting prey when my foot crosses the threshold. I am loathe to enter on those days, too weary to push open the door and descent into the pit. There are worse days, though, manic ones that he spends scribbling lists at the dining room table, circling want ads he will never answer, filling out forms for work-at-home schemes that will deplete our dwindling funds even further. It is why, for the last six months, I have put most of my paycheck into my own bank account. At least I know the money will be there when I need it, not withdrawn in some manic phase he will not remember.

Once in a great while it will have been a good day. He will be bustling about the kitchen, setting the table and frying burgers. Those days are the cruelest because they give me hope. And hope , being the thing with feathers, can quickly fly away.

And so I am tired. At night I seek solace under the quilt my grandmother made for my wedding day, burrowing myself deep into my pillows. But I am never really rested.

A BUMP IN THE ROAD

I meant to get there right away
I meant to leave without delay
But before I could start on my chosen way
    I hit a bump in the road.

The bump was long and deep and wide
It pushed my plans off to the side
And rather jarred my fragile pride
    The unexpected bump in the road.

The bump was bigger than I'd thought
And although against its pull I fought
It took me down roads I had not sought
    That treacherous bump in the road.

I bumped and jarred and banged along
I felt this way to be all wrong
But gradually I heard a different song
    From the mysterious bump in the road.

It led me down highways and byways and lanes
Through violent storms and summer rains
To straight and narrow and empty planes
    That directing bump in the road.

I climbed up mountains, down valleys, o'er dales
Through rolling green lawns and hazardous gales
Into the most hidden and secret of darkened trails
    Led by that curious bump in the road.

And after years of climbing winding paths
I found my way back to my road at last
Richer from the journeys past
    When I first hit the bump in the road.

The way I'd traveled was varied and long
But the traveling had made me straight and strong
And I'd learned to sing a joyful song
    From that blessed bump in the road.

CHAPTER SIXTEEN.

DECEMBER 22, 2000. LATE.

It is December 22 and Ron is still in the hospital. He is scheduled to be released tomorrow. His stay this time was only five days longer than predicted. I am still determined to put a good face on Christmas and a few wrapped presents sit under the tree that two church members brought to us last week. I send out Christmas cards and include this letter:

Dear Friends,

I have been searching for the Wise Men this Christmas.

On our first "married" Christmas, Ron gave me a white porcelain set of the Holy Family with the intention of adding a piece each year. But before he got to the Wise Men, the set was discontinued. Each year when I set up my crèche, I feel that it is incomplete. No Wise Men. So as I bustle about my Christmas duties, I keep an eye out for these tall, imposing figures that would complete my Nativity. So far, they have eluded me.

But I got to thinking about the Wise Men this week—not the porcelain ones, but the ones who traveled across those ancient paths. Despite our American tradition of putting the Wise men at the scene of the manger, history tells us that they were not really there. Jesus was almost two by the time the Kings from the East found Him, no longer a Babe in a manger but a toddler in a rented house. The journey of the Wise Men was not an easy one. They were not aided by maps or tour guides. They had only minimal understanding of the magnitude of their journey. There were no four-star hotels along the way to ease the weariness of their travels. But they continued on, night after night, mile after mile, with only a Star and a promise to guide them.

Our family has been on a journey this past year. Beginning with Ron's horrific accident on March 1, we have trodden paths we had never expected to traverse. There have been valleys and mountains. There were moments when we wondered if we would ever walk in the light again. But we kept on walking, guided by no more than the Light of Our Savior and His promise to us: "I will never leave you nor forsake you."

The journey of the Wise Men ended when, at last, they found the Child and "fell down, and worshipped Him" (Matthew 2:11). Then they departed unto their own countries to fool that wicked old Herod. They are not mentioned again in the Gospels, but one assumes that on starlit nights they glanced up at the sky, remembering the brilliance of the light that had set them on their journey and marveling at the intricate workings of God.

Our journey is not yet ended. In the weeks, months, and years ahead Ron will continue to heal. We pray, as we know you do, for his complete recovery. But, whatever the outcome, we have been forever changed by the journey. With each step, we have gained strength from our Savior. He is present not only on the mountaintops but in the valleys and in the waiting rooms. When others have commented on the strength the children and I have shown these last nine months, my answer has been that it is a strength given by God.

My crèche is still without Wise Men. They are still traveling on to their destination, still following the Star and the Promise. I know that they will not turn back from their journey until they have reached their appointed end.

Perhaps next year, we, too will stand in awe before the newborn king and rest from our travails. We pray many blessings upon you this holy Season and rejoice in knowing that, in some small way, our lives have touched yours.

Ron, Linda, Dennis, Bonnie, and Allen

I sign our names in cheerful green ink, forcing an optimism I no longer feel. In fact, I am quite beyond feeling. I am beginning to wonder if any of the promises I cling to are true. I need at this moment, if not a Star blazing from the East, something that will salvage my faith. Anything.

But night, as is wont, holds no answers but only the emptiness I have come to know so well.

JANUARY 1, 2001. 5:30AM.

It is proving to be the predicted shoestring Christmas,

stretched taut between two hospitalizations. The heater breaks down on Christmas Eve and Allen and I try to cajole it into working with a hammer and a wrench. I wrap Ron up in afghans, fearful of another attack of pneumonia. Around midnight, the ancient heater finally coughs into function, but I know that this is one more thing to add to the list. Where will the money come from for this?

I think of a word I have just learned: "synchronous." It means, "Occurring at the same time." My life, I muse, is synchronous. Everything happens at once and I have no time to sort it out.

Christmas vacation is a blur. Ron is too ill for much company or visiting, so mostly we sit at home, huddled in front of the fireplace and watching Christmas videos. I try to read and write, but it seems I no sooner get settled then Ron needs me for something. Often I look at the sketch I made in my journal of Ron's open wound back in November, reminding myself that the healing going on inside of him is not yet complete. Above the sketch, I have written, *If God can heal the outside, He can also heal the inside.* There are days I need this reminder.

Dennis, who supports my writing even if he seldom comments on it, has given me *Chicken Soup for the Writers' Soul*. I leaf through it, engrossed in stories of ordinary people who felt the same passion to write that I do. Even as I wait to hear from Bonnie, who has spent the night at a friend's house this New Years' Eve, I calm my frayed nerves by writing down ideas in my journal, ways that I can somehow pare my duties down and find time to write.

There is no doubt—well, practically no doubt—that given the time and the ink my computer could turn out a best-selling novel. Ideas flow across me like a river over a waterfall, banging and crashing against the rocks as they jar me at odd moments during the day, carrying me headlong into a cold, shocking plunge: quick, write that down! And sometimes the idea makes it to my journal, but often I am summoned away by the cares of my life.

The few days left of break are quickly spent. Housebound and broke, I am rediscovering simple pleasures:

The poetry of Anne Sexton, riveted by her haunting, honest admissions. I slide a thin volumes off my bookshelf one day and sit on the floor for hours, wedged into a corner where no one will think to look for me, allowing myself to be engulfed in the voice of the poet. I drown in her sea of melodic pain, feeling a kinship to one in such despair.

Knitting with warm, loopy yarn on large needles. Listening to the satisfying click of the needles against each other as the stitches slide and a single strand takes on new dimensions. The bright colors ease my worn and tired soul.

Snowball fights. One crisp, perfect night we bundle up and head into the frost, pelting one another with soft, white balls. The cold air pierces my lungs and my shouts are carried over treetops and into the quiet night. My fingers and toes grow cold and I stomp around, scooping up the snow into round balls and hurling them at my family. Eventually, we all fall together into a heap, laughing and warm and heedless of our clothes.

Hot cocoa. Sipped while reading an engrossing book that is not required for any graduate class.

Stretching. Simply putting my arms over my head and reaching my fingertips towards heaven. My bones creak, my muscles unclench. It is not as good as one of Heather's magical shoulder rubs when she sneaks into my classroom before after school care, but the tingles down my arms and back remind me that I am still alive.

Sometimes I am finding, I need to remind myself that I am, indeed, still alive. Parts of me seem to keep dying off.

JANUARY 9, 2001. 7AM.

Christmas break is really just a pause, a comma rather than a period. Ron has at least two more surgeries ahead of him, as yet unscheduled. It is rainy and foggy the first day back at school, a less than auspicious beginning. The only umbrella that has not disappeared into someone's trunk or locker is the big striped one Pop Pop used on his riding lawnmower. I am not sure how I fell heir to this treasure, but it will keep me dry as I trek across campus today. Feeling a bit like a circus clown on a high wire, I teeter out into the morning.

My car—thank God!—starts on the first try. It would not start for Bonnie yesterday as she left campus, so Ron and I needed to cross country in the falling snow to rescue our stranded child. It has not been Bonnie's week for cars. On Tuesday at man pulling out of a parking lot smashed into the driver's side of her red Tempo, pushing her car into the guard rail. Bonnie was bounced around like gravel in a cement mixer but is otherwise unhurt. We can't say the same for the car. While we wait for insurance companies to inspect the damage and render their decisions, we shift the two remaining cars among three drivers. Bonnie has hitched a ride with Christina today so I am alone on Route 452.

I do not like headlights. They pierce my corneas like miniature novas, exploding beams that burst into fireworks and reflect off rain puddles. Every day can be the Fourth of July. I squint against the onslaught of light. A pain—small and innocuous—begins behind my right temple. The pounding will increase in intensity and rhythm as the day wears on and the bottle of Tylenol in my purse will be opened more than once.

It is difficult to see the road. My headlights slice through the fog and rain and the drops sparkle with luminescence, millions of fireflies dancing in front of my car. I navigate through them carefully. The cars line up behind me, frustrated by my crawl, but in the fog and the rain all are too cautious to pass me. I am, for the moment, the leader of the pack. I drive past the spot on 452 where Bonnie's car was hit, shuddering at the thought of my daughter's helplessness. But I have driven past other places where ones I have loved have had their blood spilled on the black asphalt. Bonnie is still whole.

It is the white line that is my salvation on this dark morning, that lovely line so thoughtfully painted by highway workers. While the paint glows and reflects a hazy shadow to the right, it is low to the ground and does not grab the headlights and toss them into the air, confusing me with the iridescence. I follow the line foot by foot; it disappears into the dark now and again, rounding a corner or replaced by a curb or barrier. I panic at these moments. It is my lifeline and losing it leaves me adrift on the black sea. I flounder, searching for the marker, praying the wheels of my car still grip the road. I have gone wrong on occasion, turning into driveways and parking lots when I lost the white line. I needed long moments to regain my equilibrium, holding my breath and pulling out into the flow of traffic again, picking up the white line in broken pieces and allowing it to guide me.

It is a peculiar way to see. Strange and weird and wondrous. It is almost impossible to explain to anyone by my eye doctor, who has stalwartly tried to help me overcome this disease since I was nineteen and began walking into walls, the shadow images of my childhood now full-blown and distracting. Neil is, he tells me, president of my fan club, marveling at what I have been able to accomplish with such distortions in my vision. I have tried to explain that my vision and my view are two different things. The way I see the world is definitely distorted but my perceptions of the world are not.

I just follow the white line.

Early on, I learned to make compensations for my lack of visual acuity. I learned to tap on the back of a stair with my heel, sliding down to find the next step. To place my finger on the top of my tea mug so I could feel when it was full. To use my hands to guide me down stairs and through doorways. I guide keys into locks with both hands, punch in phone numbers by rote, drive by memory. I do not trust what I see. It is not the way the world truly is.

Perhaps it would be a gentler world if it were, if all the edges that define our planet were blurred and hidden in shadows. If there were more fireworks on perfectly ordinary days. If everyone could summon a skyrocket for their own amusement at any given moment. If each of us had a white line to follow, a sure directive for their paths.

The white line guides and once again I have traversed the thirty-mile drive to my school. I leave my car in the parking lot and carefully pick my way through puddles and ice patches. There is no line here to guide me, but memory serves. The sky has lightened a bit and while I cannot quite see the steps, I know they are there.

The thumping behind my eye has increased. The fluorescent lights in my room will play havoc with my vision. I will squint to bring my sixth grader's essays into focus and decipher my own handwriting on the blackboard. Somehow, I will find a way. The white line that I have followed into teaching continues to direct my path. It is not always an easy line to follow. More than once, I have lost the line and meandered for a while. It is a demanding line, expecting more from me than I think I can give, pushing me to limits I am not always prepared to face.

I make my way down the hall, using my hands to guide me on the stairs. Whatever the day holds, it will undoubtedly test both my vision and my view. But it is where the line has led me.

The line God has chosen for me.

JANUARY 10. 2001. 4PM.

One person sought me out today. She came at the end of English class, standing to the side and smiling at my students as they left, the room the usual hub-bub of sixth-grade confusion.

"I wanted to tell you," she began. My mind scrambled to finish her sentence with information she needed to impart, an observation she needed to make. But instead, she finished with, "you helped me."

These words fell like molten gold onto my tired ears, dripping and swirling into rivulets in my heart. You helped me. Me helped you. The meaning is the same. Something I-said-did-though-acted-demonstrated-read had helped another human being in the struggle we call life.

The details of the conversation do not matter. The way in which my words aided another colleague is important only to her. What matters is that God was able to use me, depleted as I was, as a tool in her life. Even without the acknowledgement Nicole brought to me, this purpose is a high-calling. Amid the busy day of a middle school teacher with planning periods precious and few, she took the time to come to my room and tell me.

Remember those ten lepers that Jesus healed? They had come to Him begging for help, imploring Him to have mercy on them. And He did. He said but a word and they were healed, running off in their rejoicing to rejoin their families and their lives.

But one came back. He saw that he was no longer affected with leprosy and he marveled at the unmarked skin on his hands. He turned from the road, postponing his reunion with his own family. He turned back and bowed at the feet of the Lord, giving thanks and praise.

"And what of the other nine?" asked Jesus.

The man shrugged. "They have gone," he said. "They were anxious to return to their families. They have been diseased for so long that they could not wait."

"Yet you came back," the Savior observed. Then He bade this former leper, too, to return to his own home, saying, "Thy faith has made thee whole."

I wonder if Jesus did not tuck this little "thank you" into a hidden pocket of His robe someplace and keep it for a rainy day, a day that turned so dark no one stood beside Him.

One had come back.

The other lepers remained healed. Jesus is not vindictive. But perhaps the soul of the man who came back carried him forward with more joy and compassion. Perhaps his miraculous recovery and heartfelt gratitude allowed him to reach out to others with these words, "Once there was a man who healed me."

And maybe, just maybe, one life was changed. Maybe

someone said thank you.

All it takes is one.

JANUARY 11, 2001. 8 PM.

I was behind a woman in the market today who bought a king-sized Hershey bar and a Good housekeeping magazine. I thought to myself, Good for you. Nothing like a little self-indulgence. Now, it is true that I don't really know that both these items were for her. Maybe the Hershey bar was for her husband and the magazine—which featured a picture of Kathie Lee—for a son whose school report was on the exploitation of children in sweat shops. But I like to think that these items were both for her and that they were the beginning of an evening of self-indulgence. No offence intended, but she looked like she could use a little indulgence. Tired. Drawn. Her hair a little lifeless. Wearing the pallor of winter. Much like I looked when I saw my face in the mirror this morning. I guess I could stand a little self-indulgence as well.

What is it that makes me afraid to yield to this inclination now and then? Am I truly afraid that the world will collapse without me?

Or afraid that it won't?

JANUARY 14, 2001. 10 PM.

Bonnie's new boyfriend likes to fix things. To people who live in an ancient house in constant need of repair, this young man and his tool box are a blessing. In the seven weeks they have been dating, he has fixed the outside faucet, the burners on the stove, the wobbly legs on the dining room chairs, the loose leg on the coffee table, and the outside porch light. He has rewired the outlets in the dining room and the living room, installed new overhead light fixtures in the basement, and put a new light in the foyer. He says he can't wait to get his hands on our pipes!

He asked me yesterday how long the back burners on the stove had been out and I cast my mind over the last ten months and said, "Somewhere between the ruptured diaphragm and the first infection." I am sure he thought it an odd sort of answer, but he had the good manners not to say so.

It is true, though. Out of the last twenty-four months, Ron has spent fifteen in the hospital. This means that I spent fifteen months in waiting rooms and emergency rooms. I ran on a daily basis from work to the hospital to home and back to work, squeezing in graduate school along the way. I became adept at grading papers while perched on the green plastic chairs outside the OR and doing laundry at midnight. We lived on meals cooked in the microwave or in crock pots or donated by church members. Now and again I ran the vacuum cleaner. I had the heater repaired when it conked out at Christmas, figured out how to install the window air conditioners last summer, remembered to change the oil in the cars, and paid the bills on time.

But I never once thought of climbing up onto the roof to investigate the condition of our shingles. When the overhead light in the living room quit working, I lived without it. I didn't know what to do about the leaky outside faucet except shut the water off. The vagaries of the stove remained a mystery.

My focus was clearly not on my house. It was on Ron. I Corinthians 6:19 says that our bodies are the temple of God. While my material house fell into disrepair, it was Ron's body that occupied my thoughts and energies.

Two years ago, the current state of my house would have immersed me in guilt. But God has shown me these last months that my energy is finite. I need to choose wisely where I invest it. I chose Ron. The house could wait.

Ron continues to heal and recover, although it is slow going. Time invested into repairing his temple has not been in vain. There are days when his eyes sparkle with a light I did not think I would see again. He laughs more. He will grab me and tickle me and in the manner born into all males think it funny to put his cold hands on my neck. His body is almost repaired due to God and the prayers and skills of many.

Nicholas and his toolbox are welcome visitors to our broken-down house. He honors and respects my daughter. He makes her feel good about herself and invests his energy into putting our house back in order. Nicholas brings with him a new season, a season of repair.

FEBRUARY 11, 2001. 8 PM.

Life holds no guarantees. I remember thinking this as I drive to school this morning. I heard the sound of an ambulance in the distance and my hands froze on the steering wheel. What if it all happens again? Just because we have had our share of tragedies this past year does not make us immune from another. Maybe it is God's way of preparing me, for I am not surprised when I receive an emergency phone call two hours later. Marie, our school secretary, is apologetic when she gives me the pink slip. She has carried many down to my room.

This time, though, it is not Ron. It is Bonnie, my sunshine. I call the number on the message slip shoved into my hands and am connected with the nurse at Bonnie's community college. All soothing and comforting, the nurse tells me that Bonnie is doubled over in pain and crying. The nurse suspects that she has a kidney stone. I shift into automatic, letting Marie know that I need to leave, and grab my keys and my coat from the closet.

It is starting to rain hard when I get to my car and I have trouble seeing through the windshield. I think about my daughter and the strength she has shared with me these last months. I wonder if she might have a burst appendix. I sing Sunday School choruses. I pray.

Bonnie has been raised with boys. We say it in the same tone we would say, "Bonnie has been raised with wolves." We mean it the same way. Squished between two brothers and with a parade of

Lost Boys traipsing through her life and parking their sleeping bags in our living room for months at a time, Bonnie has learned survival skills. She has a sarcastic wit and a fierce right hook. She does not suffer fools lightly. Boys who have dared to cast an eye in her direction have found that she is just as likely to tell them off as she is to date them.

Lately, since the advent of Nicholas, she has been trying to be "more like a girl." Enter the curling irons and the make-up case. Earrings and dressy sweaters. Perfume. Nail polish. All the things I have been dying to share with my daughter in which she has had no interest. Until now.

When Bonnie left the house this morning, she had on both eye shadow and lipstick. Her hair was pulled back and curled. Her cheeks were brushed with pink. She smelled like apple blossoms. She looked beautiful. But even as she left for school the hair was beginning to bother her and the lipstick needed to be reapplied.

"You know, Mom," she said, "I don't know about all this girl stuff. It might not take."

Bonnie has, after all, been raised with boys. It is akin to being raised with wolves. It has given her an inner strength that is concealed by her outward appearance. Whatever is going on inside of her right now, it cannot be stronger than she is.

MARCH 3, 2001. 5PM.

It began here, We walk down the long corridor, each of us lost in our own thoughts. We have timed this passage, sometimes making a game out of it, trying to improve upon our brisk pace as we marked the distance. But we do not hurry now or check our watches. Bonnie moves as slowly as Ron, still recovering from the severe kidney infection that sent her to the hospital two weeks ago. I blink at the light, a case of iritis and a suture wrapped around a blood vessel in my right eye causing a throbbing pain. But time does not matter tonight. This will be, we pray, the last time we make this journey and it cannot be marked in mere minutes.

The walls and the carpeting are all too familiar. We have nodded to many of the faces we pass, not knowing names but recognizing fellow pilgrims. Sometimes we have sat in waiting rooms with them, letting our Styrofoam cups of coffee grow cold as we tapped our fingernails on the molded chairs and kept a sharp eye out for green-gowned figures.

The corridor ends and we enter the main lobby. The same burgundy and pink furniture sits on the same beige rugs. There are touches of green today in token of the approaching Irish holiday. We have seen the lobby decked out for Easter and Halloween, Thanksgiving and Christmas. The seasons, too, have trudged across this floor.

One West is to our left, just beyond the bank of elevators. It is our first stop. Here we deposit the flowers we have brought to the nurses, reminiscing with them for a few minutes. There are a few quick hugs and handshakes. Several patients ambulate the halls in their blue hospital gowns. We do not linger, but head back to the elevators and up to the fourth floor.

I catch my breath here. The scene is achingly familiar; a family sits in the glassed-off waiting room outside the ICU, wringing their hands and praying. I have been inside this room too many times to count. I do not need to enter it to remember.

We circle back on our tour, past the pay phones where I dropped so many quarters, past the telemetry units and the operating rooms. They are now a part of our past.

I can talk now. My voice, scratchy for the last few days as we finished up with medical tests, no longer catches in my throat. Here is where I would lean my head against the wall, praying for the strength to go on. Here is where I would stop for a moment, gathering my courage around me before plunging headlong down the hall. Here is where I sat and cried one evening, too broken and tired to stand.

Bonnie and Allen hug me. *It's okay, Mom. We made it.*

And it seems as if we did. For the last time, we traverse the corridor, walking slowly and sharing our memories. There is no need to rush. Ron, his gait cautious and halting, walks with us. Today, he has been released from the services of Dr. Joanne Huffman and her staff.

Step by slow step, we have come to the end of this part of our journey.

BOOK TWO.

"BANG"

"When you pass through the waters, I will be with you; and when you pass through the rivers, they will not sweep over you. When you walk through the fire, you will not be burned. The flames will not set you ablaze.

Isaiah 43:2

EMULATION

My daughter says she wants to be
Just like me.
Nightly as we pray
She bows her head
Beside her bed
And mimics what I say.
Dear God, this is an awesome task
That you have called me for.
She watches everything I do
Though she is only four.

My daughter says she wants to be
Just like me.
She sews a crooked seam
A zigzag trim
On Barbie's hem
A fashion dolly's dream.
Dear God, my little ten year old
Will need these wifely arts
So she can one day be a mate
To a Christian husband's heart.

My daughter says she wants to be
Just like me.
She cuts her corners neat
And turns the wheel
The tires squeal
And I cringe in my seat.
Dear God, my child is seventeen
And has a woman's face,
So many things still left to teach.
God, grant me the grace.

There's miles to go
No time to lose
Each day's a precious jewel,

Of clothes and boys
And late-night talks
And happenings at school.

My daughter wants to be
Just like me.
The years have flown away.
A college degree
A teacher she'll be
And on her own one day.
Dear God, she has been
My sweet joy
Despite the bumps and hills.
Thank you for
This precious child
Her spirit to instill
With a solid faith
A gentle hand
A strong and loving heart
A ready smile
A freckled nose
A willingness to impart
Her love of God
Through word and song wherever she may go
My greatest gift
In all the world
Has been to see her grow.

My daughter wants to be
Just like me
As much as she possibly can.
But in every way
On every day
She makes me who I am.

CHAPTER SEVENTEEN.

APRIL 3, 2001. 8PM.

Bonnie is in trouble. Serious trouble that may affect her health and her future. The news takes me by surprise yesterday, borne on the slender shoulders of Nicholas whose concern for her finally won out over his code of silence. I am grateful—despite the battle he needed to wage with his conscience—that he came to me.

"Bonnie is obsessed with being thin," he says, getting right to the point. "She doesn't eat at school. Sometimes she makes herself throw up. And sometimes she takes her dad's medications."

Bad news takes a while to assimilate. At first his words bounce off me with a surreal quality. I listen but I do not really comprehend. I am still a little shell-shocked by the last year. Nicholas stands there, watching my face. His words begin to surround me and engulf me and threaten to strangle me. Tears rise to my eyes, but I do not let myself cry. I am stronger than that. I have been remolded of steel. I nod and walk away, climbing the steps up to my bedroom. I need time to think, to calm my racing heart and mind. To close my eyes and pretend I can make it all disappear.

Nicholas follows me and stands in the middle of my bedroom, not sure what to do with his long arms. He crosses them over his body, clearly uncomfortable but determined to finish what he started.

"I care about her. But if she knows I told you, she'll break up with me. On the other hand, I don't want a dead girlfriend."

I nod and try to clear my throat. I need to let this sincere young man know I am listening. "It's been a rough two years," I say. "Bonnie may not have told you that two years ago her dad had a nervous breakdown. Then the accident last year. She's had a lot of stress, more than your average kid."

Nicholas agrees. "And she's handled it."

"She's been my rock. But even rocks can crack. Maybe it's all gotten to be too much for her." I feel the tears rising up and stinging at my eyes. I wish this young man with his depressing news and his nervous arms would just go away. "Thanks for telling me. I'll…deal with it." I cannot, right now, even begin to imagine how, but I need Nicholas gone. He stands there for a few more minutes, hesitating. I turn away and begin to fuss with things on my dresser. Finally, he takes the hint and backs out of the room. I hear him downstairs a minute later, laughing with Bonnie. *How can she laugh?* I wonder. *Has she become so much like me that she can pretend everything is fine when the world is falling to fragments?*

I kneel by the bed and close my eyes. I have no idea where to go with this, but to God. *Dear Lord,* I pray, this is my child. *The why and the how do not matter. Where do I go from here? How do I help her?* When my heart and mind are a little quieter and my thoughts have slowed down, I am able to listen, to understand, to know that God will prepare me for whatever this task demands.

Hours pass and I stay in my room. I call my best friend Chris and Bonnie's older brother, seeking counsel. I find another spot for Ron's medication, out of the hall bathroom. Bonnie is already in bed when I knock on her door at 10:45 but she is not asleep. I snuggle down next to her, inhaling her apple blossom scent and holding her hand as she cries onto my shoulder. Confessions come easily in the night, under cover of dark. I understand that she has been terribly frightened, worried somehow that she caused the kidney infection from poor choices and an unhealthy diet. She has been reluctant to ask for help, but she knows she needs it. I am feeling guilty for not knowing that she was in trouble but, typically, she pats my arm and says, "Mom, you've had too many other things to take care of."

In the morning, the world is not nearly so dark. The sun rises and lightens the land again. Despite the long and mostly sleepless night, hope shines forth. We are talking, my daughter and I, setting some limits and looking for help.

She will eat some breakfast at home before class, at least toast and a glass of juice. She will have a light lunch, perhaps salad and fruit. And we will find her someone to talk to, someone she can trust. I will call our minister today about a counselor. Bonnie says she will enlist help from her friends, including Nicholas. As she showers and dresses, I pack a lunch for her and tuck a note into the bag. *You are my heart. You are my life. You are wonderful and unique. Do not leave me.*

I do not know if she will believe it, but I say it anyway. Not because I am her mother, but because it is true.

Nicholas has said that I am Bonnie's "avatar." It is, he informs me, a word from a video game that means the reincarnation of a Hindu god. In a more modern, technological world it has come to mean the perfect ideal.

I am far from the perfect model and I force myself to look at some of my own behaviors to see how they have affected my daughter. Her desire to be "just like me" never seemed a bad thing. Until now. She is not me. She is not my clone. With Ron's descent into mental illness, tasks often fell to me that I was ill-equipped to handle. Bonnie became my right hand, my steady and reliable source of sunshine.

Nicholas's news has made me question many of my choices. Have I given my children the stability and love they need? Despite Ron's fluctuating moods and on-going needs, do they feel secure and safe? My thoughts are convoluted. The list of things I am forced to handle has grown exceedingly long.

I think back to last October, on the occasion of our 25th wedding anniversary, and Allen's tribute to us on the meaning of courage. *But have I been too courageous*, I ask myself now, *showing such a perfect face to the world that my children think I can move mountains?*

How can anyone, even a daughter, hope to live up to that?

Maybe, I tell myself, *it is time to stop being so brave. Maybe I need to show my daughter that it is okay to be human.*

First, though, I will need to give myself permission to be less than perfect. In my musings, I come to recognize this about myself: calm makes me uneasy. I deal with chaos, crisis, and catastrophe with extraordinary skill. Nothing seems to faze me as I set out single-handedly righting the wrongs of the world. I have been saving someone for years.

But calm is unnerving. It is the lull before the storm, waiting for the other shoe to drop. I can never relax and enjoy the calm because I know it cannot last. *Let's get on with the next crisis!* My mind says. *Let's go!*

I have been running from crisis to crisis for eight years, jumping from one to the next like stones across a river. There have been very few places to stop and rest. Another crisis has always loomed on the horizon.

Now, with this latest calamity, I am feeling a little frayed, as if part of the carefully constructed and held together me is starting to unravel. On those infrequent occasions when no great tragedy claims my attention, I find it impossible to sit still. I pace and fidget, looking for things my hands can get into but unable to settle my mind on any one thing.

A while back, in an undergraduate sociology class, I read that Americans have forgotten the art of "just being." Have I forgotten it or just never had it? We buy into the good old fashioned work ethic early on. Our nation of type A personalities thinks we need to be in motion twenty-four hours a day.

I wonder what I would do without a crisis in my life. What will I fill the time with when I am no longer required to save the world? Or do I need to learn now to give up the burdens I carry? Whose shoulders will carry them if mine do not? Or do they need to be carried at all? I take these questions to Margaret, our school psychologist.

I tell her this story about me:

When I was a baby, my mother would often leave me in my playpen in the backyard as she went about her chores. One afternoon when I was about two, she completely forgot about me. She took my older brother into the house to start supper preparations while I continued to play contently in my playpen. Supper came and Mom, Dad, and Harvey ate. Perhaps Dad thought I was napping. Eventually as the evening wore on, someone remembered me. My mother rushed out to the backyard and there I was, smiling and happily playing.

It is the point my mother makes of the story that amazes Margaret. "You were always such a capable child," my mother would tell me. "Even at two, you could take care of yourself."

"So when," asks Margaret, "were you ever a child?" I ponder this. I have been an excellent adult, but somehow I have lost the child I should have been. Everything I do is for someone else.

"But there are things I want to do for me!" I protest to Margaret. "I'm working on a novel. Finishing my master's.

Writing an article on autism."

Margaret smiles. "Those are all achievements. What do you do just for you?"

I draw a blank. She suggests I make a list of ten things I do just for me. In the span of an afternoon, I can come up with only seven that are not achievement-oriented and not done for someone else. Not only is my list incomplete, but I realize how seldom I allow myself time to do any of the things on my list. So, the question is, what *have* I been doing with my time? And was it worth it?

APRIL 18, 2001. 9 PM.

Her name is Peggy but the last time I saw her face it was atop a body a foot shorter. She was a school mate of Dennis'. Many was the afternoon that he would come home with Peggy in tow. She loved to roll down the hill out front and "help" me bake cookies. Her mother worked two jobs to support them and there was no father. She had few friends, but quickly found her way down the two blocks to our house where she would join the gang of kids in the backyard making circus tents out of my bed sheets. She became one of them. Like the rest of them, she piled into the Caravan on Sundays and joined us for church. Whenever I gathered everyone around to read a Bible story, her eyes would sparkle.

Her eyes still sparkled, although they are sometimes obscured by the brown hair she wears long and straight to conceal the scars on the left side of her face. I had almost forgotten about Peggy. So many kids just like her have trooped through my life! But there she was at the video store, tapping me on the shoulder and reminding me of her juxtaposition in our lives.

She caught me up on her history. She moved away with her mother when she was ten. By fourteen, she was pregnant. By the time she was eighteen, she had married, divorced, and turned to drugs. When she was twenty-two and under the influence, Peggy ran her car into a telephone pole in an attempted suicide. She lived. The scars are a daily reminder of how low she had sunk.

"And that's when I thought about God," said Peggy. "When I was laying in the hospital, wishing I had died and afraid to look in a mirror, I remembered the stories you read, Linda. About how God loves all of us and forgives all of us. That's when I decided to make something of my life."

She now lives in upstate Pennsylvania and has custody of her twelve-year old son. She hopes to soon gain custody of her eight-year-old daughter. She works at a steady job, has been sober for four years, and is going to cosmetology school.

And she knows God loves her.

Her re-entrance into my life seems fortuitous. It has been a long and difficult week, with the revelations about Bonnie causing me to question some of the choices I made in my own life. I wondered if I did the right thing by having such an open home, always crowded with neighborhood strays. Had there been enough love for everyone or were my own children stinted?

Then Peggy tapped on my shoulder at the video store.

"You know," she said as she hugged me with a promise to come visit, "your house was the one place where I felt safe as a kid."

After all, I guess I did the right thing.

SHE IS

...two years behind the kids she

Graduated high school with and

While they will finish college this year

And face—for the first time—the real world

She has already seen it.

She has haunted hospital corridors and

Scrambled eggs for her younger brother and

Kept the home fires burning while

One parent kept falling down and

The other kept picking him up.

She is not invincible, and sometimes she cries

Because life is not fair.

But unlike her peers who are ensconced being

Ivy-covered walls and plodding through classics on

Ancient French poetry and bio-physics

She knows it.

CHAPTER EIGHTEEN

APRIL 23, 2001. 4 PM.

With a few tears and a lot of prayer, Bonnie and Nicholas have decided to be "just friends." It was, they both contend, "almost right." With two such lovely young people, both committed to God and His plans for their lives, one wonders why it couldn't have worked. What was it that was missing, keeping them from filling the missing pieces?

"Something," Bonnie has said early on in the relationship, "just isn't there."

They tried to make it work, tried to fall in love with each other. The best they could do was genuine affection. It is more, of course, than a lot of people ever manage to have. But for these two young people, it is just not enough. They deserve head-over-heels, fly-me-to-the-mood, heart palpitations and sweaty palms love. And someday they will find it. They are not willing to settle for less than what they know God has to offer them. They each know that God has designed someone out there especially for them. They're willing to wait.

Good for them. Good that they recognized that all the things that were right with the relationship did not make up for what was wrong. Good that they think they can still maintain a friendship. They still laugh together, but it is slightly hollow. However much they try to put a good face on it, it is still a loss. And our lives seem to be continually full of losses.

I, too, feel the loss. I am grateful to Nicholas, who entered our lives with a toolbox in his hands. In the few months he and Bonnie dated, he installed light fixtures in the basement and the foyer, rewired the outlets in the house, and installed a new bathroom floor. Not only have his repairs strengthened my house, but they have strengthened my daughter as well. The last two years saw her spending far too much time in hospital rooms and not enough time being young. Nicholas helped her find the twenty-something inside herself again.

Yet even as my daughter packs Nicholas into a memory corner of her heart and tries to move on, I sense in myself a sadness that is out of keeping with such a commonplace occurrence. Daughters break up with boyfriends all the time. I cannot seem to shake the notion that my daughter is doomed to seek out the wrong young men, always believing that she can somehow remake them. Nicholas, for all his gentleness, had problems with anxiety and hyperactivity. And the boy she dated just before Nicholas seemed always on the edge of despair.

"Don't you know any normal boys?" I ask Bonnie.

"And," she counters, "how would a normal boy fit in around here?"

She is right, of course. Our lives have been off-balance for so long that we wouldn't know normal if it knocked on our door. I take a long look at my daughter. She is twenty-two and lovely. She has a tender heart and a love for God. Her smile lights up every freckle on her face and her blue eyes sparkle with delight. Her gregarious personality attracts people to her. Some of them seem to be the wrong sort of people. Her brothers, I tell her, always brought home the Lost Boys. She feels the need to date them. Somehow, she thinks she can save the world.

She reminds me too much of me.

MAY 2, 2001. 9AM.

I float, a round, white balloon drifting towards the sky and the sun, slowly breathing in and out. Each breath is labored as I try to focus on my lungs. I can still feel the congestion in my chest and hear it in the rasp of my voice. An all engulfing tiredness descends on me in the middle of the day, tempting me to close my eyes even as I struggle through the last class of the afternoon. I would love to give in to it, allowing my limbs to succumb and move no more, my brain to shut down and doze for a while. Instead, I keep floating in my white balloon existence, struggling to keep both feet on the ground when what I really want is to be lifted into the air and carried away on a current, suspended above the green earth.

Pneumonia, the doctor said when I finally gave into my daughter's pleading and went. I stayed home for a few days, melting into my pillows but not really resting. Ron paces the floors. The few hours he is able to work each day do not really occupy him much and he asks me constant questions about going to school, setting goals, becoming a "better person." I am weary enough without his interference. I return to school, still in my balloon state, glad to be floating away from Ron.

It is not wholly unpleasant, being a white balloon. Nothing—no worries or cares or injuries—quite breaks through the haze. I can fall asleep at the blink of an eyelid, saving precious time usually spent tossing and turning while I wrestle with the problems of the world. Floating white balloons have no problems, except sharp points, of course. These seem easy enough to avoid as I hang in the air.

My thoughts in this white haze are not always coherent, but they are always gentle. Warm sunshine. Pink roses. Delicate china teacups. With each rise and fall of my congested lungs comes an image of rainbows and tulips, dancing just at the edge of my mind.

What am I *on*, wonders my daughter. Nothing. I stopped taking the antibiotic days ago because it made me feel out of control. Or maybe it was the fever that did it. No matter. White balloons have no fevers.

Eventually, I know, I will need to come down to earth again. Even now, harbingers of disaster lurk on the horizon. Nicholas has taken to calling every night and continually asks Bonnie if she likes him. If she says yes, he laughs and tells her she is weird. When I land again, I will probably find Nicholas' behavior annoying. I will try to remember that he is both dyslexic and

ADHD. Somewhere in the past few days, my mind recalls glancing at an article on autism and the human brain and other learning disabilities. But such deep thoughts are above my capabilities right now. Ron is experiencing his own anxiety problems. Dennis phoned yesterday to say that he is getting laid off and will need some help with the rent money. The stress is just waiting for me, piling up and trying to reach me on my balloon voyage.

Avoid sharp points, I keep telling myself. Just keep floating.

MAY 23, 2001. 8 AM.

"Eleven days" is now written on my chalkboard. Am I anxious and eager for the school year to end? I am not fully recovered from my bout with pneumonia. I still feel jet-lagged and have trouble breathing. What I need, I tell myself, is a week in the sun, basking on the beach at Rehoboth and renewing myself in childhood memories. Chances are good that I will not get it. Something always interferes with my escape attempts. Dennis needs help filling out his unemployment forms and is worried about making ends meet. I seem to find it easy to place my oldest son in God's hands, but I cannot do it with Bonnie. I continue to feel the loss of Nicholas and know that I am too wrapped up her life. But I do not know how to extricate myself.

Bonnie, Allen, and I are the survivors of the Titanic. We share bonds that no one else does. Dennis, beloved child, was more peripheral to the events of the last two years. I often think I have neglected Allen these past few months, focusing on my daughter. He says he understands. "You've been sick, Mom," he says. His Mother's Day card to me was so sweet! It said that he often though he'd like to be as "smart as you are. But that's way too much trouble!" The card ended with, "Good thing I'll always have you to help me."

I need to find time to contact the family counselor that Margaret recommended. I have waited too long already, but white floating balloons do not need to see therapists. I feel like we are all in a state of limbo. I find myself bursting into tears and not being able to name a cause. Last night a great sadness overwhelmed me and I could not help but cry. It was all over just as quickly, but I know that I need to find someone to talk to. I have two weeks left of school and then graduate classes this summer. I cannot fall apart now.

Is it all just stress and exhaustion? I get angry at minor things. I seem to always be mad at Ron. I obsess about Bonnie. I've become resentful of the choices I have needed to make for my family, choices that may not have been right for me.

I am both confused by and angry at Ron. He has turned my life upside down for so long! Each day when I drag my weary self home, he and Allen are plunked down in front of the TV. Why isn't the laundry done or dinner started? Why aren't they at the park or out back playing basketball? But I feel guilty if I complain and Ron becomes defensive. He honestly thinks that doing the dishes and the laundry once a week makes him an exemplary husband! Yesterday I yelled at him for napping on the deck after sitting on the couch all afternoon.

Lord, I need help. I recognize this. Send someone, Father, someone who can help me. I am so used to being in control, but now I cannot control either my emotions or my thoughts.

What is wrong with me?

CLOUDS

Sometimes they

Obscure the light,

Or filter it in streaks of white

But whether dark, or

Weather fair

The sun and stars

Are always there.

CHAPTER NINETEEN.

MAY 29, 2001. 11 AM.

My journal has gone missing. I suspect that I left it at church Sunday morning. Since it has my name scrawled all over it, I will more than likely get it back, but for the moment I feel totally lost without it. In the last two years, my journal has been my safe haven. I have often bled onto its pages, pouring out all the wicked, horrible things I dare not utter to a living soul. It holds my hopes, my dreams, my fears, and my dark, dark secret: I am not always a nice person. I my journal I have chronicled Ron's accident and illness and my attempt to hold the world together. My journal, unlike a novel, has no neat and happy ending. That is because this is real life—my real life, I sometimes need to remind myself. There is little about it that has turned out as I planned. My life keeps on changing, no matter how much I might want to slam the covers of my journal together and stop it in time. But I am not able to stop writing; it is the only thing that helps me maintain my sanity. For now, then, loose pages of notebook paper will have to do.

I left a message for a Christian counselor this morning. A long conversation with a friend last night helped me to see that it is really me, not my kids, which need help. The kids are fine. They are fine, my friend contends, because of me. While I was busy saving everyone else, no one was saving me. No one ever has. All the help and counseling we have ever had—and the list is astoundingly long!—has always been for Ron. No wonder I am so frazzled!

I have been compartmentalizing my life for years, tucking parts of it into neat little containers that seldom seep into one another. I can sit in a graduate class at West Chester with my cell phone set to vibrate, just in case there is an emergency call from one hospital or another. Separate little suitcases are stowed out of sight while I go about my many duties, but now the contents seem to be leaking out and muddying things, making my life a bit of a mess. I seem to always be on the verge of tears. Is this normal? How would I know? What about my life these last few years has resembled "normal"?

There are moments when I just cannot hold the floodgates closed any longer. Last Friday, I laid my head on my desk during a free period and burst into tears. I could not give a name to the cause—just the same old feelings of stress and anxiety—but my heart felt as if it would break. I cried out to God: *Send someone! I need help! Quick!*

God, I believe, heard the agony of my soul. Bonnie—bless her!—walked into my room just at that moment, on her way home from her class at college. She did not ask a single question, just gathered me into her arms and let me cry. I am sure she is worried. It is not often that she sees her invincible mother reduced to tears. She told me that it was "okay to cry. Sometimes it makes you feel better." What an incredibly sensitive girl I have raised! I do not know why I spend so many days and nights worrying about her. I worry that she will end up with Nick, who is still hovering around the fringes of her life. I worry that she will not end up with Nick. I worry that I have stolen much of her youth away from her with Ron's illnesses. I worry that the world will take advantage of her and her kind and loving nature. I worry that I might not always be there to protect her, that she spends too much time with me and not enough with people her own age. I can become so consumed with worry that my stomach cramps up and I cannot eat or drink.

I worry about Ron and his increasing weight, such a problem that he cannot stand for more than a few minutes at a time. I am angry about this, I guess. I put so much energy into getting him well again, yet he has ignored all of Dr. Huffman's advice and allowed himself to become heavy again. I am tired—so tired!—of dealing with Ron and his issues. I would really like to escape to the beach for a few days after school is out, but I dread dealing with the aftermath. My escape plans are always thwarted, anyway, just as the beginning of the school year always sees Ron is one crisis or another. He has become a gigantic burden and I no longer worry about hurting him with my shrewish tongue. I, too, was injured in the accident. He claims he doesn't know how to be any different than he is, but he will make promises to try. All of his promises are of the Mary Poppins pie-crust variety, "easily made and easily broken." If I can maintain an attitude of anger towards him, he will get his butt in gear for a week or so, clean the house and do the laundry and start supper. But the energy required to maintain my anger is draining.

I am eager for the end of school—witness the counting off of days on my chalkboard—but I am sure the summer will offer no respite. Historically, our summers have been difficult these last few years. Last summer we spent dealing with Ron's recovery issues and the summer before he was at Friends'. So I end the year with no hope. How sad!

I need help. I am sinking fast. I need to become healthier so I can keep my kids healthy. I am tired of always being so damn strong and positive about life. I just want all this to end.

JUNE 1, 2001. 8PM.

I went to see the Christian counselor for the first time today. Gary seems to be a good person to talk to. We spoke briefly of Ron's depression and disabilities, but most of our conversation revolved around me. That has never happened before; everything always comes back to Ron. I feel guilty about spending the money on myself—this is not covered by my insurance—but Ron has had more than his share of counseling and therapy. So I am going to try and not feel guilty about spending the money on me.

Gary commented that I am a "woman of incredible strength."

This has always been part of the problem, because I think I am strong enough to handle it all. He thinks a lot of what I have been feeling is stress from having so much to deal with for so long. I like his spirituality. He said his goal in counseling is always to have "God increase and self decrease." Still, it will take me a while to get used to the idea that I am not able to do this for myself.

I slept well last night until about 4PM, then prayed until I fell back to sleep. I awoke feeling as if I had had a good night's sleep for once. Bonnie went with two friends to a modeling try-out. None of them expects to get called, but it was fun to see her fussing with her hair and make-up. I am really trying to put her in God's hands.

On the way to bed last night, the kids stopped by for a group hug. Ron had already gone up to bed and Bonnie and Allen mentioned that they really do not like being alone with their dad. I am quite certain Ron heard; maybe he needed to. In some way, he seems to think I stole their affection from him due to my consistent care while he was hospitalized. "It cost me," he says. Of course it did. It cost all of us. But since he has been home, he has done precious little to win them over.

Gary asked me yesterday where I see myself in ten years. As a published writer, I hope. A reading specialist. Maybe a visiting author. It did not occur to me until this morning that none of my hazy plans include Ron. He is the unknown quantity; his actions have become unpredictable.

I am feeling better, a little stronger. I am NOT going crazy, and that in itself is reassuring. I have had to make difficult choices and I have done the best that I could.

Maybe, just maybe, everything will turn out okay. I guess Hope is still inside Pandora's Box.

JUNE 5, 2001. 3 PM.

I have gotten my journal back and stapled in the loose-leaf pages. As expected, I had left it at church. I hope that no one read it and now thinks I am one whacked out woman. Still, I am grateful that I keep a journal and that God has given me the ability to write. I can track my progress and see that I am a little further along the road today. I still worry about Bonnie and Nick and their odd relationship but I am no longer suffering physical pangs or feelings of guilt. I keep telling myself this: they are both right where they need to be. They are "sort of friends" but are trying to move on with their lives.

Bonnie still occupies so much of my thoughts, far more than she ought. I have other children, other concerns in my life. Allen needs my attention, too, my oft-neglected child. He wants to try out for basketball or track next year and he wants me to help him write a science-fiction novel over the summer. He still is not good with new situations. The Sunday School class frightens him and he says he often feels like he is going to cry. Part of this is Allen's learning disability; he does not handle new things well, but needs to be eased into them. How could I possibly have eased him into the events of the last few years?

I have thought about this logically, trying to remove my emotions from the equation. I have been trying to save my husband, myself, and my children. Perhaps I cannot save them all. Perhaps I can only save my children and myself.

I sometimes wonder why I let Ron remain at the house. Do I lack the strength to ask him to leave or am I afraid of what he would do without me? I try and tell myself this: if I could let go of Ron, perhaps Bonnie could let go of Nick and what I think may be her codependency on him. I so want to solve this problem! I have been solving problems for years. Why should this be any different? Aren't I in charge of the world? I blame myself—probably more than I deserve—for the demise of her relationship with Nick. I am so obsessed with my daughter! This cannot be healthy, but I am incapable of stopping it or changing it.

A TREE BOUGH HANGING OVER JOHNNY'S WAY

It has grown far from its home,

This golden-leafed bough

Shimmering with red, orange, and gold.

It arches over the road,

Shading the path

With the colors of the sun.

I drive beneath, marveling that

So many leaves and shoots

Have emerged from this one tree.

The wind blows gently, rustling

The leaves, shaking the branch

But the bough

Does not break.

Why have I?

CHAPTER TWENTY.

JUNE 13, 2001. 7PM.

The blow-up at our house begins as a simple discussion, or so I think. Bonnie had been home all day, trying to get the house in order and the laundry done with little help from the guys. Exasperated, she tells me about it when I get home from work. With my usual penchant for problem-solving, I decide a family conference is in order.

It actually begins calmly enough, with the four of us gathered around the dining room table, my notebook in front of me. Maybe it is the notebook that does it. I always want everything in black and white, neatly written down and ordered. I sometimes forget that when you deal with a bipolar, you seldom get order. I point out that I will be heading off to graduate school over the summer and that Bonnie will be working full time. The guys are going to need to do more around the house.

I mention to Ron—and in hindsight it is not my wisest move—that the dishes were piled high in the sink when I got home on Tuesday. He begins to shout at me that he had done the dishes and I am just attacking him. I ask him to quiet down and talk, not shout, but he keeps right on yelling. I get mad and throw my pen across the table and yell back at him, even though I can see where all this is going. Getting mad at him like this is never helpful. Again, I sometimes forget the rules. He stands up and pounds his fist on the table. Now we are both acting like temperamental three year olds.

I grab my car keys and say, "We don't need to stay here and take this."

"Then leave!" Ron shouts. "Just get out!"

So we do, running out to my car a few steps ahead of my manic husband. We slam and lock the doors and Ron catches up to us, pounding his fists on the hood of my car and shouting. Ultimately, we are able to pull away and, lacking any real direction, head to church. Joan and Lisa are working in the office on Sunday's bulletin and they welcome us in, offering tissues and shoulders to cry on. We sit in Pastor Lowe's office for a while, hashing over the events of the last nine years. I do not think talking about the situation will do any good. It never does. It just makes me feel very, very sad that Ron's illness has done this to all of us. Pastor's attitude puzzles me. He tells me that, given Ron's physical and mental problems, there are things I just need to put up with. Should being afraid of my husband be one of them?

We go back. I am not sure it is the right decision, but my mind is filled with regret and some semblance of hope. There is, I tell myself, always hope. Maybe, just maybe. Cross my fingers and hope. Ron is calmer when we arrive back home, but he has called his parents and they are there, offering support to him but none to me. The things we live with are difficult enough without the usual lines being drawn and sides taken. There is surely enough blame to spread around, but what good does it do? Nothing is solved. Nothing ever is, but eventually peace reigns again. On most days, it is the best I can expect.

Later on in the evening I call Dennis, looking for an impartial view from an almost outsider. I have raised a smart and tender young man. He thinks part of his dad's problems is knowing I have made a success of my life and Ron has done little with his. As always, I worry about making the right decisions for Bonnie and Allen. Dennis assures me that whatever decisions are best for me will ultimately be best for them. Bonnie is paramount in my thoughts. Does she make the wrong decisions about men in accordance with what I have shown her? Does she put up with erratic behavior in the boys she dates because I put up with it from Ron? Dennis, bless him, tells me that Bonnie is still very young and inexperienced and just makes stupid choices sometimes. She may continue, he says, to make stupid choices. I need to let her. It does not mean that she will end up with the wrong guy.

So it all comes back to the same issue of letting go and trusting. This is so much easier said than done! I feel that I am a foreigner to myself right now. How could I have survived Ron's accident but be unable to survive the recovery? Am I just exhausted from the events of the last few years or is this my new life and the way I will always feel? How depressing the latter would be!

JUNE 15, 2001. 4:30 PM.

I enfold people. This is what my counselor has told me. It is, Gary says, part of my servant quality that I bring people who need some tender care into our home and make them members of our family. It is why I found it so hard to let go of Nick even after Bonnie had moved on. To me, he was still a Lost Boy who needed help. Gary assures me that there is nothing wrong with this reaching out to others, that it becomes wrong only when I become so consumed by the problems of others that I make no time for myself. But this is what my life has been like, with Ron's problems always crowding out my own needs.

I told Gary about our blow-up and he thinks Ron's tendencies are, like most men, to put up defenses. Our family structure is necessarily different owing to his disabilities, but Ron still wants to be the man of the house. Gary suggests a "short term" commitment, Ron and I each writing down three things we need from each other this coming week. At least it is something positive to do.

I need to make myself believe that all will be well. I put too much credence into little things, looking for signs and then bending them to my own interpretation. For instance, at supper last night I became convinced—for no reason at all—that someone would call and ask Bonnie out. I spent the evening biting my nails to the quick, feeling the flutter of anticipation in my stomach each time the phone rang. Then Christine called around 10PM and asked Bonnie to go to a wedding with her on Saturday. So much for my premonitions!

My journal continues to provide me with more support than I am able to get from human beings, or even at times from God. At a recent Pennsylvania Writing Project workshop, a suggestion was made about using bright colored pens to lighten our moods. Since mine decidedly needs lightening, I've treated myself to some gel pens in rainbow colors. I am hoping these new pens will keep me from writing the same depressing thoughts.

The peace I felt a few days ago was only temporary and has evaporated. I have a hard time concentrating on any one task. Even watching TV is beyond my ability to focus. My mind is always, always wrapped around Bonnie and as hard as I may try, I just cannot hand her over to God. My friend Deb suggests that I am preoccupied with my daughter because I see so much of myself in her. This is no surprise to me. I do not want her to make my mistakes, to live my life. I do not want her to settle for a man whose emotional needs will never allow him to grow up. I am reconciled to my own state. I married whom I married. He is who he is and is, except in a manic state, a gentle man. But Bonnie deserves so much more. I cast daggers at happy couples who dare to walk past me hand in hand. I so much want this for her! I have to continue to believe that God has plans for her or go crazy with worry. I may well go crazy anyway.

JUNE 29, 2001. 10AM

JABEZ PRAYER JOURNALS #1

The small book, *The Prayer of Jabez,* is enjoying immense popularity right now. I hear about it in church on Sunday night and buy both the book and the devotional on Monday. I am constantly seeking answers. Along with my new colored pens, I am now armed with all the tools I need to turn my life around. I desire, as Jabez, to give my life and stress over to God. If this long-ago Old Testament man did it without benefit of gel pens, so can I.

This is the prayer of the little-known Jabez:

Oh, that You would bless me indeed

    And enlarge my territory:

That Your hand would be with me,

    And that You would keep me from evil (I Chronicles 4:10)

The devotional asks me on page one, "What is your portrait of God?" and I respond in purple ink: *I think of God as loving but stern, someone who wants the best for me even when I don't know what that is. But I also think God has given me the ability to take care of myself. At some of the most difficult moments in my life, I have felt God's strength, but I rely on my own abilities a great deal of the time. I usually think God has more important things to do than watch my every step!*

Maybe I am wrong about all this. Exodus 34:6 says, "The Lord, the Lord God, merciful and gracious, longsuffering and abounding in goodness and truth." Does this mean that God *does* want me to "bother Him" about everything and rely on myself for nothing? Today, I begin praying the prayer of Jabez for the first time and making my heartfelt request to God:

Oh, that You would bless me indeed
    And enlarge my territory;
That Your hand would be with me,
    And that You would keep me from evil
Beneath the prayer I write, in pink gel pen:

Bless me, Father, with a clear mind and a pure heart. Help me to be the kind of wife Ron needs, the kind of mother my children need, the kind of friend my friends need, the kind of teacher my students need. Let my influence for You extend beyond my small circle, Lord. Let me have opportunities to speak for You in ways I cannot even now imagine. Keep me and guide me, Lord. Keep me from evil. Let me in no way serve the enemy or hinder your will.

JUNE 30, 11AM.

JABEZ PRAYER JOURNALS #2

The Lord's blessing is our greatest wealth; all our work adds nothing to it. (Proverbs 10:22)

Jabez's prayer asked for what God wanted in his life. Contrary to my original thought, it was not a selfish prayer based only on his needs. In praying this, we put ourselves totally at God's mercy. Our own will often obstructs what God wants to do in our lives. God wants to give us so many blessings but cannot because we do not ask. It's the old free-will clause, "You do not have because you do not ask" (James 4:2).

Is my stress level any lower now? It is lower than it was before I began reading *The Book of Jabez* but still much, much higher than it should be. God may want to give me many blessings, but my life is certainly not blessed by stress! So if I seek a blessing from God, that must mean that God desires me to be stress-free.

I visualize what my life would be like without stress. I cannot remember how it feels. But I can commit to my journal—in green ink, this time—a prayer that asks God to lift the cloud under which I now live.

Dear God, like Jabez I ask You to bless me—a lot! I want for my life what you want for it. Yes, I currently carry a lot of pain and stress. This is why I need Your blessing SO desperately and seek it with such urgency. Bless me, God. A lot!

JUNE 30, 2001. LATE.

JABEZ PRAYER JOURNALS #3

What is the main reason I have a hard time asking God for His blessings and believing He hears my prayer? I guess I have always thought of a blessing as an Old Testament thing, Jacob and Esau kneeling before Isaac and asking for their father's blessing. I haven't really considered it as having God's hand upon me in the literal sense. Yet, that is just what God wants to do; put His hands upon us and bless us.

I seem to be a little less obsessed about Bonnie and find that I can put her into the back of my mind now and again. But it continues to be a source of stress for me and stress is something that God—who wants to bless me—does not want me to have. How to handle it? I am afraid that God must be getting very tired of reassuring me, but He is infinitely patient. I think I have learned this much, at least: my own anxieties and desire to control hinder God's ability to act, all due to that free-will clause.

JULY 1, 2001. 3 PM.

JABEZ PRAYER JOURNAL #4

Lord, thank You that You have plans for a nobody like me! Now I beg You to pour Your extraordinary favor on me today. Bring to my mind the "small thing" You want to bless in my life.

I have continued to call out to God to bless me—a lot!—and extend my territory. I have little notion of where He may take me and, typical of me, I am uncomfortable with the idea that it may be someplace I do not want to go. On the other hand, I have not particularly enjoyed being where I am of late, so what have I to lose?

There is an idea growing in me, a thought about the journals I have kept for the past two years. They are full of my pain and my faith and moments where only the ability to put words onto paper kept me moving forward. I think of these journals as a walk in the valley. Does God want me to write this and share it? I am scared of writing it, of ruining it, of others seeing it and my pain. Above all, I am scared of facing the pain again. But, if God calls me to do it, then I will try my best. I do, though, hope that God has other plans to extend my territory!

JULY 2, 2001. 8 AM

JABEZ PRAYER JOURNALS #5

Oh, that You would keep me from evil!

This prayer, according to The Book of Jabez, is for God's supernatural ability to protect us from Satan's influence. Success, after all, brings the greatest opportunities for failure. Most Christians prays for strength to endure temptation, but Jabez prayers that the temptation might be sent away. Even Jesus asked for this, "deliverance from evil." (Matthew 6:13)

Satan is wily. He wants us to doubt our own wisdom, using just enough of the truth to deceive us. We are so easily deceived! We need protection from His deception.

This is written in blue ink in my journal:

Lord, keep me from making the mistakes I am prone to when temptation comes. I confess that what I think is necessary, smart, or personally beneficial is too often only the beautiful rapping of sin. So, please, keep evil far from me!

Satan wants us to doubt our own experiences. Someone has said that, "Your danger is not being on the edge of the precipice, but in being unwatchful there." How easy it would be to fall over and lose our footing! We need God to spare us from serious misjudgment.

Lord, keep me safe from the pain and grief that sin brings. Protect me against both the dangers that I cannot see and the ones I think I can risk because I try to do much under my own power. Protect me, Lord, with Your power.

SHATTERED

Shattered into pieces

Scattered by the wind

It will take the King of Heaven

To put me together again.

CHAPTER TWENTY-ONE.

JULY 4, 2001. 9AM

JABEZ PRAYER JOURNALS #6

You shall be called by a new name, which the mouth of the Lord will name (Isaiah 62:2).

These are the names Our Father wants to call us:
His Chosen (John 15:19)
Mine (Psalm 50:10-12)
Beloved (Deuteronomy 33:12)
Sought After (Isaiah 62:12)
Friend (James 2:23)

What wonderful names, showing how much He cares for each one of us! But this is the name I call myself: Overburdened. On all sides, I feel as if I carry too much. Yet I realize that many women carry as much—or more—than I do. Has my "too busy" attitude kept me from accomplishing more with my writing? Has my "I can solve it by myself" attitude kept me from truly throwing myself on the mercy of God?

Yes. Yes. And yes. God favors those who ask. He holds back

nothing from those who earnestly long for what He wants. In education, we often talk about the "spiral curriculum", revisiting the same concepts each year but on a higher level of understanding. I've discovered the same to be true in graduate school. Bruce Wilkinson, author of *The Prayer of Jabez*, says the same thing is true of this prayer. You continue to receive the four-part blessing, but in more and more abundance. These are my specific prayers, written in red:

Dear Lord, I desire a lessening of my stress and a trusting attitude that God is in control of my life, my finances, my family, and my career. I ask for an extension of my territory as a teacher and a chance to influence others for You. Aid me in my writing, Father, if the completion of this book be Your will. Keep me from evil, even the evil of my own thoughts and leaning on my own strength and wisdom. Keep me from actively seeking anything except what You want for me.

JULY 5, 2001. 10 AM

JABEZ PRAYER JOURNALS #7

And now try me in this, says the Lord of Hosts, if I will not open for you the windows of Heaven and pour out for you such blessings that there will not be enough room to receive it (Malachi 3:10).

We can never use up our quota of blessing. How exciting! Nor will the blessings God gives to us ever take something away from another. God has more than enough to go around. Has my life changed in the seven days I have been saying and praying the Jabez prayer? Yes. And no.

Yes, I feel calmer and more confident. There are moments when my old buoyancy, long buried under the care of my life, rises to the surface again and I feel for a moment that everything really will be alright. I still awake at odd moments of the night, consumed with worry and obsessing about Bonnie and her odd relationship with the equally odd Nick. My picture of God has changed somewhat. I know that He doesn't want me to lean on my own power but trust in Him in all things. Most of the time I can avoid conjuring up scenarios in which everyone in my life behaves the way I think they should, thereby resolving the problems of the world. I am trying to be kinder to myself, giving myself more time to just sit and relax, an art I have all but forgotten.

And no. It all feels so tenuous, like a thread stretched too tight that is holding together for the moment but will eventually snap. I can keep myself in one piece for a while, then I will find myself breaking apart and scattering to the wind. I cannot really afford to keep seeing the Christian counselor and I am afraid that anyone else will think I am nuts. This is not the image I have carefully projected over the years. I have been the strong one, the one who is able to handle whatever comes her way.

So I am riding on a seesaw right now, sometimes up and

sometimes down and mostly struggling to just stay on. Writing is my solace, but what I write—even in rainbow gel colors—often does not make sense. The fear that is still at the essence of my journals is my concern for Bonnie. My worries about her have often take prominence over my thoughts and prevented me from being more productive in other areas. I try—I really do!—to lean on God and look for answers to my prayers. Sometimes I convince myself I see answers coming to pass, but there are always mere mirages that disappear when I move my head.

I used to consider myself a very brave person. I did not back away from the many tubes and machines that surrounded Ron's body in the hospital. Even though it was difficult, I learned to clean and care for his open wound. I do not back down from a challenge. I have managed these last few years to take care of my family. But I think perhaps I am not as brave as I need to be. If I was really, truly brave, I would cast all of my cares and worries onto God and leave them there, walking away instead of continually rehashing them and picking at them like a festering sore. Despite what I say to others, despite what I often write in my journal, I doubt God's power to make all this right again. I think that it is all just too broken.

AUGUST 6, 2001. 11AM

I have somehow ended up on the beach here at Rehoboth and I hardly know how I got here. But this is the one place in the world where I have always felt peace. I left the house at 8:15 this morning after another sleepless night spent crying and praying. My daughter crawled into bed with me, holding me close and offering comfort. I had no words to tell her of my agony that would not frighten her even more. So, at 8am, while she slept, I rose and dressed quietly, looking in on my sleeping children. Not on Ron. If I am to save myself, it will be for them.

What did I hope to gain as I got in my car and drove away, seeking the sun and some peace? I had no plan, no purpose. I just knew that I could not go on any longer in the same unhealthy state, worrying and agonizing and obsessing about things over which I have no control. I remembered the words of a visiting nurse who came when Ron first returned home from the hospital. "All the rules are different now," she said. "It's hard to trust again."

Hard? Try impossible. I have spent most of the summer trying to trust and find peace. The emotional pain is suffocating me, much more than I can bear. My burdens are too heavy. I have been trying to tell people all summer that I needed help, but either they do not see it or are unable to give it. Everyone seems to expect that I will just keep going and going and going. Where? For what?

Is God listening? I ask myself this question as I drive down Route 13. I have prayed so hard for Ron, yet he remains a hollow man. I have struggled to commit Bonnie to Him but I continue to be confused by it all. Once I controlled the world, but now nothing seems to be in my control any longer, not even my own feelings.

What is worrying me? Why is it so hard to put it into words?

Many of the demons are nameless though they are real. Sitting on the beach, here by the ocean, writing in my journal in blood red, I list some of the anxieties I *can* put a name to:

Ron and his lack of improvement. My worry that he will never be any better. My own waning strength. What will happen to the kids if I collapse? Who will take care of the house and the bills and my family? Bonnie and her choice in men. What if she marries someone who will drain her, the way my marriage has drained me? Is she strong enough to handle it? Am I?

Naming them does not help, but for a few moments I am doing something purposeful. I walk along the beach, kicking my toes through the sand of my carefree childhood days, wondering why I have come to this frightening, emotional place. Climbing up the rocks where my brother and I fished for baby sharks, I listen to the lap of the waves and the hum of the breeze. God is not in the clamor of my daily life nor in the obsessions and anxieties that threaten to consume me. I feel that I am drowning, being sucked into a whirlpool that keeps pulling me deeper and deeper into the black ocean. I kick furiously, struggling with the weight of the water until my head is in the air again, just barely. But He is here, in the still small voice inside me that still struggles to be heard.

He loves me. And He cares that I am in such pain. The temptation to give up is strong, but God's will is stronger. I have but one chance left. I need to turn it all over to Him.

But I so like to be in control! I've had to be in control these past nine years. I've had hardly a moment to rest. How do I suddenly take the strength that I have and turn it over to God? I have been like the water, eagerly filling in everyone's cracks and spreading myself too thin. My strength is a thing of the past. It is time to let go and move on.

I will. I can. In my more lucid moments, I know that I can do this. I can survive. I do not yet know what it all means. The me that comes through this fire will not be the same me that went into it. I have been the good girl, always the good girl, forever patching up quarrels or giving in. I handled arguments among relatives and even played peacemaker from a hospital bed. I am the dependable one who remembers birthdays and anniversaries and always tries to do the right thing. The most outrageous thing I have ever done is grab my car keys and drive 100 miles to the beach without leaving a note. This is my life. No one else's. And I need to live it without this pain. I cannot control anyone else.

But can I learn to control me?

BOOK THREE

"BOOM"

"My comfort in my suffering is this; your promise preserves my life."

Psalm 119:50

MOUNT VESUVIOUS

A scream begins

Deep in the bowels of agony and

Burns its way up the esophagus

Until it erupts

Like Mount Vesuvius

Linda Waltersdorf Cobourn

WEIGHT

The crashing weight has

Pushed me down, lower

Than a limbo stick.

Burdens picked up over the years

One by one

                              And added to

The growing pile upon my back.

I stagger under the load

Hardly faltering, picking up more and more until

It all topples over

And I fall

d

o

w

n

CHAPTER TWENTY-TWO.

AUGUST 30, 2001. 9 AM.

So what is it like here, on the other side of the padded walls? It is a little odd but comfy, the Club med of psychiatric wards. There is a large and lovely community room. Each patient has a private room with a bath. My responsibilities here are few: Get well. Be sociable. Move on. This is, after all, just a stopping place, only one more in the long line of waiting rooms that litter my past.

Summer is gone. What a waste! Perfectly good sunny days spent in graduate classes and used up with worry and things I could never control. Bonnie and her relationships. Ron and his own demons. Who was I fooling? God is in charge and always was, even when I refused to acknowledge it.

Ron doesn't quite get it. Yes, he knows that he is a large part of what brought me here. Perhaps that is not accurate. Rather, it is my reactions to Ron and his illnesses. I have been taking on far too many burdens in an attempt to help him heal, and in the end I only fell ill myself. Ron, there is no doubt, needs to learn to function as a more independent person. He needs to have a chance to fail or succeed on his own. His illness cannot continue to consume me as well.

Life goes on outside of these walls. Allen is home doing "Allen stuff." Bonnie has enlisted a girlfriend's help in keeping the house running. Ron shuffles out from his nightly visit, head hanging down, for once the one being left out of the locked ward. There is a lonely drive ahead of him. No one at home he can depend on.

For me, this is a respite. Recharge. Regroup. Take a long, deep breath and learn to face the world again. This is only a temporary bump in my road. For Ron, the bump has been a long, wide pit. He may never be able to climb out of it.

Was he ever really independent? It is hard to remember. Dennis thinks he has a memory of a dad from fifteen years ago, laughing and smiling and better able to cope with the world at large. We have pictures of Ron from the "before" time; he is happy and active. The older children show them to Allen now and then, trying to introduce him to the father he never really knew. Ron was—still is—a gentle soul. Pure, innocent, faithful, true. He was a man who would never willingly hurt another. On some level, he is still those things.

I have no doubt that I, back at the farm, will be better off for my respite here as a human being, a wife, a mother, a teacher. I know that in a day or so I will go back to the real world. But what about Ron, forever caught in the limbo of T.S. Eliot's straw men, unable to choose between heaven and hell?

I have no wish to scream this morning. There is no need. I will try and figure out how to keep my life balanced and still fulfill my many roles. It is permissible, here, to say all things as long as they are honest.

Here is my terrible confession, uttered only in this place: the days I have been least stressed in the last nine years of the roller coaster ride have been those days when Ron was hospitalized. Oh, sweet relief to know that he was in someone else' care for a while and the burden was no longer mine! It is a socially acceptable way to get rid of a burdensome spouse: hospitalization. Hospital stays have happened often enough in the last nine years that I have had some vacations in which to breathe. There was two weeks in October for gallbladder surgery, four days in March for throat surgery, three days in April for an anxiety attack that pretended it was heart, five days in June for a mental crisis, then a long and peaceful fourteen weeks spent at Friends' Hospital during a summer that seemed to span forever. The kids and I packed lunches and drove to the lake, all but forgetting Ron except for nightly phone calls and Sunday drives up Roosevelt Boulevard to visit him behind high and locked walls.

When Ron returned home, I allowed myself to believe that we might have a normal existence. But what is normal, anyway? Who remembers? The car crash on March 1 was the end of that hope. Almost, almost, in my darkest hours I could wish that he had not survived. Enough is enough. Could I survive? But he didn't and I did and the anticipated two week stay predicted by Dr. Huffman after the accident stretched itself into sixteen and plopped itself—again-into summer. But this time there were no peaceful trips to the lake, but frantic runs to the emergency room. By August, we were well ingrained into the routine: two days hospital stay for a hernia, two weeks for an infection. The open wound that Ron brought home in October was worse than anything I had ever seen and I had to clean and change the dressing three times a day, biting back bile and trying not to look at it. Two more weeks in December and another surgery meant more wound care for me. What a Christmas present! Then an endless parade of outpatient visits. Too much, too much! How does one person carry it all and still teach fulltime and care for her children and home and go to graduate school and maintain her own sanity?

Scream? Who has time to scream? But the scream builds up inside of you, breaking you down, destroying you piece by piece.

Until you fall.

AUGUST 31, 2001. 7AM.

I am watching people this morning while I wait for the community meeting to start. Most of these patients have mannerisms that mirror Ron's: continuous motion, nodding off, difficulty forming thoughts into words. I sit among them, however briefly, thankful I am not really one of them. I have a real life outside. I am thinking of school this morning. Will I be there for the first day on Tuesday? If not, the world will probably go on without me. Call it exhaustion or stress of anxiety. For once, I need to put me first.

I still want happily-ever-after. I still want a whole family. But the Ron I married—the kind, gentle man with the winning smile—no longer exists. He died on March 2, the victim of a horrific car accident. I need to let him go, grieve his loss, and move on.

I talked to Dr. Mechanick today, the weekend psychiatrist. He is the latest in a long line of people who have looked at the last nine years of my life and said, "Wow! How did you survive?" The answer is simple. I survived by being strong. Maybe too strong. He says that I do not really need to be here—he would send me home today—but I do need a chance to regroup. I am clearly not depressed, just overwhelmed.

Dennis and Laura came to visit last night, bringing their wry humor into the room. Dennis finds it amusing that a friend of his from school is also here. "You're really fine," my son said. "You just OD'd on Dad." He grinned at me before he left. "Geez, I knew I had one loony parent. But two?"

I am a little scared this morning, wondering how I will pull it all together. I keep so many balls in the air! Still, it does not all need to be solved today. Or tomorrow. One step at a time.

I am getting to know some of these patients. Karen is a social worker who says she is glad there is another "intellectual" in this merry band. She says it took her a long time to admit she needed help. And Sondra is an art teacher who has asked if we can talk privately later. She said when I first arrived, she said to herself, "That woman is not like the rest of us. She does not belong here." But, for the moment, I do belong here. The world can come crashing down on anyone who is trying to be Atlas.

We talked in group this morning of ways to face our own emotions and how difficult it often is. I spoke of the mask I wore for so long of the competent wife. I do not want to wear it again. Others here have also worn masks. Sometimes we are our own worst enemies.

Dennis suggests that I use this episode to my advantage. "It's worked for Dad for nine years," he points out. Every now and then, my son advises, I should become agitated and mutter strange words to myself, referring obliquely to "the psych ward."

There is an amazing sense of community on this side of the locked doors. Like all of the other waiting rooms I have been in over the years, people here have been torn from their lives. No one has intentionally made the choice to be here. Most of us have been carrying far too many things for far too long. We have lost part of ourselves along the way. We played "Bingo" in the common room last night and it was an absolute riot. We cheered each other on and plotted to make sure that everyone won at least once. Bob, who joined our ranks yesterday, became our focal point as the only one without a prize.

"This one's all about Bob!" we said as we began another round. "This one is for Bob!"

Joanne, one of the staff, laughed. "If your doctors could see you all now," she commented, "they'd send the whole lot of you home! None of you seems the least depressed."

"What about you, Bob?' we asked.

"I'm great!" he shouted. "I think I'm cured."

Later on in the evening, Sondra and I played our own made-up version of ping-pong. We named it wolley-pong because it sounded funny. Troy ran in circles around the hallway, ducking beneath the desk of the nursing station so he would not be caught. Randy, Dennis' friend, went about collecting money to order pizza. Two pizza places and a Chinese restaurant will deliver here. The crazy ones also get hungry! Gretchen and Virginia sat on the coach and gossiped and flipped television channels.

More laughter all evening long. "Aw, Linda," said Sondra with her lovely Argentinean accent that makes the "I" in my name sound like an "e". "You're so good for us. Your humor is contagious."

If laughter is the best medicine, then everyone in this room will soon be well again.

SEPTEMBER 1, 2001. 9 PM.

Going home, going home. Tomorrow, says Dr. Mechanick. *You've done great. You're going to be fine.* I believe it. The others here are surprised at my early release. But not really. *Home? You're going home? No one leaves so quickly. Then again, you never really did belong here.*

They say it without rancor. There is no jealousy among them, no I-wish-it-could-be-me attitude. They wish me well. They believe in my ability to put it all back together again. If I can do it, with all of the burdens I carry, there is hope for them. We need to do the best we can to take care of ourselves, but sometimes we all need a hand. This is also what Ron needs; not to have me continually prop him up, but to get support from others with similar challenges.

Back to school on Tuesday. I am not feeling at all panicked. There will be an extended homeroom and an assembly. I will meet only three of my four sections. I will have absolutely nothing copied or planned, but life will go on.

Mary, a therapist, asked me to share with the group this morning the secret of my early release. Simple secret: community. Support and love each other. Ask for help. My release from Bryn Mawr has been quick, but the release from my own demons will take much longer. I will need help to conquer them all. I hope that I am brave enough to ask for it.

IN THE CIRCLE

I am living my days more calmly
In the circle of God's love.
I am channeling my cares
Into prayers that will rise above.

I am sleeping much more peacefully
In His protective arms.
I am trusting more in God to keep
My loved ones safe from harm.

I've been outside the circle
And found it dark and bare.
Outside God's loving circle
Is the weight of stress and care.

Lord, stay my wandering feet
And keep me by thy side.
For if I leave the circle
I'll have nowhere to hide.

Nowhere thou won't find me
And call me to thy side
Nowhere thou won't seek me
Nowhere left to hide.

Keep me in the circle, Lord
Don't let my wanderlust lead.
Outside your loving circle, Lord
There is naught that I need.

CHAPTER TWENTY-THREE.

SEPTEMBER 20, 2001. 4PM.

The one activity in physical education class at which my high school self excelled was gymnastics, in particular the balance beam. I amazed myself as well as my classmates, who saw me as the intelligent egghead, when I discovered that I could not only balance on, but turn and jump and somersault on, the balance beam. What my astonished classmates did not know was that the fear of being up off the ground did not bother me because I could not actually *see* the ground. So, how could I tell how far away from it I really was?

I was always good at balancing. Most of the time, I still am. For many years I have effectively balanced work, children, home, and school. I have hardly ever dropped a ball, until last summer, anyway, when a whole bunch of balls came tumbling down, bouncing around me. It was not a happy time.

I am learning to balance again. I teeter now and then and drop the occasional ball. I am trying to learn if the ball I dropped is one I really need to pick up, or one better let go. Sometimes, the act of bending over is enough to make me topple. A lot of things just don't seem to be worth the trouble anymore. Keeping a spotless bathroom and making beds and drying the dishes are just not worth juggling anymore. I am remembering what a friend told me years ago; "Think of yourself as having a finite amount of energy. You need to spend it wisely."

While I have become pretty good at balancing, I have never been especially good at waiting, despite the proverb that says, "All good things come to them that wait." Where is the virtue, I often wondered, in sitting on the sidelines and waiting? Much better to be in the thick of the action, getting things done!

Yet, in my heart, I longed to be like Mary, who sat contentedly at the feet of Jesus. What perfect tranquility she found in listening to Him! I imagine her cozily curled up on the floor by his feet, her knees drawn up beneath her, her hands at rest on her lap. Her shoulders are relaxed and at ease; on her face there are no worry lines or wrinkles. She is a woman of perfect peace. Her life holds no stress. She is at the feet of Jesus and that is the only place she needs to me.

Compare this woman to her sister, Martha, who bustles about the kitchen banging pots and pans, her face red and hot from the cooking fire and her exertions. Her hair is in disarray, her apron stained. She tenses her shoulders and knots her brow when she sees her sister sitting so calmly, then shouts like a fishwife, "Come and help me!" Martha is tense and the lines on her face make her look older than she is.

Ah, I long to be like Mary, but I know that I am more a Martha. Or was. I am trying to learn the art of waiting on the Lord.

Some days my mind is totally at peace and I hear strains of gospel music in my ears. *He is able to do much more than I could ever do. God is good, all the time. He brings a song of praise to this heart of mine.*

I have been waiting—not always patient and calm, like Mary—but waiting, nonetheless. Waiting on the Lord. And while at first the waiting seemed arduous—haven't I already spent enough time in waiting rooms? Shouldn't I be exempt by now?—it is becoming easier.

Somehow, Ron and I have survived this latest round of crises. How do we always manage to keep going and putting the pieces back together again? One piece at a time. Slowly. Carefully. Waiting. Nothing is to be gained from rushing. In his own way, Ron tries to take care of me. He makes me laugh. He keeps me from taking my own life too seriously. He reminds me to make time for my friends. He reminds me that waiting gives us time.

OCTOBER 7, 2001. 7AM.

Driving to school this Indian summer morning, I steer around the bend by a farmhouse and notice that the fog has lifted and now hovers twenty yards or more off the ground. It is a strange sight, like a cloud that has dropped near the earth and become too entrenched by gravity to escape back to the sky. In just a moment, I will be driving under it. I hesitate. The blackness has begun to life from my soul, but I still need to guard myself, fearful that at any moment a sight, a sound, a smell might trigger a memory too much to handle and send me spiraling back into the deep gulf. I have spent too many days already trying to climb out of it, inching my way out of the abyss and sometimes slipping back again, struggling to reach level ground. I am doing better now, my new therapist and my friends all say. I nod, believing that it is mostly true but aware that my clamber out of the abyss is not yet complete. The dark void is still a part of my soul; I am leery of it.

I am passing under the layer of fog now, and the rising sun is shrouded by the gray mass rolling down from the hills. It is eerie. The ground beneath me is solid and the wheels of my car still make contact with the street. Yet I feel that I am somehow floating, my soul rising from my body and up through the roof of my car, into the layers of gray fog. It is moist and cool, I imagine, but not cloying. I do not feel trapped or frightened. I can drive through this and come out into the sunshine.

NOVEMBER 2, 2001. 3PM.

I like to know the endings of things, and I do not really know how this story will end. It is the reason I became a writer, to control the endings of my stories. In fact, I generally know the outcome of my characters first and then construct the story around it. Once in a while, though, my characters will surprise me. They will refuse to act the way they are supposed to. They will want to make their own decisions about the outcomes of their imaginary lives.

There are several plot lines running through my life right now. Ron and I are trying to figure out a new relationship. Allen is getting to know a different sort of dad. Dennis and Laura are moving towards a life-time commitment to each other. Bonnie and a new beau are exploring the depths of a budding relationship. And I do not know any of the endings. It makes me vaguely uncomfortable.

When I pick up a new book to read, I always flip to the back. I want to make sure the main character survives and is thriving. I don't invest hours of worry into a character that gets knocked off on page 292. Knowing the ending has never stopped me from enjoying the story.

But real life is not a book. I still tend to construct "happy-ever-afters" in my head, but I realize that it is not within my power to make them happen. In the last scene of the movie, *Pleasantville,* the woman says, "How will this end?" and the man replies, "I don't know. Isn't that wonderful?"

I am not sure that it is wonderful. I do not know the answers to any of the plot lines now twisting through my life. Will my offspring find everlasting contentment with their current loves? Will Ron be able to fully recover from the accident and illnesses and return to work? Will I ever finish my Master's in reading and become a published author? Tune in next week, when life may change again. I am uneasy about it all.

But, uneasy though I may be, I have come to know that God

loves us all. He has planned out the perfect path for each of us. The ending is not within my control, but God knows what it will be.

And isn't THAT wonderful?

REFLECTING

I see myself as a prism.

Reflecting.

Refracting.

Refining.

The light of the Lord.

If my planes and angles

And beveled edges

Cast out a spectrum of colors

The light you see

From me

Is only a dim reflection

Of Him.

CHAPTER TWENTY-FOUR.

JANUARY 1, 2002. 11AM.

I cried a bit in Meeting for Worship today, but not because I was sad. Sometimes the joy within me needs to spill over because my heart is just too full to hold it all. It's been a year—a whole year—since Ron was released from the trauma surgeon's service and sent home to heal. Naively, we thought this was the end.

Little did I know that I would need to heal as much as Ron. My scars are not visible, but they run just as deep. It has taken me a while to get used to life without a crisis. A ringing phone need not mean that someone's life hangs in the balance. Holidays do not need to be celebrated in hospitals. People can leave my presence and arrive back home without the assistance of an ambulance.

Ron has begun to heal, although the damage is great and he will never be the same man again. I, too, have begun to heal. I cannot ever again take for granted the blessings of family and faith. Each day offers a new beginning and a sense of gratitude.

Sometimes, the joy just spills out!

There is a scene in *Lord of the Rings* where Frodo is pierced by the sword of a Dark Rider. The dark magic of the sword sends him into a shadow world from which he will never be able to return if the poison fills his system. He will become, as the Dark Rider is, a wraith.

I have been to the shadow world. Nothing is clear there, yet some things are far too clear. The shadows are large and menacing, looming over everything. They block your path, stepping in front of you at every turn. Yes, they are only shadows. You know that. You know there is really no substance to them. If you were brave enough, you could push right through them. But you cannot make yourself do it. The very thought of reaching out and into the void of the shadow is overwhelming. You simply cannot touch it.

Frodo is saved from abandonment into the shadow world by elf-magic. For the rest of his life, though, the shadows lurk around the edges. He can feel them creeping up on him at times. It is tempting—often too tempting!—to give in to them. But he knows that if he does, he will be lost forever.

Elf-magic will not save me. Prayer will. God will. I am out of the shadow world, walking in the light. But I know that the shadows still lurk around the edges. I need to force myself to physically turn away from them.

I cannot let them win.

JANUARY 24, 2002. 10PM.

There was a famous football coach—I forget who—who said to his team, "Back to basics, guys. *This* is a football."

Often we need to return to the basic tenants of our faith. They are the rocks upon which we stand. Satan would try to topple us with his lies and schemes, so we need to hold fast.

I have had a great week, so it was predictable that Satan would try to pick at me in my most vulnerable area, my daughter. She saw Shawn on Monday night, talked to him on Tuesday and Wednesday, and went to Bible Study with him last night. He calls every day, always late in the evening. So, what is there for me to worry about?

Nothing. Everything. He hasn't been here since Sunday, and he is a frequent visitor. But they are both, I remind myself, adjusting to new schedules at work. He seems to genuinely care for her, but his friends and activities seem to come before her. She says she does not mind, but I find it hard to trust his words. It is none of my business, I tell myself. She is an adult. But she is still my daughter and I will not see her treated shabbily.

I try not to allow this to destroy the trust I have struggled to build up in Shawn. I think through it logically. Do I doubt his affection for her? Not when I see the two of them together, not when she tells me that she trusts him. But, yes, I guess that I do. I guess that the words they say do not ring as true as either of them would like.

JANUARY 29, 2002. 8PM.

I saw David, my therapist, yesterday. He says I am "healed"

and do not really need his help anymore. He'd like to see me in about three months to "check in". I have, according to him, "walked out of the valley." Or, as I see it, crawled out. There were times when the going was incredibly rough. Now I marvel at how far God has brought me.

It has been hard work, this climb. I needed to let go of much of my self-sufficiency. I had to share my burdens with others. I had to let down my guard and let people in. I had to learn to trust again. What has brought me through? Prayer and my journal, both tools God provided to help me through.

I was telling David how, more and more, the kids from church congregate at our house to play chess. The other night there were eight of them, ranging in age from 16-25, scattered throughout the house engaged in a tournament. A little unusual, I said to David.

Yes, he said. But there is more going on at your house than chess. Your family is healing.

It is true. In many ways, the horror of the last three years is finally waning. The scars are fading. We are starting to feel whole again.

David asked me about my eye condition. He always does. I told him about my latest trip to the eye doctor. My vision is no better, a little worse, but I manage.

"Why," asked David, "do you always smile when you talk about your eye problems? Why do you minimize it?"

"Because," I said, "my vision does not define me. It is not who I am. I do not allow my vision problems to dictate my life."

Granted, it is part of my life and has been for thirty years. But it is like having brown hair and dimples, just part of who I am. Hardly worth commenting on.

The other night I was sitting at the dining room table, reading a text for a graduate text and using my giant magnifying glass. Mike walked in. "Gee," he said, "I don't think I'd want to read if I had to use that."

"At least," I said, "I can read."

Praise God for that! Whatever obstacles have thrown themselves in my path, God has always given me tools to overcome them.

Even magnifiers!

JANUARY 30, 2002. 7:30 PM.

Peace. Like a river. Like a restful nap. Like a comfortable silence. Yet in the midst of my busy life, it is often hard to hear the God.

I am a doer. It is probably why I am such a good teacher, why I can multi-task and keep so many balls in the air. But in "doing" I sometimes forget about just "being." I am always so eager to solve the problems of the world! Unfortunately, my way of solving things can interfere with God's plans.

I wanted to be the one to help Shawn with his car loan, the one who helped him pull it all together. I wanted to be the heroine! But I forgot to stop and ask myself if a new car for Shawn was what

God wanted. Wasn't my will taking the glory away from him? I have said it to Shawn many times this past week as he has used our computer to track down past tax transcripts: let go and let God. It has been easy advice for me to dispense, harder to take.

Shawn told Bonnie he is fine either way. He came close to selling his first car at the dealership yesterday, so he is feeling better about his job. I would also like to feel better about him and Bonnie.

Let go. Let God.

FEBRUARY 2, 2002. 9AM.

Nobody got the perfect prince. The saying goes, "You need to kiss a lot of frogs before you find your prince." The bitter truth is that no man is the perfect prince. As wonderful as any man can be, he still has frog qualities that have yet to evolve.

And that's okay. We are not to lean on our husbands or boyfriends more than we lean on God. The men in our lives are, after all, just men. They leave the toilet seat up. They snore during movies. We love them anyway.

Ron is not a perfect man. I never really thought he was. He is, though, a man who strives to do the best he can for his family and God. Despite his physical and emotional problems, he has always had a heart for the Lord.

There have been some changes lately. Ron's return to fulltime work, even the adjustment to third shift, has made him feel, he says, "like a real man." I wonder at the stress the long illness and recovery put on his psyche. But then, I wonder about the damage to each of us. How did we survive?

We just did.

Shawn, too, has his faults. I am very quick to point them out to my daughter. She is not yet ready to see them. He is no more ready to see hers. But they are there, the frog qualities that will keep him from being the perfect prince.

It is just these frog qualities that we find so endearing. Shawn always misses a belt loop. Ron misaligns his shirt buttons. It is just proof of how much they need us in their lives. God did not put perfect people into the Garden of Eden. How different the world would be if He did! He could have, I suppose, but He chose not to. Would perfect people have had any need for each other, or for God?

It is our imperfections that draw us to each other. We have holes and deficiencies that only our soul mates can fulfill. Ron and Shawn are both wonderful Christian men. Part prince. Part frog.

I try to convince myself that they are gone, these nagging doubts about Shawn and his commitment to Bonnie. I still pray he will not hurt her, that he really loves her. God continues to hold my hand. I know, at least, that *He* loves Bonnie.

REST

You have fought long and well,

The Father said,

And the battles have all been won.

But it's time to bow your weary head

And rest in the care of my Son.

Lay your burdens down gently at my feet

I'll keep them safe from harm.

Then sink into quiet, peaceful rest

In the Savior's loving arms.

But I'd battled too long

And battled too hard

To quickly let it pass.

God needed to wrench my

Burdens away and

Retrieve them from my grasp.

I'll continue to carry them,

Thank you, Lord.

They're my burdens, after all.

God's care and love

I chose to ignore

I would not heed His call.

My shoulders sagged, my heart grew faint

My mind became clouded with grief.

At last I cried out to my loving Lord,

Father, I need relief!

And with a Father's patient care

He slowly pried away

My fingers from each heavy care

And at His feet they lay.

Now rest a while, my Father said.

You need some time to heal.

Finally, I laid down my head

And allowed myself to feel

The peace of God's all-knowing love

His mercy and matchless grace

The blessings of life from heaven above

And His glorious, beautiful face.

Someday soon, I'll call you back,

Into the world's great fray.

For now just lay aside your pack.

Rest, and wait, and pray.

I now wait in peaceful and quiet repose;

The burdens have taken their toll.

I will be ready when next God calls.

His love has made me whole.

CHAPTER TWENTY-FIVE.

MARCH 8, 2002. 4PM.

My daughter is my Achilles heel. She always has been. It is not doubt the reason that God gave me only one daughter and sent numerous sons my way, the Lost Boys included! I have wanted Bonnie to avoid the mistakes I have made: marrying too young and dropping out of college. I've wanted the sun, the moon, and the stars for her. And she, acquiescent soul that she is, has been pretty much willing to let me run her life. Personality adaptoid, Dennis dubbed her, because she was never really sure of who she was and tried on the identities of others. None of them really suited her. So, she tried to be me.

Is there any greater flattery? I, proud mama bear, had a daughter who did not disdain me but wanted to model herself after me! But she is not me. School work is hard for her. It always has been. For the last four years I have been trying to push her through college. Maybe it's been my dream, not hers.

She is a sweet and caring person. Her faith and her morals run deep. She has c charming innocence about her. She sings with the voice of an angel. She is fiercely loyal to her family. Her brothers—both biological and adopted—try to guard her. In the past six months, with the advent of Shawn in her life. God has been trying to pry my fingers away from Bonnie. It has been a difficult job. One at a time, slowly, He has practically had to break them off my hands.

She is not me. She is her own person, unique and wonderful. And she is trusting God to lead her steps. He cannot do it if I continue to stand in His way.

Shawn has asked for our financial help in replacing his car engine. I feel awkward about it, but I know he would not have come to us if he had another option. It is God's money, I try to tell myself. Not mine. It is, I try to convince myself, an investment in Shawn.

"No one's ever done anything like this for me, ever," he says. "I look at your family and I think, 'So this is what it's like to be part of a Christian family.' This is what I've missed." Shawn confessed his amazement that we are not pressuring him to set up arrangements to pay us back. Maybe we should. But I never lend money expecting to get it back. It is God's money. If He wants to send it back to me, He will.

God is being incredibly patient with me. There are no guarantees that Shawn is "the one" for my daughter. He may depart from our lives and I will need to let him go. Since Ron's accident, I try to keep people I care about close to me. It is not easy for me to let anyone go.

MARCH 12, 2002. 8AM.

I am a self-confessed Martha. I admire the traits of Mary, who sat so contentedly at the feet of Jesus, but with the responsibilities of both a working mother and a graduate student weighing me down, I am much more Martha than Mary, doomed to a life of service. Sigh.

But there is a different view of Martha, the changed woman who learned to be content in her service. As she serves supper to Jesus in John 12:2, there is none of the familiar whining or complaining we saw earlier. There is no bustling about, much encumbered with things, as there was in Jesus' earlier visit. She does not insist that Mary leave her place at Jesus' feet and help out. Jesus needs to give Martha no gentle rebuke. She is content with her piece in life.

Do we choose our own piece or is it chosen for us? I am a Martha. I will always be a Martha. But I am no longer the Martha of Luke 10:38, so busy that she misses the best part of life. I am becoming—with God's help—the later Martha, the one who is content with her service to the Lord.

I am a teacher. I serve my students.

I am a mother. I serve my children.

I am a wife. I serve my husband.

But above all, I am a Christian. I serve God.

And if that service is something as mundane as scrubbing kitchen floors, I do it. And I am content.

Or trying to be!

MARCH 15, 2002. 7AM.

She is back! says my friend Monica at dinner last night, patting my arm. *Our Suzy Sunshine has returned!*

And I had realized this myself just the other day, thinking of Bonnie's broken hand that resulted from a fall down a flight of stairs and how fortunate it is that I have two weeks off on Spring Break to take her to doctors and type her papers and drive her to school. I was cleaning the bathroom when the thought first struck me. I sprayed cleaner on the chrome faucets and declared to myself, "I'm back."

Susie Sunshine has returned, bringing her own brand of unique optimism to the world. The endorphins in my brain are once again busy sending out happy signals. My cheerfulness is once again driving people crazy.

How can you be like this? People ask. So infernally cheerful! The simple answer is, Because of Christ. My sins are paid for. I have an eternity waiting for me.

Susie Sunshine reigns!

MARCH 21, 2002. 11AM

I am still growing into myself, still becoming the person God wants me to be. Every day, though, I get closer to a more Christ-like being. There are days, sadly, when I take a few steps backwards.

Simple joys uplift me. During the dark winter months, I came to appreciate the people who left their Christmas lights on all night. As I drove to school each gloomy morning, they were beacons of hope to me, little pinpoints of stars that had drifted down from the heavens to land on trees and bushes. I was still piecing together my fragmented existence, but they beckoned my onward. Don't give up, they seemed to whisper. You can do it.

It is lighter now when I leave in the mornings. The sun has not yet broken through but the sky is lightening. I wear my sunglasses because the glare snags on my damaged corneas and makes me squint. I have a thirty minute drive to school and my Christian radio station fades halfway, just as I pass Garnet Valley. Sometimes I pop a CD in, but more often I just push the "off" button and enjoy the silence. My life is hectic; there are not many moments for reflection.

This is the third year I have watched spring encroach along these roads. Daffodils stand up above the ground, their golden yellow a stark contrast to the brown earth and the dead grass. Azalea bushes sprout tiny yellow buds and here and there a purpose patch reveals wild violets and Johnny jump-ups. The world is renewing itself.

Renewal. I have been renewed along these roads. I have been reinvented. My life is not what I thought it would be. I have stopped railing against the Fates that have brought to much difficulty my way. I have not broken under the trials. I have learned to bend.

In metaphoric terms, I think of myself as a crystal prism. I take in light from many sources. My life is full of angles and planes and complicated patterns. But I reflect a rainbow of colors. The tragedies have not made me bitter. I have not lost my faith. Indeed, I have learned to rely more and more on God. The joy of the Lord is my strength. It is not my own strength I lean on daily. It is God's. If my prism reflects any light at all, it is His.

Sometimes, as I am driving hither and yon, I look at the sky and think of it as God's canvas. Who but God could blend together so many shades of gray and blue and white? Who but God could make the canvas shift and continually change?

Yesterday, the sky to the west had a bank of gray thunderclouds piled one of top of the other, looking like mountains in the sky. I marveled at them and their place in the heavens. Who but God could have put them there? Frequently, these darkening skies are backlit by a heavenly light and the rays of the sun shine through any gap in the cloudbank. When they were small, I told my children that this was the window the angels used to peek down on us.

I still need to believe it.

APRIL 2, 2002. 10AM.

In the two years since Ron's accident, I have come to accept the reality of this statement: not everything can be fixed. There are parts of Ron's body that will never work again. His lungs are damaged, his diaphragm does not work, his spleen has been spliced, his bladder doesn't function correctly, and his memory is often erratic. Like the King's Horses and Men, the doctors and nurses have been unable to put all of my Humpty Dumpty together again.

Time to move on.

His mind is clearer, sometimes free of the mental illness that has shrouded him for years. He smiles and laughs more often. In losing part of his physical self, he has gained some emotional stability. It seems a good trade. I tend to always think of how the last few years have affected me, and then I stop and think of how they have affected him. He can no longer work for more than a few hours. Breathing is sometimes hard. Playing basketball with his son is not possible. Physically, many things no longer work.

But there is still new growth. God has chosen not to complete the repair of Ron's body. The damage was too grievous. But He has saved Ron's mind, brought him out of the shadow world in which he lived for nine years. Ron reads his Bible more, interacts with others more. He no longer scares me with his violent outbursts.

New growth. Like the buds beginning to poke their heads up out of the ground, like the blossoms on the dogwood trees, like younger, tender shoots saved from a dying willow.

We begin again.

DROWNING AT SEA

Drowning at sea,
    Is very easy.
The waters, dark and slow
    Begin to ebb, begin to flow.

                                               They close overhead.
                                               They block the sun.
                                               They pull you down.
                                               Soon, you drown.

Gulping air, your lungs will sear
The waters soon
    Compress
    Your chest.

                                               You cannot cry.
                                           You cannot scream.
                                               Water is now
                                               Your only means
                                 Of buoyancy, of hope, of life
                                     But water has become
                                               The strife.

Drowning at sea,
Is very easy.
The more you struggle
The more you sink.

                                    Into the black, forgiving ink.

CHAPTER TWENTY-SIX.

APRIL 1, 2002. 8 AM.

This morning the cloud cover is holding in the spring warmth and allowing us to enjoy an early April day without jackets. We may not see the sun today, but that does not mean it is not there. God, too, is always there, whether we feel His presence or not. I need to remind myself of this again and again.

Bonnie had a difficult day on Monday, finally realizing she cannot graduate until December. How I long to shield her from this hurt! But she needs to grow and learn, and sometimes that involves pain.

Shawn needs help with his car insurance. I am not certain how much help is proper to give him, since he and Bonnie have no formal commitment between them. I really need to pray before making yet another loan to this young man. They are becoming more and more frequent.

I write this letter in my journal, not sure that I will ever share it with my daughter.

My Dear Daughter,

On my way to class today, I was thinking of you and praying for you. I began—as usual—to regret the circumstances that robbed you of two years. Perhaps, I started to think, it would not have been so difficult for you if you had had the chance to go away to college, as Dennis did, and be insulated from the horror by distance.

What, then, would I have done? You were my right arm for two years and more, my angel and my rock. I may have appeared to be the very pillar of strength, but it was an illusion. Many days, it was your own strength and love that supported me and kept me moving ahead.

So, yes, I would spare you from any additional pain if I could. Any mother would. But that would have denied you so many experiences that made you into the unique person you now are. How many girls your age know how to do the emergency room run or keep their younger brother calm while Dad undergoes yet another surgery? How many know how to emotionally support an exhausted mother? How many know how to bend their knees and pray fervently that God's will be done?

You are, darling Bonnie, more than a college degree or blue eyes or freckles. You are a strong and faithful young woman with talents as yet untapped. God has a wonderful and mighty plan for your life. I cannot wait to see it unfold. I pray that I will be able to let you go when it is time, when God brings the right young man into your life. While we wait, darling child, I thank God for the joy of being your mother.

Mom

APRIL 4, 2002. 9AM.

There is a sign on my daughter's bedroom door this morning:
I'm driving myself to school today.

After five weeks of being forced awake at 5:30 AM to catch a ride with me while she sat in the passenger seat, her hand in a cast, she is now able to manipulate her hand enough to operate her car. She doesn't need me to drive her anymore.

It is, in some ways, a relief. Less stress on me. An earlier arrival at my own school where I can spend precious moments reflecting and planning for my day. But a part of me will miss the early morning conversations—centered mostly around her current boyfriend—that we shared on our drives. I have, for the time being, done my job with this one.

She can drive herself.

I, too, can drive myself this morning, my own beloved Toyota back from its five week stay in the shop. It has been freshly painted and detailed and I revel in its sparkle this morning, listening to a new Steve Green tape and counting the yellow daffodils that grown along the roadside like bits of scattered sunshine.

It is good to be driving again. As we leave winter behind and move into spring, I find my heart joyous as I drive along the now familiar road. My life is coming back into balance again, but I am not the one behind the wheel. God is.

He steers my course. He steers Bonnie's, as well. And I need to let Him. Let go. Let God. This is a phrase oft-repeated and oft-written as I work through my own anxieties and learn to trust again. Joy fills me.

It is noticeable. The other day, Margaret said to me, "You have been awfully chipper lately." And I acknowledged that I have been feeling better, that once again I can find joy. I do not know what the future holds. I do know that there will be more difficulties ahead. This is the Christian walk. God will see me through.

There are only a few scant pages left in my journal, begun in November as I took the first tentative steps towards my own recovery. I flipped through the spiral notebook yesterday, rereading some of the entries, noticing how more poetry and colors decorated the pages as my spirit lifted. Thank God for my journals and the ability to write!

It is well with my soul. There are still external pressures, still much to do in my life. As I come to the end of another school year and a difficult semester at graduate school, I am physically tired. But my soul is light and airy, thirsty for a closer walk with God, eager for what lies ahead.

I'm driving myself to school today.

And as I drive, God is my Pilot. His hand is on all that I do. Today, Lord, I will let You drive me to school.

APRIL 16, 2002. 2 PM.

Relationships—true, deep, lasting relationships—make us vulnerable. We cannot curl ourselves up tightly, protecting our beings, and open our arms at the same time. In other words, we need to trust. For people who have been deeply hurt, trust does not come easily. We do not like pain; we try and shut ourselves off from it.

I am still learning to trust God again. It is a long, slow process. While my faith in Him remains constant, I have had enough hurt for a lifetime. Where was the loving God when so many burdens were shifted to my shoulders? Where was He through all of Ron's surgeries?

And the answer is: He was holding me. He was carrying me. He was weeping along with me.

Some trust in chariots. But we trust in the name of the Lord our God. God is worthy of trust. He has proven it again and again.

And what of Shawn, this young man who has courted my daughter so patiently? Can I find it in my heart to trust him completely? I want to. I try to. But, always, something nags at me, gnawing away at the trust I would like to give him. Perhaps I am being too hard on both of us. I am not completely ready to trust anyone, even God, again.

APRIL 19, 2002. 11 PM.

I feel squeezed sometimes. Lots of times. Most of the time. And the problem is always the same. Time. It never feels as if it belongs to me. It is divided in daylight hours of 43 minute segments distributed among 62 students. In the evening, it is gobbled up by cooking, cleaning, schoolwork, and family. Where is my time? Time to write, to dream, to think? At the end of the week, I am a deflated balloon. I have fulfilled my duties, done what was expected of me, but I have found no time for me.

Will I always feel so pressured?

REPOSE

Still and quiet

Is my heart though my feet seem to scurry

In a thousand different directions and my

Hands seldom rest upon my lap.

I am a study

In movement, dashing from one task to

Another as the day propels me forward,

From home to school to class and back.

My body is seldom still.

Even in repose,

I toss and turn in the night, my

Mind abuzz with worries and ideas,

Reliving the events of my day.

Still and quiet.

Stop my perpetual motion today, Lord,

And let me listen to your world, let

Me hear your heartbeat,

Even as my heart rests

Still and quiet.

CHAPTER TWENTY-SEVEN.

APRIL 25, 2002. 6 PM.

I pull into the parking garage at 4PM, knowing the shifts are changing and finding a spot will be difficult. I head for the upper levels, keeping a look-out for white-garbed figures headed to their cars. My sunglasses are still on although the garage interior is dark, but removing them will mean rummaging in my purse for "inside" glasses and juggling a quick change.

I find a spot on level 3, a pleasant surprise. I remember many afternoons when I was forced to drive all the way up to the roof, then take the elevator back down, go through the out-patient pavilions, then back up the elevator. Today's trip will be simpler.

I lock my doors manually, wishing I had not misplaced the clicker to my Toyota, then remind myself of the many times I left my ancient Celebrity parked here and unlock. Always untouched. My oldest son would chastise me if he were in the passenger seat.

"Who's going to steal this heap?" I would say and he would shake his head at me.

"These are the type of cars that chop shops want, Mom. What would you do if you came out and your car was stolen?" I would shrug, too many more pressing things to worry about.

I am alone on my errand today, although companionship was offered. It seemed like something I needed to do alone, facing down my own demons and making them relinquish their power over me. I have not been in this garage for over a year, but the memories are still sharp and clear. They are memories I have struggled to forget.

I walk up the short rise to the elevator, push the down button. The door opens quickly. I am the sole passenger on my descent to the first floor and my thoughts race. The first time I did this…the day before Easter…On Bonnie's 21st birthday…There are a jumble of dates and days, of holidays in the lobby, of food hastily eaten in the cafeteria. The ride down is brief. The elevator doors open and I walk up the hallways. Here is where I met Uncle Robert and Aunt Shirley one day. Here is the guard who smiles, sure he recognizes me.

"How are you today?" he asks, as if he has just seen me yesterday. We shared many yesterdays in this corridor, pausing for a moment to exchange pleasantries before I headed off to One North or Three South or the Telemetry Unit or the ICU. I nod and smile. "Fine," I say. "Really fine."

"That's good," he says and smiles back at me. "Have a nice day." A banal remark, but one that often encouraged me to keep putting one foot in front of the other.

I am at my destination in just a few steps beyond the guard's station. My errand today is not in the hospital proper, but in the out-patient pavilion where my eye doctor has his office. I reach it five minutes before my appointment time, my dark glasses still one. I pull them off and tuck them into my purse, then straighten my shoulders and open the door.

Life has returned to normal. This is just a visit to the eye doctor, not a life-or-death quest. Beyond the door there is nothing to fear, no tubes or wires or clicking machines. Today's visit will herald no emergency surgery. It is just a visit.

I am learning to live without a crisis.

MAY 15, 2002. 7 PM.

Question: How do you eat an elephant? Answer: One bite at a time.

There have been many "elephants" in my life lately: school, my vision, Ron's medical problems, Allen's LD. But the solution has always been the same: take one bite at a time. Or, since elephants are really an acquired taste, one step at a time.

For many of the current "elephants" in my life, the step-by-step journey is almost over. The school year, begun in September with so much grayness, has only six weeks left. My graduate degree, the plodding activities of four years, is just nine credits away. Bonnie has begun to talk about going away to college next year. I might be ready to let her go.

One step at a time. One bite at a time. Elephants are not really unconquerable.

They just look that way.

MAY 22, 2002. 9PM.

Bonnie and I seem to be always attacking each other these days. It takes very little for her to become exasperated with me and vice versa. I try to blame this on a lot of things: stress, over-work, tiredness. But the truth is really this: she is growing away.

In most regards, it is past time. At twenty-three, she is an adult and should be independent. The circumstances of the last few years stole her early twenties from her, so in many ways she seems younger than she is. I tend to treat her that way, too. Once content to pretty much let me run her life, there is a new determination about her these last few months, especially since she started dating Shawn.

In some ways, he has been good for her. He has helped her regain much of the gaiety of life she lost while Ron was so terribly ill. He has shown her how to have fun again, and introduced her to a new crowd of people. In my heart, I know that someday she will leave my home for one young man or another. The thought hurts. Bonnie and I literally saved each other when women of less determination and strength would have drowned. Even as she plans for a life apart from me and Shawn becomes more and more pivotal in her plans, the bonds forged of pain and fright will never really be broken. They will, indeed, be stretched. Perhaps to Millersville University next fall, where she would like to go. Or even to Kansas, where Shawn longs to return.

Some of my friends' children have wandered far from the Lord. Ron and I continue to be blessed by our children and the close contact they have with us. All accepted Christ as Savior at a young age and all are baptized. Even Dennis continues to regard our house as "home." The children coined a phrase: "Home is where, when you get there, they have to take you back." But each of them must, at some point in time, leave home. This stretching hurts, especially in my current relationship with my daughter. Is she ready for life on her own? Have I taught her enough? Have I taught her what is important?

Yes. And no.

I have taught her family and faith and love. I have taught her commitment and integrity. I have taught her to dream. Yet there is still so much to teach her! How to life on a shoestring budget without help from Mom's check book. How to balance a mortarboard on her head. How to walk down the aisle without tripping over her wedding train. How to rock a baby to sleep.

I want to let her go, and I am trying to pull my hands away. I want to trust her heart to God and to Shawn, but always something holds me back. Even last night, when Bonnie asked Shawn to attend church with us on Sunday, he balked at the commitment and suggested that it was best they each attend their own church for a while longer, until they are ready to make a choice.

Even as she struggles to pull away from me, I know the bonds will continue to hold. Despite the bumps we now encounter in our relationship, I believe the best times for us are still ahead. Despite growing up and away, she will never really be gone from me.

JULY 7, 2002. 8AM.

"Restore to me the joy of your salvation!" Psalm 51

Remember it? That first moment when you knelt by your bed and asked Jesus into your heart? For months, God had been planting seeds, sending people you way to tell you the good news: Miss Scipione, Debbie, Dawn. And your soul, bound up for years in church tradition, thirsted. You hunted and searched, spending days digging into your Dad's Bible, writing favorite verses on index cards and storing them in a file box.

Your poetry, too, reflected your growing interest in the spiritual: sunrises described as God's watercolors, thunderstorms speaking of God's power.

Gradually, the truth—the wonderful truth!—began to dawn. God loved you. You! He knew your name. He knew how many hairs were on your head. And he had sent his Son to die for you. It was just that simple; no penance to be made, no special prayers to say. Just you and God.

Remember the joy that flooded your soul? Like the ebbing waves as they carried the stones away, leaving the beach sand soft and pure, salvation washed over your soul, taking away every evil word and deed and thought, leaving you clean and whole.

In those first moments that you breathed as a born-again Christian, no worries or burdens clouded your mind. There was nothing but the overwhelming, all-encompassing love of the Savior that wrapped around you like a soft, silk cocoon, so palpable that you were sure others could see it. You wanted others to see it!

In those first days—maybe months—your soul continued to thirst and you continued to feed it with Bible study and fellowship and song. You knew, for the first time in your life, real joy.

Then you became an adult. A wife. A mother. The things of the world began to intrude on your joy. Finding time for Bible study became an exhausting chore. There were bills to pay, meals to cook, children to raise. All too soon, it seemed, you found yourself with too many burdens weighing on your back, too many worries clouding your mind.

But the joy of your salvation—that small nugget planted thirty years ago—was still there, parched from neglect but still alive. God sent others your way—Chris, Deb, Vi—who helped to water the dying seed.

Slowly it grows again, struggling to crowd out the worries and the burdens with the sheer and utter joy of it.

JULY 20, 2002. 9 PM.

It is just three rooms—really, two rooms and a galley kitchen—but the sunshine floods the front room through bay windows, only one of which actually opens. Still, it is the sheer light that they love, the white walls waiting for his artwork, the shelves ready for her books. The bedroom faces a brick wall. She will hang a brightly colored curtain, then. The side windows abut another building. No one will look out them anyway, because it is the front window and the big room with the wooden floors and the brick fireplace that have called to them.

Ron and I spend a day shuttling back and forth, from the house Dennis lived in with two roommates post-college, to this second floor walk-up he will share with Laura. It is their first home together and as we struggle with boxes and bags and canvases and furniture up the long, narrow staircase, just barely angling the sofa through the door and past the kitchen wall, I remember.

First words. First steps. First day of school. Wasn't that just last week? And now here he is, a strapping six foot ten scenic design artist wearing a Cookie Monster T-shirt and maneuvering a queen-sized mattress down the hall with his younger brother. The three years he lived on Fairhill have been packed into cardboard boxes or shoved into black garbage bags. Step by step, we carried them up, depositing them on the beautiful hardwood floor in the sun-dappled front room. Along with his things are hers, sundresses mingling with blue jeans.

The hallway becomes crowded with spillage from the front room and my giant of a son grins. "Well, it WAS a big room." He sits among the bundles, content to let them be for the moment. Later, when Laura comes home from work, they will begin the sorting and the organizing and the ordering. For now, chaos reigns but it belongs to him.

I rise up on my toes to kiss him good-bye, one single tear sliding down my face. First tooth. First report card. First home with a woman not his mother.

We leave, Ron and Allen and me, down the dark, dingy stairwell, back out onto the street of a not-so-terrific neighborhood, knowing that our son still sits in that patch of sunlight in the front room.

His own sunlight.

AUGUST 9, 2002. 8AM

Give me a molehill. Any molehill. Or an anthill, for that matter. I will find a way to make it into a mountain, a high and unconquerable mountain, taller than Mount Everest. It is a bad trait of mine, one I am working on. But the molehill-to-mountain mindset is still at work.

Shawn has just returned from his trip to Texas chaperoning three young ladies—two of them former girlfriends—to visit their dying grandfather. Bonnie was upset by his sudden decision to take the trip and the impact use of this vacation time would have on Shawn coming to the beach with us later in the summer. But she swallowed her worry and kept seeing him. Now he sits at my kitchen table, munching pizza, and imparts the news, rather casually, that he is quitting his job. This time, he is going to work at the shoe store with Joe. The news takes us by surprise, of course.

It always does, blurted out in his typical "I've already made up my mind" style. His reasons make some sense: more money, more security. But this is the fourth time in less than a year that Shawn has changed jobs. He then launches into his plans to go to Lancaster Bible College in January to get away from his "annoying and demanding friends" and his growing desire to return to Kansas where life was "peaceful" despite the psycho ex-fiancée he left behind.

No doubt about it, this is the one that will give me the gray hair. In more quiet and lucid moments, when my mind is not busy building mountains, I trust the relationship between Shawn and my daughter as part of God's plan. Wait, God whispers to me. You just need to wait.

Waiting is not something I am particularly good at. I am a woman of action! I watch my daughter's face as Shawn imparts his news. She is stricken, once again left out of his planning, but she recovers quickly, congratulating him on his new position. She will, she reminds him, be at Millersville in January, not at all far from LBS. He smiles at her, patting her hand, assuring her that yes, it will all work out nicely.

But I see his face as he turns away from her and back to his pizza. The mountain looms ahead.

AGAIN

Let me breathe again,

That first joy, that first taste

Of my salvation.

Looking not ahead

To the strife that is my daily life

But only inward

To You.

To once again revel

In the beauty of a world created

Only for me

And a sacrifice made

For my immortal soul.

I am free

Again

And forever!

CHAPTER TWENTY-EIGHT.

AUGUST 24, 2002. 10 PM

I am lying on the bed in my room, having given up the pretense that I was actually watching Stephen King's "Rose Red." Allen is spending the night at Jonathan's, so I am free to let my mind wander over the last twenty-four painful hours and hash and rehash them all. Not that it will do any good. Not that it ever does. Not that it will stop me from still doing it.

I have just gotten off the phone with Shawn, whom I would have cheerfully strangled if I could have gotten my hands through the telephone cord. It is unfair to blame all of the last day's events on him, but it makes me feel marginally better to try. He has called for two reasons: to see how Ron is doing after an episode this morning forced him back into the psych ward at Crozer and to see how Bonnie is "holding up." To the first I give a vague response. It is not like a report on his temperature and blood pressure will determine how he is doing. With the cyclic nature of his bipolar disorder, the best we can do is wait it out. Shawn wants to know if Ron's episode this morning had anything to do with him. The mother of Lost Boys until the end, I assure him it did not. It is only half a truth.

Last night, during a thunderstorm that shook the shingles of the house and downed limbs and wires, Shawn broke up with Bonnie. She arrived home around 3AM, a wet and bedraggled little girl who had not see the coming of the runaway train. I think I saw it. I remember thinking about their relationship lately like a house of cards, ready to by knocked down by the slightest breeze. There was something different in his manner the last two weeks, a distance between them. After driving our "extra car" for six month months while his was having the engine repaired—a repair we paid for—he suddenly bought a Honda from a friend and returned our relic. He managed to visit us at the beach for one day out of our vacation, arriving two hours late. He came over for dinner one night last week, but left early, claiming that he was recovering from a "flu bug."

"Bonnie," I tell him, "is out with Rich and Kelly." I want him to know that she is not sitting around crying her eyes out for him; most of the tears were spent by 6AM. I want to say more to this young man. I want to tell him how hurt my daughter is, how hurt we all are. Why claim our family as his and take to calling us "Mom" and "Dad"? Why seek our financial help with no plan of a future? On the other hand—and there is always another hand—part of me is relieved. This young man was way too much trouble, from his financial problems to his tangled past to his family relationships. At least thirty ex-girlfriends dot the landscape behind him, compared to the two or three young men Bonnie has previously dated.

He told her, last night, that he is "not ready to commit." He has, he says, too many problems to solve in his life, problems he does not want her to be a part of. It sounds almost noble. But things with Shawn are never what they seem. There is probably more to it than I—or even Bonnie—know at the moment. . "I think she's okay," I say. "She misses you."

"I miss her, too," he says. "Maybe I'll call her cell phone." And I want to tell him not to call—ever. That the polite and proper thing to do would be to drop off the face of the earth with the courtesy of her last boyfriend. But there is that of the lost puppy dog about Shawn. I cannot quite bring myself to taunt him. Instead a murmur something that passes for a closing, then add, "God bless" and hang up the phone.

Ron's side of the bed is empty once again. I have packed a suitcase for him and I will take it up to the hospital after church tomorrow. The routine is oh-so-familiar and I am oh-so-tired of it. He is not, the doctors say, responsible for his actions. So that, as usual, leaves me to be the responsible one, to make decisions that are best for me and my children. We are all worn and frazzled right now. My own tenuous grip on serenity has slipped again. The locked doors that have closed behind Ron have closed on my heart as well. I do not know where all of this will end, or if it will ever end. I do not know what is right and what is wrong.

But I do know this. I have made a decision from which I will not waiver, no matter what pressures are brought to bear upon me.

When Ron is released from the psych ward, he will not come home.

SEPTEMBER 3, 2002. LATE.

I lie down and sleep;
I wake up again because the Lord sustains me.
I will not fear the tens of thousands drawn up against me on every side. Psalm 3:5-6

As always, it is at night when the demons like best to strike. They poke at me with white-hot irons, stabbing me on all sides. *There is no hope,* they whisper to me with their fetid breath. *Life will never be right again. Everything is hopelessly wrong and cannot be fixed.*

I try hard to ignore them, to turn over in bed and fall back asleep. But the demons often force me up and I flip on the television set, or pick up a book I cannot read. Sometimes I wander about the house, looking in on my children and standing and windows and looking out, wondering how other people are faring with their lives and certain it must be better than I am doing with mine. I need help, but who does one call at 3AM?

My fears are double-sided and linked inexplicably together. I am once again walking too close to the edge of the abyss, afraid I will tumble back in but unable to stop it. *Ron will never be well,* the demons whisper. *He will never return home to be a husband and a father. You will spend the rest of your life alone. If you had been a better wife, this would not have happened.* I am tired, I plead. I have struggled for too many years. I cannot do it anymore.

Bonnie and Shawn will never figure it out, the voices continue. *The past year, what looked like love was nothing but lies and deception. She will never find happiness. Never.* They are still friends, I counter. She is still young. There is someone for her.

With the support of my pastor and encouragement from my parents, I have convinced the doctors that Ron needs more care than I can give to him right now. I do all that I can. I arrange for him to have six weeks at American Adult Day in Drexel Hill, a program he went into after he left Friends' three years ago. I assure him that he can come home on weekends and we will try to become a family again. When he is discharged from Crozer, he goes to his parents' house. It is not the ideal arrangement, but it is the best I can do for the moment.

Taking Ron to the Crisis Center—again—was hard. Telling him he could not come home was hard. Going through each day without his presence, sleeping alone at night—sleeping at all!—is hard. Allowing him to work through this on his own without jumping in and trying to solve everything for him, leaving the outcome up to God, is hard. There are no guarantees of happy endings, but I am assured of this: God loves me. And Ron. And the kids. He knows what He is doing and I need to step aside and let Him do it.

School begins again. I will need to somehow plow through

this last semester of graduate classes and keep teaching at Westtown, help Allen through his junior year in high school and do what I can for Bonnie. She is not going back to college this fall; her world is just too fragmented right now. It is time for me to compartmentalize again, something I am becoming way too good at.

Be with us all, God, I pray. *Make our ways straight and our paths clear, because nothing else makes any sense right now.*

SEPTEMBER 12, 2002. 7AM.

It punches me in the morning like a fist to my stomach, two thoughts railroading into my brain at first consciousness:

Ron is not here

Bonnie will never be happy.

I cry out at the pain of these losses. It is after the first blow, the first gasp, that my mind can begin to rationalize.

Ron is not here because he is ill and needs help.

Bonnie is still very young and has every chance at happiness.

Even with my rational mind in control again and soothed somewhat by a hot shower, I push the thoughts into the pit of my stomach so I can walk and talk and act like a teacher, but the thoughts lie there, hard and bitter. Breakfast is an impossible task.

I gather my energy from my students, feeding on their exuberance and making my way through the day, class by class. I am here. I am now, I tell myself. Later on tonight I will face my problem again, but in the classroom I can keep them at a distance. Sometimes, I can even manage to laugh.

My rational, analytical thinking propels me through each task. I tell myself that it will all be as it should in time. But things are not turning out the way I wanted, and I pound my anger into my pillows at night. Sleep comes hard, despite the prescription from my doctor. Peace is fragile and evaporates quickly. I try to write in my calm moments and hang onto the peace. I try to thank God for the things I still consider blessings in my life!

Open your heavens, Lord, the storehouse of your bounty! (Deuteronomy 28:12)

SEPTEMBER 17, 2002. 10 AM.

I am not dancing. Not yet, anyway. But I am on my feet this morning. If my steps are not quick and light, they are at least firm. One foot in front of the other. One step at a time, I remind myself. I exactly where I need to be at the moment. I have been reading *Beyond Codependency* by Melody Beattie, and I am trying to apply some of her sound advice to my own life. After almost six hours of uninterrupted sleep last night, I feel better, but still tired. I could sleep for days.

Reading through Beattie's book has helped me to see the truth about myself. I have been Ron's caretaker. I thought I was doing the right thing for him but, as Beattie points out, caretaking

NEVER works. I have been caretaking Ron for years, particularly since the accident. It is understandable, but still the wrong thing to do. Now he needs to learn to take care of himself.

I have also been the caretaker of my children, particularly Bonnie, to the point where I needed to be a part of everything she did, even her relationships to young men. I "caretook" Shawn, making him feel obligated to me. It is time to stop being the caretaker and let go of all of them, time to really pull my hands away. I need to let the people in my life work out their own problems, without me at the helm.

I am making small moves, still waiting for the answers to big problems. God continues to show me he cares in small ways. A hug from Judy. A pat on the back from Mary. A card from Sheila. An e-mail from Vi. Encouraging words from John. These are gifts from the Father, scattered over my days like refreshing raindrops.

There is still a deep ache in me, a wonder at what my marriage may become and loneliness for the things that cannot be. But we are all coping and putting it back together as we have done many times before.

Small moves. One step at a time.

NOT DANCING

Not quite dancing, Lord

But I am moving on.

Not quite singing, Lord,

But my heart can feel the song.

Not quite strong enough, or feeling that I can

But knowing and believing that You have a perfect plan.

I'm still a little fragile, Lord,

I'm still a little raw.

My steps are still so faltering

Sometimes I fear I'll fall.

But I know Your hands are guiding me

I know Your love is true.

When I cannot see the road, I can still see You.

The days may bring an onward storm

Of sorrow and of pain.

My faith may grow in leaps and bounds,

Or my strength begin to wane.

But I'm gathering my forces, Lord,

The sky is not so gray.

I'm taking time to heal

I'm taking time to pray.

I'm not quite singing, Lord,

Though the melody is sweet

I can't quite hear the lyrics

Or feel the measured beat.

Not quite dancing, Lord.

But the song is in my feet.

I know in time the steps will come

And make my song complete.

CHAPTER TWENTY-NINE.

SEPTEMBER 21, 2002. 11 AM.

A new journal to add to my growing collection. A new beginning. I love starting a new journal because it is full of possibilities for happier endings. I spent much of the last two weeks rereading entries from the past year, picking at the old wounds, and sorrowing over what I have or have not done. But today, in this journal, I begin anew. The past is past and cannot be changed, no matter what my mistakes might have been. What matters is now.

Shawn called Bonnie at lunch yesterday to tell her he would meet her at the bowling alley last night with the Bible Study group. They seem to be easing into their friendship, talking on the phone and meeting at group activities. Bonnie seems fine with it. I am trying to keep my distance.

The distance has to be good for us both. I was overly involved in Bonnie's relationship with this young man. Every missed phone call, every late arrival, tore at me. I doubt I could have survived the torment much longer. I think that, on some level, Shawn cares for Bonnie. I need to continue to let go and let God. Easy words to write, hard words to follow. Eventually, Shawn and I will need to make some arrangements for the repayment of the loan. I hope he is honorable enough to uphold the commitment.

From all reports, Ron is making some progress. I know he is not yet ready to return home. I am just beginning to heal, to sleep again. Bonnie, Allen, and I are adjusting to our new lives and our new roles. Ron's return too soon would shatter our hard-won and delicate peace. I missed his phone call yesterday as I was not home yet. I kind of missed talking to him. There are no rules to follow here, so I just keep putting one foot in front of the other and following God.

I am sleeping better, from 12:30 last night until 6 this morning with no interruption. Bonnie was out bowling with her group—including Shawn—but I was not concerned. She is an adult. John, my resident encourager here at Westtown, is keeping a close, brotherly eye on me. I thank God for his support!

I saw the therapist my insurance company uses for intake sessions yesterday. I am waiting to see now where I will be sent. This needs to be my time to heal and recover and see where the next steps take me. Before, I was on the brink of recovery but I stopped taking care of myself too soon and allowed the world to pull me over the edge. I will not let Ron force me into doing anything before I am ready. I will not try to force Bonnie into anything she is not ready for either. One step at a time.

The Bible has this to say about fear: "For God has not given us the spirit of fear, but of power, and of love, and of a sound mind"

(2 Timothy 1:7). I have known for months that the anxieties and fears are overblown in my mind, products of my own obsessions and issues with codependency. Once in a while, when I allowed it, a sense of peace would flood over me, assuring me that all was where it needed to be.

These days, I try to free my mind up for these fleeting, precious moments! God is still in control. Step by step.

SEPTEMBER 23, 2002. 7AM.

We must clothe the skeletons of our lives with the flesh of His love, or we shall perish. These words from Catherine Doherty have seen my daughter through the last few days. She has chosen the purer, higher ground. After spending a pleasant evening—as friends—with Shawn on Thursday, she found out inadvertently that he has been seeing someone for the last few weeks. The news was blurted out to her by the very girl he has been spending time with who called Bonnie's cell phone and announced, "Shawn and I are dating!"

She is hurt. Word around the group is that he was "cheating" on her for months, frequenting places where he should not have been and not being honest with her. She prays for him every night, not to come back to her but for his current state of confusion and walking away from God. She asks her friends to pray, too.

Some of them cannot. The hurt they all felt by Shawn's actions run deep. She understands, she tells them. One day they will be ready. In the meantime, she surrounds her friend with prayer.

What an example she is, flesh of my flesh, child of my heart. What a strong Christian woman she is becoming, feeding not her own pain but on a friend's need, channeling negative feelings into the cleansing power of prayer.

She e-mails him to tell him she is praying for him and that she never stopped. It is a surprise to me when I log into my own e-mail this morning and find that he has responded to my inquiry about the debt. His words are full of pain. He claims that he is in enormous distress and just wants the pain to stop. I do not doubt his pain.

God is still in control. Whatever the outcome, we want His perfect will. We will continue to pray.

Ron will be released from American Day tomorrow, then home to his parents for a while longer. I am making no sudden moves. Johns says he admires my strength in doing what I know to be right, as hard as it may be. He says he would like to be president of my fan club! I am afraid that position is already taken by my eye-doctor!

SEPTEMBER 24, 2002. 7:30 AM.

I come to school this morning because everyone needs to be somewhere. Westtown continues to be an oasis of caring people and a job I love. It is always hard to come here, to pull myself out of my slump and make the forty-minute trek. I listen to Christian music along the way, trying to ease my mind away from my chaotic life.

Will my life ever be easier? Or will each day bring a new brand of heartache? I cannot even escape into sleep for long, the prescription the doctor gave me wearing out around 4AM. Cobwebs of sleep still cling to me. I am beyond exhaustion.

Ron is back in the hospital again, a heart event landing him in the telemetry unit. We have been there before! He may be released in a day or so, and I am once again being put under pressure to bring him home. I try to spend time at the hospital with him, but I just find it hard to see him there again. My palms get clammy and I feel jump. My father-in-law is upset that my visits to Ron are so brief, as if my presence ever makes a difference. Add this to my list of crimes!

At Westtown, I have forbidden myself to worry. I try to leave these burdens in the car and concentrate on my students and on me.

SEPTEMBER 26, 2002. 9AM.

I am feeling pretty well this morning, or at least not weeping, crying, or panic stricken. My definition of wellness has changed! I had some energy last night and cooked supper, did laundry, made banana muffins, and studied. Deb called around 8, broken-hearted that she had just broken up with her gentleman friend. We talked for a long while, depleting the energy. I went to sleep at 10:30 with no trouble, no tossing or turning in the night. I awoke around 4:30 AM and Bonnie was instantly on my mind, but I fought the urge to wake her up. I prayed for a while and fell back to sleep until 5:45. I was actually laughing in school this morning as we all compared our wedding photos in honor of Alicia's nuptials!

I am trying to take positive steps to help myself. I have an appointment with the counselor at 3:00 tomorrow and I am having blood work done on Thursday at 4:00. My doctor suspects that I am anemic. Bonnie, too, is moving on with her life. She made several phone calls last night and is getting together with friends on Wednesday. The Lost Boys were all over last night with Ben and Jerry's ice cream to soothe our woes. There was lots of laughter and silliness!

I continue to be convinced that prayer works, although not always in the ways we would imagine. My fears that Ron would return home too soon have been circumvented by some continuing heart problems.

One step at a time. It has become my mantra. It is starting to look as if we might make it through this latest crisis.

SEPTEMBER 27, 2002. 3PM.

It is the afternoon, the end of another school day. Almost time to go home. I have had another good day. That makes two in a row. I am on a streak! I feel a little more like my old self, less anxious and nervous and upset. This does not mean that my problems have all been solved.

Ron is still living away from us, still in the hospital but returning to his parents' when he is released so there will be someone to take care of him during the day.

Bonnie is still feeling lonely, missing the close relationship she had with Shawn.

Shawn has yet to make arrangements to repay the loan.

In fact, the same problems still exist. So why am I feeling better, concentrating more, laughing sometimes? I have felt anxious and obsessed for two years, seldom having a break, but in the last two days I have noticed a slight improvement.

Is it the Kava root my physician recommended for stress? The care and concern of colleagues and friends? Concentrated prayer? (Is that like concentrated orange juice?) The realization that I am ultimately the only one who can make changes in my life? That the way I feel does not have to depend on the circumstances in which I live?

My new counselor, Annie, is a kind and caring woman. She marvels at the strength I have shown the past three years. She assures me that it is no longer necessary for me to be that strong.

There is still a great deal of sadness in my life. When I awakened at 4:30 this morning, I missed both Ron and Shawn, but there was no desire to scream, no sudden feeling that I had been punched in the stomach. And even through the cloak of sadness, I can see some positive things.

Ron is slowly improving.

The Lost Boys are keeping us laughing.

Bonnie is reaching out to friends, moving on with life.

Perhaps I am just a cock-eyed optimist, what my friends call Susie Sunshine, but I feel the beginnings of hope once again.

A DIFFERENT LIGHT

(Inspired by Marie during Meeting for Worship, 10/23/02)

Shadows cast along the plane

Of nose and chin

An air of disdain

A tilt of a weary

And graying head

A sagging spirit

No words were said

No smile, no twinkle, no cheerful tone

Melancholia. Just leave me alone.

And then the light began to shift

To move along a different line

And what I thought I'd seen before

Was noticed at a different time.

The light so brightly lit her face

All lines of care

Were quite erased

The years that had seemed so

Heavy-felt

The wrinkles and cares

Just seemed to melt.

A change of light was all

This transformation took.

I am so glad I stopped and waited

For that second look.

CHAPTER THIRTY-ONE.

SEPTEMBER 29, 2002. 8AM.

We have this hope as an anchor for the soul, firm and secure. It enters the inner sanctuary behind the curtain. (Hebrews 6:19)

I am feeling a little less settled this morning, but not really anxious. I have an appointment with Annie at 3PM. Bonnie is handling some distressing news today and this are much on my mind. Because her security clearance has not yet come through, she cannot work as a teacher's aide at Pennel right now. We got the needed forms for her to fill out and she needs to send them in and head to the mall in search of an interim job. I am certain there will be growth in these trials, but she says at the moment her life sucks. No job. No money. No boyfriend.

We continue to talk about Shawn at length, not that it does either of us any good. Shawn is not responding to her e-mails, nor anyone from the Bible study group, but she still needs to gain some closure on this relationship and lay it to rest. This, too, is a growth experience, albeit painful. In fact, before I left for work today she said she was going to attempt to "straighten out her life" on her own, since I could not seem to do it. She was actually miffed at me!

Most of my adult life, I have handled things for people. I have been the one in charge. After Ron's accident, I leapt into overdrive, taking on too many burdens and too much responsibility. I tried to pretend that the team was "God and me" but really I thought it was just me. Now it needs to become just God.

I have to learn to trust God so that He can work out all the adverse circumstances in our lives and that He knows ultimately will be best for us. I am trying not to focus on my problems, but on Him.

Maryann called last night and offered to go to Covenant with me on Sunday. Tomorrow I am meeting Debbie for supper. I haven't seen her in the twelve years she has been overseas. We had alarms installed in the house yesterday. The young man who came to fill out the paperwork told Bonnie she was a sweet girl who could have any guy she wanted and that she should not even consider taking Shawn back.

I hope she listens!

SEPTEMBER 30, 2002. 10 AM.

For almost four days now, my world has been a better place to live. I am climbing up slowly, inch by painful inch. I will probably slip back down now and again, but it still seems to be a steady ascent. I could not have remained in the pit much longer and survived. It was destroying my soul.

I slept for almost eight hours last night, deep and untroubled sleep. My mind did not race and soar but settled easily into rest. I took the morning off to complete some blood tests my doctor wanted. Time to take care of me!

Since the same problems still exist, I do not know why I feel improved. I feel the faint buoyancy of optimism again, just the beginning bubbles around the edges of my mind. Things will be alright, I tell myself. Trust in God.

There is an Amy Grant song on a tape Bonnie made for me that goes like this:

It takes a little time sometimes
Baby, you're not going down.
It takes a little time, sometimes
To turn the Titanic around.

Many aspects of my life have resembled the sinking of the ship. God's timing is inscrutable, but seldom fits in with our human expectations. My family has been ill for a long, long time. I have compared us to the survivors of the Titanic, but it's not really over yet. We still struggle to keep our heads above water and save ourselves from drowning. It will take more than a few days!

Slowly, I see the changes taking place. My stomach no longer clutches and churns. I can think of something other than Bonnie without forcing my thoughts away. This week, I found myself once again able to read, to cook, to study, to do laundry, to sing, and to laugh. Small things, maybe, but important in a life that has lost so much.

OCTOBER 3, 2002. 9 PM.

The Evils of Gossip. Sounds like a sermon, doesn't it? Gossip can be as damaging as a hurricane. Last night, Bonnie and Shawn had their final "relationship talk," bringing closure to the chapter. She was clear in telling him that she would not date him again, but wants to remain friends. Bonnie asked him point-blank if he ever cheated on her. He says he heard the rumors, too—that he had been two-timing her since July—but none of them were true. He claims that he really wanted the relationship to work out but felt that it was going nowhere after five months of dating. When she tells me this later, a faint bell rings in my head. If Shawn really felt this way back in February, why come to us for financial help and continue to drive our car? I choose not to mention this.

Bonnie has learned much. Shawn said that during their entire relationship, she barely talked. Now she knows how to make her feelings known. So as Shawn exits the stage, another Bible study boy stands ready to take his place. I am living in a soap opera!

OCTOBER 5, 2002. 11AM.

I am wearing a pink rubber band on my left wrist, all but hidden by my wristwatch. It is there in case I need to snap it, a suggestion made by John when I tell him I still get the occasional panic attack. "Snap it hard," he says. "It will bring you back to reality."

Panic attacks, says Annie the Therapist, are caused when our minds take us to things that are not happening. We need to remind ourselves that we live in the present, not where our minds often lead us. I gave the band a few tentative pulls yesterday, testing it. I felt the sting of the elastic against my wrist and wondered if it would really be enough to keep me from the grips of panic: the palpitating heart, the clutch of the stomach, the disarray of the brain. Would a good, sharp sting to the wrist be enough to convince me where reality lay? I don't know because it hasn't happened yet. Yesterday, I had not need to pull on the pink band. I did not snap, in any sense.

Snapping back. I have always credited myself with my quick recoveries from life's setbacks, bouncing back abominably fast from childbirth and surgeries, loss and pain. Perhaps I bounced back too fast, never really giving myself a chance to heal.

Like with most things in life, I need time.

OCTOBER 11, 2002. 8 AM.

Someone left a rose on my desk this morning, a brilliant pink that survived into October and now graces my desk with its beauty. Someone cared enough about me this morning to take the time to clip this rose and hunt up a glass to hold it, to carry it to school and to leave it on my desk. Someone cares about me today, and that may be enough to get me through.

WEIGHT

The crashing weight has

Pushed me down, lower

Than a limbo stick.

Burdens picked up over the years

One by one

And added to

The growing pile upon my back.

I stagger under the load

Hardly faltering, picking up more and more until

It all topples over

And I fall

d

o

w

n

CHAPTER THIRTY-ONE.

OCTOBER 13, 2002. Early, before anyone else is up.

It has been six months since I have worn it, that slim band of gold Ron placed on my finger in a different age. It still sits in a heart-shaped box on my dresser. My eternity band alone adorns my finger, that circlet of diamonds that symbolizes a lifetime together. I think that I will always wear it—whether on my right hand or my left—for Ron will always be a part of my life.

But I can find neither the courage nor the compassion to slip the simple gold band back onto my finger. It stands for a commitment I no longer feel, a future I can no longer envision. It binds me to Ron, with his carpetbag of problems, in a way I am not yet ready to be bound. Perhaps I never will again. Since Ron's first hospitalization in a mental ward, I have worn the ring off and on, torn always between my survival instincts and my sense of duty.

I no longer feel the duty. For now, for today, the ring does not belong on my finger. What it once means no longer applies. What it may come to mean has not yet been seen.

I am still waiting.

OCTOBER 14, 2002. 11AM.

When I am feeling depressed, anxious, obsessed, or lonely, my journal bears the brunt of my feelings, holding them secret on its lined pages, shut safely between cardboard covers. I pout in all out in ink, opening up my veins and bleeding over the pristine white pages. A lot of the last few weeks have been morose entries, describing the pain and heartbreak of living. I chronicle my life in these spiral journals. They are therapy bought cheaply in any store, yet prove an invaluable tool for me. I reread them, shuddering sometimes at the pain the words recall. *Four weeks*, I think, *since that happened.* Or, *this time last year.*

But it is not all sorrow in my journals. Here, too, is my hope, carved and curved into letters and words, sometimes crafted into poems. Like the small, last voice in Pandora's Box, the hope flies up at me, flapping its incessant wings furiously in my face. **Look at me! Look at me! God is still in control!** And part of my buoys up, bobbing to the surface like an inflatable ball, colorful pageantry amid the dark and treacherous ocean.

What do people without journals do? What do people without God do? When a soul is hurting and broken, when a heart is torn in half, to who does one call if there is no God in the universe? Where does the pain go if not into the pages of a friendly and non-judgmental notebook? It is too much for a human being to carry around!

OCTOBER 22, 2002. 11 PM.

I did not want to fight with her so I lagged behind when she walked into the video store, then returned to the car and drove around the block to cool off. She knows just how to push my buttons—always!—and her stubborn nature will surely be the source of my future wrinkles.

"Tony's mad at me, "she said.

I agreed. "You started it, and then you clam up and won't tell him what is wrong."

"I know. But he'll get mad at me."

"So he'll get mad. Then he'll get over it."

She stomped away from me in a huff.

Fifteen minutes later, I pull back up to the video store, expecting to see my contrite daughter waiting. She is nowhere in sight. I search the aisles. No Bonnie. The nearby supermarket. No Bonnie.

I call home. "Bonnie and I got separated, "I say, giving only the sparsest of explanation. "Has she called?" The answer is no. Neither one of us has our cell phones. I continue my search, my panic rising. I drive home slowly, on the off-chance she has started walking.

I pick up reinforcements at home, Tony and my cell phone. Allen is instructed to "man the phones," a command he is used to. Ron has already gone off in search. Tony and I head back to Blockbuster's, slowly scanning the sidewalks. I begin to pray audibly. My panic rises.

She's got to be okay, I whisper, *she has to be okay.*

We search the shopping center, looking into each store. Tony, too, starts to panic. I go into the video store to look once more and when I come out, there is Tony standing off to one side, his arms around my daughter.

"I would be lost without you," he tells her, and I realize that he echoes my feelings exactly. I would be lost without her.

OCTOBER 24, 2002. 2 PM.

One problem I have lately developed is no longer trusting my own instincts. I used to so clearly know what God was telling me! Now, I vacillate, unsure if God is talking to me, if I am talking to myself, of it the devil is whispering his insidious lies. I am not sure if this is a problem Annie can help me to solve.

I was SURE of the promises I thought God had given me for Bonnie, so sure that I ignored my instincts about Shawn. I knew he was wrong for her, yet I allowed the relationship to continue.

Annie would stop me here. *Wait a minute*, she would say. *Was it your decision to make? Isn't your daughter an adult?*

True, I might concede. *True, too, when I did try to caution her, when things started going wrong, that she would not listen.*

Lose the guilt, then, Annie would advise. *Not your fault.*

Back to MY problem, then. Or is it my problem? Things are no longer clear to me. Bonnie is enjoying Tony's company, although she is not sure where the relationship is headed. She tells me she doesn't need to know yet.

"When he gets a job and keeps a job, maybe I'll date him," she says. She admits that they are currently more than friends but that Tony will need to prove himself to be anymore. He is not at ALL what I want for her.

My continued preoccupation with her resulted in a crying spell yesterday and my pink rubber-band did little to help. I would like to lay the blame at the ballet-slippered feet of an aerobics classmate who heard about jobless Tony and thought I should intervene. I just shrugged. "It's her decision," I said with more conviction than I felt.

Later on, I began to dwell on it, like the dog and his proverbial bone. How far does guarding my daughter's heart go? She's not committed to Tony in any way and has told him that she is not ready for anything more. She insists that he will need to work on his future and getting an education before anything else happens. Tony has made some strides in the last few weeks, but she knows he may not be able to keep it up. His erratic history indicates as much.

But she seems happy right now, no longer moping around the house and listening to an old phone message Shawn left weeks ago. Last night, during my crying jag, Dennis mentioned that he is "damn glad" she had broken off with Shawn. "He's slime, Mom. He always has been. I wish it had ended differently, I wish she'd been the one to hurt him, but in the end he would have hurt her even more." He hopes, he added, that her current state of contentment does not depend on Tony.

I hope so, too. I think she came to that place before Tony was any part of the picture, but nothing is clear anymore. She does seem to have replaced Shawn rather quickly—as Shawn did her—and I am not the only one around here who is worried! Looking back at my invaluable journals, I can see that it was only 22 days ago that she shut the door with Shawn. Tony is a very new part of her life.

Frankly, I think she is wasting her time on this one, but she needs to follow her heart.

What, then, of my own heart?

OCTOBER 29, 2002. 9 PM.

No doubt about it, my bank account will never be an object of envy. Somehow, though, there is always enough. I manage to feed, clothe, and shelter us, make needed care repairs, occasionally indulge in a movie or dinner out. These are all part of God's provisions.

Even more than material things, though, God provides for me and mine what we need in the way of support and encouragement. During the darkest of times, He sent various comforters our way. And now as the sky becomes lighter, He is providing us with companions and friends.

This weekend, I actually found myself enjoying Ron's company. It all seemed right, somehow, all of us together. I missed him when he left on Sunday. I am starting to look forward to the times I will see him again. On Friday night, for instance, we plan on going to see *Santa Clause II.*

Bonnie and I tease each other about "our guys." The phone will ring Sunday morning at 9AM. Tony, of course. Later on, when it rings again, Bonnie will say, "Mine already called. Must be yours."

We are getting back into our joking moods, hugging and kissing and teasing. Saturday night at supper, Tony commented on my lovely china and I told him it was my grandmother's, that Ron and I never had good china.

"Sure we did," said Ron. "I bought you a set."

"When?" I asked. "When we went to the Pottery Factory on our honeymoon? That wasn't good china."

"No," he said, "the set we had in the kitchen.'

"That your mother got from the supermarket? That wasn't good china."

"No, the pink set we had."

"That was not good china."

"The label said it was china."

" Doesn't mean it was."

Tony turned to Bonnie and said, "Look, it's us in twenty years!"

Lord, I prayed, *I sure hope not!*

OCTOBER 31, 2002. 10AM.

I remember the paralyzing fear and how hard it was to make myself get out of bed in the morning. I remember forcing back the tears and crying out in agony to God. Would my life ever be right again? The pain was constant on all levels: physical, emotional, spiritual. My body was exhausted, my stomach churned, my head pounded. My thoughts were always clouded with grief. I wondered if God heard me, if he cared.

To think that I lived in this state for such a long time, under such bondage and burdens! But my journal—which holds my very spirit—confirms the months I spent in the wraith-liked state. March of 2001, it was, after Ron's major physical crisis was over. I began to clutch onto things with the illusion of control, wanting to order the destinies of those around me and prevent even the smallest measure of hurt.

But life and growth always hurts. As Jesus refines our images to be more like His, He chips away at our imperfections. We hurt.

Letting go of it all was a difficult thing to do. I look at the list John suggested I write on September 18 of all the things I worried about for so long. It is long! But, one by one, I give each worry over to God.

CASTING

One by one

They are flung

By His great and mighty arm.

They slowly sink

Into the drink

Where they can do no harm.

Satan's attack

Has bowed my back

And made me doubt my soul.

God's saving grace

His loving face

His Son's death made me whole.

Cast away, into the deep.

Cast away, my burdens sleep.

When I bent my knees to pray.

Jesus cast my sins away.

CHAPTER THIRTY-TWO.

NOVEMBER 2, 2001. 8PM.

Annie pointed out to me in our session yesterday that I have made tremendous strides in a very short amount of time. She is particularly impressed that I have done so with no help from medication. She tells me that I am a "strong and amazing woman." In her counseling, she says, she sees many women who are in relationships they would like to change. They seldom have the courage to do so. But I did. I had the courage to make the changes and the wisdom to wait it out.

What Annie says is true. I am strong and amazing. According to my mother, I never give less than 100% to anything I set my mind to. But it is not all because of me. I am strong and amazing because of God.

Bonnie knows that "Footprints" is one of my favorite poems. She gave me a plague for our wedding anniversary, a reminder that there have been innumerable times in the last few years when God alone has carried me through because I lacked any strength.

I do my best to explain this to Annie, that my "miraculous" progress is not because of my own power, but because of God.

Annie says she recognizes this spirituality in me. It may not be her own belief system, but it is good to know that she can see it in my life.

People keep saying that I look and sound so much better, but letting go is a continuing challenge. I struggle again and again. Still, I am on the way back up again, not just acting as if I am better—something I became very good at over the years—but really getting better. I hope that in changing, I am also becoming wiser.

Once more, I dare to embrace the future, not at all certain what it may hold.

NOVEMBER 11, 2002. 11AM.

Feverish dreams and a wave of dizziness assault me this morning so I call in sick and spend the day sleeping. I need to pray, again, and bring my worries before the Lord. But exhaustion engulfs me. Perhaps the weeks I could not sleep are catching up with me!

I am much burdened by my concerns for Bonnie and feel quite overwhelmed. Satan knows just how to attack me—through my daughter! But I have come too far in the last two months to allow him to so easily topple me. Bonnie has matured and is starting to take control of her own life. Instead of retreating after the break-up with Shawn, she has found out who she is and what she wants. She assures me that her relationship with Tony is in her control.

Tony thinks he loves her. Maybe he does, but she is not sure what she feels for him. It is too soon to make any commitment. I wonder just how much change this young man is capable of. He has made some progress in the last few weeks but he has not yet gotten a job and always seems to be in danger of getting thrown out of his house.

After another nap, I turn to my source of wisdom, the Bible: *DO not be anxious for anything, but in everything, by prayer and petition, with thanksgiving, present your requests to God. And the peace of God, which transcends all understanding, will guard you hearts and minds in Christ Jesus. (I Philippians 4:5-6)*

It is like a recipe, I think: How Not to Worry.

1. Do not worry. Pray
2. Talk to God. Tell Him what you want.
3. Be thankful.
4. Let God guard your heart and mind.

How often, though, is "worry" foremost in my mind? I will worry, THEN I will pray, but God's word tells us to skip my first step. Don't worry. Plain and simple. God is not recommending a mindless abandonment. He is not telling us to be irresponsible or ignore our circumstances. But He is trying to save us from spending our time and energy unwisely. Worry takes both. If only we could take the time and energy we use on worry and put it to prayer instead!

Don't worry. Pray. The first step. And tell God what you want. The second. Have a conversation with God as if He were sitting in your living room.

But prayer alone, says the next step of our recipe, does not seem to be enough. We also have to be thankful. For what? Anything. Everything. at the moment. The ability to pray, for even when our hearts are too heavy, the Holy Spirit will pray for us.

Wow! God thought of everything! Yes, God covered all the bases. Jesus taught us to pray and was our model for prayer. The Spirit will pray for us when our own hearts cannot. So we stop worrying. We pray. We give thanks. Then what?

One more step. We let God have it. We keep our grubby hands, our emotions, our human interference, away from it. We let God guard it. We leave it in His hands. And we walk away.

But walking away doesn't mean that we don't continue to pray about it, again and again and again, as often as we need to. But we do not let it take over our hearts and minds. These are now guarded by God.

It is so easy to let worry overtake us! Our world is laden with sin. We are human. But God's recipe guarantees that we do not need to worry.

Ever!

NOVEMBER 15, 2002. 11AM.

I never fail to cringe when I place one in each eye, my lid wanting to blink and keep the foreign object away from the sensitive surface. The eye wants to protect itself from invasion, but every day I force these hard pieces of plastic into my baby blues.

There is a sting of pain. Tears well up. I gasp. It hurts! My vision is blurred for the first few seconds as tears cover my corneas. I wait it out, blinking. And gradually the tears subside and the stinging stops and my vision clears. I breathe deeply. These contacts are in for the next ten hours, when taking them out will bring a degree of relief equal to the pain.

Some day, I promise myself, I will not need these. In Heaven, my vision will be 20/20. But here on Earth, where I live at the moment, my vision is a lot less than perfect. Without aid, my left eye is 20/80. On a good day. And my right eye is off the chart, somewhere around 20/400. My peculiar vision has impacted me my entire life. It has made me see things in a different light and in a different perspective. It is not always a bad thing!

But one of the bad things about these small, round plastic things is that they disappear quite easily. Looking for them is frustrating. But I have found the secret to finding a lost contact lens!

1. Pray. The moment that annoying piece of plastic pops out of your eye or slides from your finger, commit the darn thing to God. In the vastness of the universe, amid billions of people, the blue-tinged circle is not lost to God. He saw it fall. Rest assured that while one contact lens in the vastness of the cosmos is not a big deal, it is to God. Because it is to you.

2. Stay calm. Panic will not help anything. It is somewhere and, with a reasonable amount of effort, it will be found. Calmly look around the immediate area. Sink. Floor. Your clothing. It probably won't be there. Life isn't that easy. But looking will give you the illusion of doing something purposeful and eliminate those areas to search later on.
3. Refocus. God has this matter in His capable hands and now that you are calm and relaxed, He can work. Retrace your steps and ask Him to direct you. Keep praying. Think of unlikely places it could be. The bottom of the hamper. The top shelf in the closet. Remember that while the little buggers can't technically walk, they do tend to bounce!
4. Forget it. Yes, you heard me. God do something else for a while. The lens will not move if you go have a hot cup of tea and squint at the newspaper.
5. Praise God. Whether you find it or not. Actually, I have always managed to find it—in the hallway this morning—but even if I had remained lost, I would have thanked God for His help. At least I think I would have. Even in small things, there is His higher will at work. We need to trust that.

NOVEMBER 19, 2002. 6PM.

Almost. It is almost finished, this Master's Degree that has occupied so much of my mind and time for four years. One more presentation, one more paper, then the class work is over. No more evenings trucking up to West Chester University, sitting in classes that do not always have a bearing on my real life. There will still be the comprehensive exams in February and the Praxis exams in March before—yay!—graduation in May.

But life cannot always wait for a major celebration such as this. My tired, flagging body needs it not. I need to mark my last class at WCU in some way, shape, or form. Dinner with a friend. A new book. An evening out.

People often say how much they admire what I have done, cramming graduate classes with a fulltime job and a family, Ron's illnesses, and my own eye disease. But I have always tried to be clear that I have not done it under my own power. I have down it with the power of God.

This trek through education actually began a long time ago, back when I first registered for classes at Neumann College, then found out that I needed a cornea transplant. Well-meaning family and friends gave me advice.

"Your eyes are important," they said. "Cancel your classes." Even my dad, who believes me capable of just about anything, didn't think I could do both. Even my minster didn't see it happening.

Be sensible, they all said.

Sensible? Me? I totter back and forth between sensibility and insanity, the over-abundance of endorphins in my brain usually bearing me up in an annoying good humor while I continue to handle the many challenges life has handed me, burdens I was never trained to handle. Be sensible, everyone said. So I did the sensible thing. I dumped the whole mess on God.

And God told me I could do both. So I did. Not alone, never alone, but with His infinite love and mercy.

So it is almost done. Two more weeks, two more classes, then a brief chance to relax before moving onto whatever challenges God still has in store for me!

THE TOOLS I'VE GATHERED

My grandmother gave me knitting needles, each click a reminder of the homely arts she taught me while making sugar cookies. My grandfather gave me a jar of marbles, the light from the sun catching the colors and throwing a rainbow across my kitchen.

My mother gave me the independence of her Powhatan tribe, the strength to face my own emotions and the tenacity to hang on when life gets tough. My father gave me a tire jack and jumper cables because no woman, he said, should be left stranded by the side of the road, waiting for a man to come and rescue her. He taught me to rescue myself.

My brother gave me laughter and camaraderie throughout our childhoods, our relationship now elongated by 500 miles and distilled to weekly phone calls.

My husband gave me permission to grow, never expecting my apron strings to be tied to hearth and home.

My daughter offered her comforting arms during the season of tears and uplifted my heart with song. My sons come from the Polar Regions, opposites who share blue eyes and dimples but did not share a childhood. My oldest left me his dreams and his truth when he went to seek his own. My youngest gave me patience and family and wonderment.

And from my greatest, dearest friend, sister born of the spirit, I received love that was unconditional and forgiving, the kind rarely seen by earthbound men.

I have, from time to time, laid these gifts aside, then found cause to pick them up again. Now I carry them with me always. They cut my path through life.

CHAPTER THIRTY-THREE

NOVEMBER 22, 2002. 4PM.

A solid, secure building depends on them. Cornerstones, carefully hewn and squarely laid, support the rest of the structure. My job, as both a teacher and a Christian, is to help others lay their cornerstones. Sometimes, they are crookedly or awkwardly placed. They need to be removed and the work begun again.

How often, though, do my words tear down rather than build up? How often do I look on the outside—rather than inward, as God does—and judge a man by what I can see?

Ron is really trying to change himself. He's becoming more responsible for himself and the housework these last two months. Admittedly, he has a long way to go and his housekeeping skills are not on par with mine. He will never be rich or successful in the eyes of the world. And while I may occasionally long for a life filled with a few more luxuries, I know material things are only temporal and do not really bring happiness. How quickly theft or fire or the economic climate can change such things!

It is Ron's heart that I struggle to see. Emotionally, I cannot tell if there has been growth. He seems quiet most of the time, a little sad unless he is talking. He spends far too much time watching TV or just sitting, simply staring into space. I know he feels he is making progress with his new therapist, but is he ready for the commitments of being a husband again?

I myself feel that I am doing well. I had a good session with Annie today, although when I arrived at her office I wasn't really sure what we were going to talk about. I felt a little blue this morning, not quite on top of my game. Was I worried about Ron? Tony? Allen? My final paper for grad school? It was hard to focus on it all, so I drove around for a bit before I went to Annie's office, listening to some Christian tapes and trying to let the music calm my soul.

I kept thinking of what Debbie had said yesterday, that I had everything to lose and Ron had everything to gain if I let him come back too soon. I realized in my wanderings that I wasn't ready to take that risk. I had worked too hard at freeing myself from the emotional baggage that came with being Ron's caregiver. I also had Allen's words ringing my ears: "Dad's not ready to be an adult yet." When I asked her, Bonnie concurred. And so, I thought, where do we go from here?

I opened up this can of worms to Annie, who assured me that right now I need not change the situation. With the advent of the holidays, with the pressure I am under to finish my final paper, study for my comprehensive exams, and take the Praxis series in the spring, it is not a good time to make any changes. And that is okay. Perhaps when I have graduated and things are calmer, when my life is less stressed by studying and exams and deadlines, then will be time to make some changes.

I told Annie how well Ron had handled the phone

conversation with the Sears salesperson yesterday that didn't seem to understand that we were picking up a TV. Instead of getting flustered or upset, he calmly read off the serial number and the salesman's name. Annie says this showed how capable Ron was of handling circumstances even though it was hard for him. This, she said, is an encouraging sign. I told Ron how well I thought he had handled it.

I have finally made up my mind about this: I will not be his caretaker again. I enabled him before to continue being "the patient." I did not let him make any of his own decisions and in doing that I did not allow anyone else to make their own decisions either. I ruled the world! I saved everyone! And then the burden of carrying the world on my shoulders like Atlas became too much for me and I began to crack.

What I need to do, says Annie, is to find tools that will help Ron become an adult. This is not enablement, she assures me. This is permissible. I asked Annie if I should meet with Ron's therapist and she seems to think it is an excellent idea. She, too, would like to meet Ron. While she cannot be our marriage counselor, she says she can help steer us in the right direction. Annie feels that with slow, positive steps there is every possibility that Ron and I will be able to work things out and reconcile our marriage.

I left Annie's office feeling better, but still unsettled. So many things left to do for my graduate degree! So many loose ends in my life! But, cautions Annie, one thing at a time.

Ecclesiastes 9:10 has this to say about time: "Whatsoever your hands find to do, do it with all your might, for in the grave there is neither work nor planning nor knowledge nor wisdom. I have seen something under the sun; the race is not to the swift or the battle to the strong, nor does food come to the wise or wealth to the brilliant or favor the learned, but time and chance happen to all."

What is worth building up—in this case, a marriage much damaged by illness and accident—is worth building up slowly, one stone at a time.

Another of Annie's suggestions to put into play: Ask the kids what their definition of an "adult" is. How would they like their father to act? What do they expect of him as a dad?

Along with my daily prayers for my family, I continue to pray that Tony will find a job. I know he is trying, but God seems to be delaying the answer. It is because Tony is still "becoming"? In the three weeks she has been seeing him, I have seen some changes in this brazen young man. He is softer spoken and less boisterous around us. He thinks before he speaks. And while he still tends to brag—not that he has much to brag about!—it is often quelled by a look or a word. Annie says that a full half of behavior modification is knowing how the behavior affects others and thinking it through.

All things being equal, who would I rather see my daughter with? In retrospect, all Shawn really had going for him was a job and a car. And given the propensity he had for switching jobs, the former was not always a sure thing. If Shawn stood next to Tony with only his heart and soul, who would come out the winner?

Shawn always seemed to carry his past on a ponderous chain like Jacob Marley, never unable to forget the rattle of past sins. Tony, too, has a troubled past. Bonnie was never really first with Shawn; there was his car, his gaming, his friends, his finances.

But if I had my choice—which I clearly do not—I would combine Shawn's personality with Tony's devotion, add a dash of maturity and stability, keep the lovely eyes both are blessed with, and season it all with time. Bonnie is naïve, but not blind. She sees the good in everyone. I complained about this annoying trait to my mother last week. "Would you want her any other way?" asked my wise mother.

No. She is my angel. I need to learn to trust her.

NOVEMBER 26, 2002. 11 AM.

She said it more kindly, of course, because she is a very kind person. But the admonition was clear: butt out. I had asked her how she felt about Tony, if she loved him. She nodded and said that part of her did, and would I please just stop asking her questions all the time and let her enjoy the moment?

I have tried very hard to keep my hands off of this relationship and to speak only when something seems awry. Like all the time. I had asked her weeks ago if she would stop seeing Tony if her father and I asked her to. She thought a moment, then said that she would but she hoped we would never ask her to because it would make her very sad.

For years, my journals have carried the details and fears of Bonnie's relationships with the "Lost Boys." Regrettably, they also document my interference, beginning with Nick and my penchant for coming up with things for him to do around the house, and ending with Shawn and my propensity for trying to keep track of him. All of these things were done, of course, out of love for my wonderful daughter. And she never once became angry or upset with me, never backed away from me. The survivors of Titanic stick together!

I want what is best for her. In my mind, that means a man who is settled and educated, a Christian from a stable home with a family and career. Someone who will love her exclusively, second only to God. Every guy she has dated had fallen far short of the mark. Even so, I have often struggled to help her keep a relationship alive after it should have died a natural death.

I can learn much from my dear daughter, though. What God wants for her may not be what I want for her. Since before she began to date, she has prayed about her life mate. For a while, I thought Shawn might be it. He seemed to have many of the qualities she was looking for. But as time went on, problems surfaced. She was never first in his affections. His car and friends always came ahead of her. He was late for everything and often canceled dates. He did not want her to meet his family. These were all red flags. Still, I thought Shawn might be her salvation and rescue her from our home where Ron's depression frequently makes living difficult.

I should have known that God never gives half a loaf. With Him, it is all or nothing. I was hurt—possibly more than Bonnie—when Shawn ended the relationship and took up with Joy five minutes later. I felt we had all been used. We had given our hearts, our home, our help to Shawn and he had walked away.

My daughter is a better person than I am. She was able to forgive him and take steps to become his friend while I continued to seethe.

But what, I continue to ask God, of my daughter? Surely He has someone special for her, someone perfect. Except that no one is perfect. Not even her. Tony was supposed to be a distraction, someone to keep her from being lonely. I want desperately to interfere, to demand that she stop dating Tony. But I have no option but to wait it out. She assures me that she prays every day about the relationship and where it is going.

What is money and materials things? Is not love more important? Doesn't the Bible say that it is better to live in a hovel with love then in a palace with a contentious woman? My mind turns to Bonnie a hundred times a day and I can think of little else. How can I pull my mind away?

Friends advise me to let her make her own mistakes, that few things in life are irreversible. Tony may be just a rebound, but she will need to work it out on her own. Do I project my feelings and insecurities onto her relationship with Tony? Are my emotions about Ron mixed up in this? I have been so preoccupied with her since Ron's accident! Three years, three young men. Is she learning anything?

Am I?

NOVEMBER 28, 2002. 10 PM.

I have avoided the piles of strewn clothing on the floor of my daughter's room and am now perched on her bed, my ear to the phone. Downstairs, my offspring and Laura are playing a loud game of Mario Carts, careening into one another with delight. We are back from Thanksgiving dinner at Mary's. Tony was quite pointedly not invited. He has left six phone messages on the answering machine, each a shade more desperate than the last. Her brothers and Laura tell Bonnie to ignore him; he's not worth the trouble.

My mother's voice is on the phone, soothing and calm. She and Dad went out for dinner, a practically unheard of event. Mom is a homebody. But she had a good time, she says. She even "had a piece of pumpkin pie and I haven't had that since my mother died." I struggle to pay attention, half of my mind downstairs, hoping Tony will not show up. "Are you still coming tomorrow?" Mom asks. Yes, I say. Since my parents have retired to Rehoboth Beach, we have spent the weekend after Thanksgiving with them. The tree-lighting, Mom continues, will be at the boardwalk on Saturday. Their neighbor Doug will lead the carols singing. It will be cold, Mom reminds me. Bring warm clothes.

We chat for a few more moments. I am tempted to tell Mom

my worries about Bonnie, but I have mentioned them before. Her advice is always to let her make her own mistakes. Mom has never once criticized my own choices. She knows my adult life has not been easy, but she believes I know what I am doing.

The conversation winds down. I am glad we are leaving town for a few says. Perhaps it will give Bonnie some new perspective on Tony. "We should be there around 11," I tell my mother. "See you then, "she says. "Love you."

"I love you, too, Mom," I say. And I hang up the phone.

Linda Waltersdorf Cobourn

A PRAYER FOR MY DAUGHTER

Lord, it is so hard to let go of her;

This child has been through so much with me.

She has been my angel, my rock my right arm.

But she is not really mine, Lord. She is yours.

You have instilled in her a forgiving, nurturing spirit

And a pure and loving heart.

She is still a work in progress but no longer a child.

A woman. Her love is hers alone to give.

Guide her, Lord.

Let me only love her.

CHAPTER THIRTY-FOUR.

NOVEMBER 30, 2002. 9AM.

Saturday morning in Rehoboth. I have done the breakfast dishes at Mom's sink, looking out at the end of Silver Lake that abuts their property, a view Mom loves. It is just cereal bowls and coffee mugs and little plates for the Pillsbury cinnamon rolls that Mom bought and thought we would all eat together this morning after Black Friday. My brother, Harvey, teased me about the orange icing but has eaten two anyway. This is Mom's sink, I think. It will always be Mom's sink. And suddenly, I need to be outside, watching the ducks, walking where Mom loved to walk.

It is bitterly cold and everyone in the house is still getting themselves ready for the hospital vigil. Dad has left already. I walk down to Silver Lake, down to the ancient wooden bench that once sat in PopPop's garage on Washington Street and that Nanny threatened to have hauled to the dump on a weekly basis. It did make it there once, I recall, but PopPop turned around and retrieved it. Now the plain bench, showing at least three different layers of paint, sits at the edge of Silver Lake, a place for Mom to rest her bad hips while she watches the ducks. It has always been

Dad's dream to have a house on Silver Lake and while Harvey and I are astounded at the speed in which our parents sold the family house in Swarthmore and ran away from home, I am glad they had these years at Rehoboth, within the sound of the ocean's lapping waves and the whisper of the pine trees. They have been contented here. Mom has her ducks to feed and worry about, especially in the spring when the turtles eat the newborn ducklings and drive the duck families away. Sitting here on the bench that is part of PopPop's past, I watch the ducks swimming now, remembering the night Mom stayed up and watched a baby bird cling to the nest his mother had plastered to our attic windowsill. She worried all night as the wind blew and the rain fell that the baby bird would be tumbled from its nest and die. But God smiled on the infant bird and in the morning it was still safe in its nest.

I talk to the ducks for a few minutes, telling them about Mom. She won't be coming down to feed them anymore, but Dad will make sure they are kept supplied with bread. Then I heave myself off the bench—it's really too cold to be sitting—and walk back up the hill, the dry leaves crunching under my sneakers. Tears are frozen to my face by now but I cannot go back inside. Not yet. I continue up the driveway, up to School Lane, down to the old high school where Harvey and I rode our bicycles over the paths and around the school. A soft, summer wind brushes past my face and I hear my brother's voice calling to me: "Linda, watch me! Can you do this?" Laughter resounds. There are tennis courts where we brought our badminton rackets. There are the swings and the tower where we played weather station. Then around the corner, past the condominiums that were not here thirty years ago, through the stand of pines and picnic tables where students lucky enough to live at the beach eat their lunches outside, to the bridge across Silver Lake.

The bridge, too, has changed, from the roughly-hewn planks of wood my mother used to fear for us to ride across to a sturdy structure with rails. The old bridge would hold only one bike at a time steered carefully down the narrow planks. We would hold our breaths while we crossed it, Harvey and I, not really fearing the splash into the water—all of three feet deep—but knowing Mom would panic if we came home drenched. Mom never liked bridges and often drove miles out of her way to avoid one.

In recent years, though, Dad has convinced Mom of the safety of this bridge. Almost every night, they have walked across it, hand in hand, stopping part way to admire the lake and the turtles and the ducks and their own good fortune at being together after so many years. Now, Dad will walk it alone.

Across the bridge is the small park that was a golf course when we were young. Balls would sometimes sail across the narrow expanse of water and we would collect them in our bike baskets, bringing them back to the house on Washington Street to be used in our own miniature golf courses. Along the pathway from the bridge are two stone benches, one in memory of Nanny, one for PopPop. Dad says he often comes here to sit and talk to them, although he has not yet come to tell them about Mom. I cross the bridge now, stopping at each bench to caress it and read the name engraved on each stone. Elva M. Waltersdorf. Harvey R. Waltersdorf. I tell them what Dad has not been able to yet, that Mom will be joining them shortly in Heaven. Across the bridge. Up the path. Around the school, the echoes of my summer childhood calling after me. They will all be ready by now to return to the waiting room outside the ICU. *Let me be strong enough*, I pray. *Let me be strong enough for Dad and Harvey and Mom today.*

NOVEMBER 30, 2002. 8 PM.

It is Saturday night and the hospital has become a place of limbo. We sit at Mom's bed, holding her hands, taking turns in shifts of two. Occasionally, I can persuade Dad to get some soup or some coffee if I agree to stay right by her side. We post bulletins to those in the waiting room outside the critical care unit but there is little new to say. She is still with us. Still alive. Dad is holding up. Dad rattles off the names of people I should call, numbers I will need to look up. Those in the waiting room flow in and out of Mom's room, never staying long, saying their own good-byes. The boys cry a little, but most of their emotions remain locked inside. Bonnie, Laura, and I do not mind weeping.

There is strange comfort here. Dad and I sit with books open on our laps, but we seldom read. And we seldom talk as the hours wear on. Mostly, we just are. Harvey paces sometimes, never sure where to sit or what to do. He talks into Mom's ear, saying, "Honey, it's Robin. It's me," using the boyhood name abandoned years ago. In this room with the glass walls we are children again. Mom and Dad. Rob and Lin. If only we could remain here forever, locked into this limbo. Nothing would ever change.

But Mom begins to make struggling sounds; her breath is coming hard and I run for the nurse who suctions her breathing tube. My father stands with his hands on Mom's shoulders and turns to me. "Your mother is going to give me the devil when I get to Heaven," he says, "for letting them hook her up to this damned thing. She didn't want this."

I nod. "Yes, she is. And you're going to have to take it because you know she's right." Harvey and I have both read Mom's living will and we know that she did not want to be kept alive by artificial means. But we do not blame Dad for wanting to give his wife of 52 years every chance, even if it is only prolonging the inevitable.

DECEMBER 1, 2002. 2PM.

It is Sunday, December 1, the first Sunday of Advent. At 11:25 this morning, we took Mom off the ventilator. Just dad, Harvey, and I were present, telling her how much we loved her. The rest of the family—my husband and kids—had stayed back at the Rehoboth house this morning. They loved Mom, too, but knew that these last good-byes were meant for the smaller family unit.

The decision to take Mom off of assisted breathing was not easy, but it was right. After the major stroke on Friday morning ruptured a blood vessel into her brain, there was irreparable damage and no viable chance of recovery. We waited out the twenty-four hours recommended by the neurosurgeon, prayed over our decision, and talked about what Mom would have wanted. The CT scan taken right after the stroke and compared to the one taken in early November showed us all we needed to know: Mom's brain was so filled with congealed blood that areas of it were quickly shutting down.

I have the oddest thought while Dr. Young is showing us the CT scans, the way the brain is sectioned, the areas where the blood has cut off functions. *This*, I say to myself, *is fascinating. I'll have to remember to tell Mom about this.* And then I remember, of course, that I cannot tell Mom this because it is Mom's brain we are talking about. Ever since Mom and Dad moved to Rehoboth, I have saved up interesting bits of information to relay to my mother during our weekly phone calls. Who will I tell these things to now? I wonder and for a moment it seems to be the greatest of tragedies, the fact that there will be no one with whom I can share my stories.

Chris-whose-last-name-I-can't-remember is in charge of securing organs for transplants and he comes into explains that Mom's organs cannot be harvested unless the cause of death is brain death. This is news to all of us, not information we have gained from "ER!" we are all saddened that one of Mom's last wishes cannot be fulfilled. Dad is given a memory box in which to put mementos of Mom.

"Would it be sacrilegious to take a lock of her hair?" he asks me.

I assure him it would be fine and then go off in search of scissors and a plastic bag which the nurses are happy to supply. I slip a few locks of Mom's hair and seal them into the baggie, then use the pink comb and brush set Bonnie bought in the gift shop two days ago and comb her hair back from her face for one last time. I wondered how often in my childhood she had combed my hair, brushing it softly back, and I try to make my strokes gentle and loving.

"You want her rings, don't you?" I ask Dad and he nods. The wedding band, put on 52 years ago, has become so loose in recent years that Mom has slipped another, smaller band in front of it. We try soap and lotion but finally have to resort to the ring cutters from the emergency room. I put the smaller ring into another plastic bag, but Dad stops me from taking off her wedding band.

"I put it on her," he says. "I'll take it off." And so he does, kissing her finger before he removes the ring. "With or without this ring, Betty," he says, "you will always be my wife. Nothing has changed." And for the first time in 52 years the ring is off her finger and joins the other one in the memory box. We add her Medic Alert bracelet to the box and shut it.

DECEMBER 1, 2002. 5:00 PM.

It is just growing dark outside when I last leave the hospital and the promise of snow in the air nips at my nose. I have postponed this leave taking as long as I can; now the red streaks of the setting sun on the horizon make it unlikely I will return home before dark, but will be driving in the twilight, the time when my vision is at its worst. But I am still reluctant to make my departure. A hundred times I am tempted to turn back and resume my vigil by Mom's hospital bed, holding onto her fragile hand, listening to her labored breathing, knowing that before long her brain will stop transmitting signals to her heart to beat and her lungs to breathe.

I cry on the drive home. Mom no longer inhabits the body in the bed in BB Hospital. Dad and I have debated this issue last night at her bedside. Is she already in Heaven or is her soul still lingering? We have come to no conclusion, but the doctors tell us that is as if "the lights have gone out" for Mom. The nurses, though, seem to think that even those who are comatose can hear voices somehow, so we have kept up a cheerful line of chatter. And sometimes we cried and told her we will miss her dreadfully. Before I leave for the last time, I kiss her cheek and assure her that I will take care of Dad.

Harvey has already left for his long, lonely drive back to North Carolina. Both of us have volunteered to stay with Dad, but he insists we go back to our lives. He will sit alone by his wife's side until the end. His goodbyes will be private.

DECEMBER 2, 2002. 8:00 AM.

I have just returned from school where I told the principal about my mother. He has sent me home. The light on the answering machine is blinking.

"Linda? This is Dad. Mom passed away at 6:45 this morning."

DECEMBER 14, 2002. 10:00 AM.

There is something comforting about the rituals learned in my childhood; genuflecting at the altar, bowing on the padded kneelers, reciting words learned in long-ago catechism classes. Though my beliefs have grown and changed and I have left much of this ritual behind me, I am still able to take consolation in the smell of the incense rising to Heaven. So many images of Mom assail my senses! Sitting next to her during Sunday morning mass, the hats she kept carefully in hat boxes on the top shelf of her closet perched on our heads. Mom fingering her white rosary beads, kneeling in the pew while I--years away from my first communion--play with the doll that is attached to my white winter muff. Mom taking me around the Stations of the Cross at Easter, the sunshine streaming in through the stained glass windows. And now I kneel, remembering her, letting the familiar words of Father Ray's recitations wash over me and comfort me. I have no words of my own now; the tears are too close to the surface to risk speaking just yet, but the ancient words of the Catholic Mass for the Dead seem to say it all for me. I am comforted.

Mom is gone from our physical presence. We formally bid her farewell today. But here in the front pew of Saint Edmund's on summer Sundays to come, I will feel her spirit. She will continue to touch me in a thousand ways.

Godspeed, Mom. We did all we could for you in our finite human ways. When we knew we could not save your life, we tried to give you a dignified death. In the days to come, I will continue to do things for Dad, things you would have done if you were still here.

And your love will guide me.

DECEMBER 21, 2002. 10:00 AM.

I am a motherless child. The words of the song echo in my head today as I go about household chores: laundry, shopping, cleaning. I rearrange the Christmas Village, organize the gifts, to hang the Christmas stockings although I am not really in a Christmas mood. I made a dark joke at breakfast this morning, commenting on how the excitement of the holidays frequently made Mom sick.

"She topped that this year", I said. "This year, for the holidays she is dead". But I apologized at once to Heaven, and to Mom who was certainly listening. Maybe I am coming into the anger stage of grief, mad at her for leaving me too soon, before I was ready to face the world without a mother.

I almost welcome the pain, the pinpricks of it that stab at me in the odd moments of the day. I test it now and then, like one tests a sensitive tooth to see if it still hurts. It is proof that I am still alive, that I can love, that my mother really did exist and was not just a beautiful dream I have awakened from.

There are reminders of her everywhere. A song, a word, a color will remind me of her and bring the smart sting of tears to my eyes. Sometimes--in school, for instance--I can fight them back, but sometimes I am so choked up with my grief but I have no choice but to let its spill out of me, over the lids of my eyes and down my cheeks, damn the make-up. Some days are harder than others for no explicable reason. Wednesday was one of them, a day in which I met Mom at every turn. We were hosting three groups of preschool students for the annual Holiday House and on the second group I broke into tears when Monique walked into my room with a cup of tea. She hugged me and told me to go take a break, she would take over. I found some solace in my own cup of tea in the faculty room, sat in the office and talked with Pat for a few moments, rejoiced that I had caring colleagues who understood what I was going through in some way.

Sometimes, I just need to cry. I tried to explain this to Ron, who feels the need to hold me when the tears start. But there are moments when my grief is too personal to share, when I need to curl up in my own little hole and just weep from my childhood and the memories of it that died with Mom. Only she held the moments of my birth in her mind and in her body, only she knew what it felt like to hold me in her arms for the first time. As much as he might try to understand, I tell Ron, he cannot, he has not lost his mother.

Dennis called today, wanting Christmas ideas and knowledge of our plans. I have no plans, not really. It seems too ludicrous to be concerned with gifts and parties when I've just recently watched my mother breathe her last. It will be a low-key Christmas, I tell him. Don't go overboard. And he concurs that he, too, does not much feel like celebrating. There is an awkward moment at the end of a conversation. I say," I love you," quickly and he says, "Me you, too". Am I dying myself? Dennis has not admitted to a loving me since he was 10. Bonnie tells me he has been calling her cell phone every couple of days, just to talk. We are all trying to stay connected.

DECEMBER 31, 2002. 4:00 PM.

Life boiled down to the essence. It was a message preached by Pastor Watt not long before Thanksgiving. It is what we are living now. Life boiled down to the essence. Do and say the important things and hang the rest. Live in the moment, pray for the future, let go of the past. Even as others offer their sympathies at Mom's passing, I never fail to say this: I have peace with her. Every conversation we had since our relationship with boiled down to once a week phone calls ended with "I love you". These were the last words I said to my mother on Thanksgiving night, at least the last words I spoke to her while she was conscious. That was at 9:00 PM on Thursday; less than 12 hours later, she'd slipped into a coma from a massive brain bleed. I hoped that my last words were still in her ears.

I am, I've told everyone who cares to listen, running on my last cell. For years, my life has been in upheaval. Mom's death has been the final straw. I'm not quite broken, but bending. I sleep soundly and deeply when time allows, but awaken still craving more sleep. It is not avoidance but true exhaustion. It is both physical and emotional.

Where are Ron and I right now? I am not sure. He met my therapist last week. I will meet his on Monday. We need to find ourselves a marriage counselor and see where we go from there. I have returned my wedding ring to my hand, although it is on the right hand, not the left. Still, it has been resurrected from the jewelry box. Perhaps our marriage will be resurrected, too. For right now I'm too tired and drained to think.

Sometimes I think of Mom has my own guardian angel now, although I know that the angels are created beings. Still, it is comforting to think that she can still hear me and understand me. I ask her questions, knowing what her answer would be. And I ask her to watch over me and my children.

One of my last conversations with Mom was about Bonnie, and the maddening way she has of seeing the good in everyone, even if the odds and everyone she knows says otherwise. She is, I had complained, a much better person than I and, my mother wisely concurred, she is right. Will Bonnie be right about Tony? She thinks that he can turn his life around. My prayer is just that she will not be hurt in the process.

It is a comfort just to be able to write. My thoughts are sometimes disjointed. My memories come in spurts and out of order. Writing them down helps me to heal and helps me to hang on all at once.

In time the pain of Mom's untimely death will dim. I am most afraid of that, of her passing becoming just another commonplace event in my life. But as long as I can write down the feelings, as long as I can capture in words the emotions of the last few weeks and the coming days without her in my life, her importance in my world will continue.

JANUARY 4, 2003. 5:00 PM.

In my childhood years, I always asked my mother to keep the Christmas decorations up until after my January birthday. Once in awhile she would comply, but most of the time the tinsel—so carefully wrapped around newspapers and saved from year to year--and the trappings of Christmas were removed shortly after New Year's Day. Even as the mummers strutted their gaudy staff down Broad Street, Mom would be packing the red and green glass balls back into their boxes, returning our house to normal.

When I married and had my own home, I resolved, my tree would stay up until my January 7 birthday, a bright beacon for a day often snowed or iced out.

But today I took down the tree and the decorations and packed them away for another, perhaps happier, year. Mom's death hangs like a gray cloud over the holiday season, never really allowing joy to surface. Even the gaiety of the house ornaments, hastily put up the afternoon of Mom's passing in a vain attempt to keep myself from thinking, seemed false.

I need to move past Christmas, I told my family. I need to put it behind me and move on, ticking off the first holiday without Mom with a lifetime left to go. The little Angel Cheeks knickknack Dad gave me at Mom's memorial service alone survived my Christmas purge. She sits on my mantel now, holding her "I love you" sign among the Valentine trinkets put up to hurry the year along. The note Dad wrote and placed on her says, "In Memory of Mom, 12/2/02". I do not need the note to remind me.

IN MEMORY

Yellow roses carefully laid
Against the gray granite
Mark the warmth that was
Her smile.

Her spirit does not rest
In the cold gray of the granite
But in the summer sunshine
Of the yellow roses.

Elizabeth Virginia Bates Waltersdorf

December 7, 1928 to December 2, 2002

CHAPTER THIRTY-FIVE

JANUARY 13, 2003. 11:00 PM.

I have mentioned the "D" word today, both to myself and to my children. The reality is this: Ron is really no better. Well, perhaps a smidgen. I have definitely OD'd on Dad, as Dennis would say and need some distance for a while. In the seven weeks since Thanksgiving, he has been here five, both because of the holidays and Mom's death. It is time, I told him today, to go back to the former arrangement; here on weekends only. I need time to regroup.

I called in sick today, too upset to go to work. So many things are preying on my mind! My mother's death is slamming at me from every side. Yesterday, at my birthday dinner, I was helping Dad pick out the granite for her tombstone. Her tombstone! That comps are just three weeks ahead and then the praxis series. Dennis and Laura have made it clear they do not like Tony. I am having so much trouble adjusting to it all!

Then, of course, there is Ron. I have tried so hard to save him. But I can't. Can he save himself? It doesn't seem so. I reread the poem Judy gave me, "Journey", by Mary Oliver. It reflects what I have come to know is true: the only life I can really save is mine. I think that I'm finally strong enough to do that.

Allen suggests that Ron go back to his parents for a few weeks, then we have a family meeting. Good, clearheaded suggestion from my teenage son!

I had a good talk with Bonnie and Tony last night. I am trying so hard to see his heart! He talked about wanting to let go of his past and move on with life, become a better person.

I am feeling a little bit calmer. Time to study for a while.

JANUARY 14, 2003. 11:00 AM.

Another day at school although I am not feeling particularly well. It was impossible to eat this morning as my stomach constantly churned. I am not as low in spirits as I was in September, but I can feel myself sinking down again. My boat feels so overloaded and I am so exhausted!

My panic makes me think of irrational things: should I e-mail Shawn and asking what he sees between Bonnie and Tony? Is she in any danger? When have any reassurances from that quarter helped my peace of mind?

I talked to Debbie for a while last night. She seems so in control of her life right now, although I know it is not always been that way. My own life is so erratic by comparison! One thing I know for sure: any major decisions need to wait until after the comps on February 1.

Bonnie has reminded me that Laura might not have been my first choice for Dennis. True, I might've handpicked a church girl, perhaps a Sunday school teacher, someone who could cook and keep house. But I have grown to love Laura with all my heart. She is exactly what Dennis needs. Bonnie says that I need to give Tony the same chance to prove himself.

This is what it boils down to. This is what it always boils down to: put it in God's hands.

JANUARY 21, 2003. 9:00 AM.

I am incensed with myself this morning because I have spilled tea on my journal and other papers that were important to me. My first inclination was to cut out the damaged ones and start again. But I decided that perhaps I could use a reminder that I am not perfect and do not need to be perfect.

I spent some time talking to Judy this morning. She is dealing with her son's psychological issues and faces a lot of what I face. We talked about being codependents, about being controlling, and trying to make ourselves responsible for other people's actions. Judy said she has been learning about just letting the obsessive thoughts go. Not letting them control her. I told her how often a single thought will dominate and ruin an entire day. I will need to talk with Annie about these issues at our session tomorrow, both my codependency and my need to detach from

Bonnie. I anticipate that it will be very hard yet necessary thing to do.

Another thing Judy and I have in common is this; we want to write the dialogue for the people in our lives. We want to have them behave the way we want them to behave. I have been guilty of this, but especially where Bonnie's boyfriends were involved. They never followed the script or responded as I thought they should!

I miss Shawn's presence in our lives. Whether he was good for Bonnie or not, I'd gain some stability from him in what was a chaotic time. I acknowledge that we would not have made her a good husband. All of their conversations were driven by him. Not one iota of the relationship was really about her. I did the foolish thing and e-mailed him regarding Tony. He has not yet responded. Perhaps he will be wiser than I and ignore the crazy woman. I will, however, continue to pray that he will be convicted of the debt he still owes us. I still feel a pang when I see him and Joy together, which is thankfully seldom. They probably did not mean it, but their actions hurt Bonnie. Again, only God can handle that.

Tony's job situation remains uncertain. The schedule at Shopp'n Bag seems twisted up. I'm concerned because he is not more worried about it. Admittedly --and this is hard-- he can be sweet at times, making attempts to get me to relax and let go of my stress. He causes a great deal of it. I told him he should let more people see his sweet side instead of carrying on his macho act. If this another Lost Boy crying out? The woods are full of them. I've often said this to Bonnie: her brothers bring home the Lost Boys, but she dates them.

Let go and let God.

This is easier said than done, but my continued worry and control never seemed to get me anywhere. Why not give it a try? It is not a lack of faith, just a matter of retraining myself. In *Codependent No More*, Melody Beattie talks about how our tendency to control hinders God from working. I imagine a mother trying to get a child into a snow suit while the child's legs and arms continue to flail. The task would be accomplished so much easier if the child would just be still! So what I think of as helping God is likely having the opposite effect.

Let go. Let God. I'm feeling middle of the road calm today, about a 7 out of 10 on my designated Stress O Meter. Maybe I'm beginning to back away from the abyss. I hope so. I have been sleeping better at night, keeping a candle lit. I like the flickering light and the gentle scent.

I need to stop rescuing people. Ron is well able to rescue himself. He has, as Annie pointed out, a team on his side. I do not need to be his cheerleader right now. And Bonnie neither wants nor needs my rescue attempts. I attempted another rescue yesterday, when Shawn replied to my e-mail. He said he saw growth in Tony but did not think he was ready for a serious relationship with my daughter. He didn't think Bonnie was in any danger, but suggested I keep an eye on the situation. My solution, of course, was to try and make demands.

Judy and I talked about our need to change our expectations for our children. Perhaps her son will not go to college, but she will be happy if he is settled in his mind and content. Perhaps Bonnie will not meet and marry the perfect man, but be content to live her life as a single woman.

JANUARY 24, 2003. 8:00 AM.

The Stress o Meter today: maybe an eight. I should approach the weekends with peace, but I always allow something to disturb it. Maybe I can do better now I am learning to detach from Bonnie.

I hugged Tony yesterday, not just the side squeeze I've been giving him for weeks now, but a real around the arms hug. It is a step. I'm really concerned about his job situation. Make it a matter of prayer, not worry. I already have the recipe! I do not think I am the one to remind him of our agreement: steady employment by January 31 or he can only see Bonnie on Sundays. May be it needs to come from her. Anyway, God is in charge here.

Chris called last night. Her kids are being deployed to Fort Dix. I told her I was trying to detach from Bonnie and let her make her own decisions. She agreed it was about time. It is very possible that Bonnie will get hurt, but she is strong and will survive. I taught her that much, at least.

For the first time in a long time, I feel almost content. That is not to say that anything in my life is radically changed. The same problems exist. But I am not --at least today-- consumed by them. My mind is clear. My stomach is not churning. I do not have the fight or flight adrenaline rush that proceeds an anxiety attack. I'm concentrating on the present and feeling calm. And I'm telling myself, at least for today, that the negative thoughts are all only negative thoughts. They have no power to hurt me.

Only the end of the world is the end of the world.

Ron's battles with depression and containing absence from our home are not the end of the world.

Tony's lack of a plan is not the end of the world. Only the end of the world is the end of the world.

So this week ends on a more positive note than last. I'm letting go and that is good. It is hard. It is slow. And what is God doing, with my flailing hands out of the way? Ron seemed a little better. More focused. Dennis spoke civilly to Tony. Bonnie is happy.

The biggest change will be in me. I've been care taking of other people all of my life, always subjugating my own needs to the needs of others. Now, I am trying to do what is right and good for me, trusting that what is good for me will also be good for my family. I've lost a little weight. I sleep better at night with my lit candle. I've pulled out my knitting again. I'm reading a book by a favorite author.

About a year ago, when David said I was better and did not need to see him anymore, I was on my way to being well. But I didn't follow through. I allowed too many other things to overtake my emotions. I went right back to rescuing.

My mind still turns to Bonnie. I pray for her happiness, but God, not me, needs to guide her. As much as I love her, He loves her even more.

SHATTERED LIFE

My life has many jagged edges, Lord,

Sharp places I am loathe to touch.

It hurts too much.

I have tried to patch and glue them

But they always break.

My heart will ache.

I bring these broken shards to you, Father,

To replace or repair or renew.

I give my shattered life to You.

CHAPTER THIRTY-SIX.

JANUARY 25, 2003. 9 PM.

O, Lord of hosts, who is strong like unto thee? Or to thy faithfulness round about thee? Psalm 89:1-4

What a difference a week can make! Melody Beattie, in *Codependent No More*, says that for codependents, putting ourselves first is out of the question. I have begun to change that this week, trying very hard to take care of myself and putting my needs—both physical and emotional stability—first. It is not, I am finding, as selfish as I thought. If I fall apart, those who still need me in their lives will fall apart as well.

The kids have been trying to encourage me to relax and let go of my stress. Even Tony has joined in these endeavors, making me hot tea, helping Allen clean up his video games. And, thus far, it has been a good week. *I can do this,* I keep telling myself. *I can learn how NOT to be codependent and how to detach myself from Bonnie. I almost managed it last year. This year, I will.*

My days are somewhat calmer. I have less obtrusive thoughts. I breathe more deeply, particularly if an anxious thought crowds in on me.

Only the end of the world is the end of the world. Thoughts are only thoughts. They cannot hurt me. For the moment, I am right where I need to be. For today, everyone is safe and fine.

This has become my mantra. And, amazing, it seems to be working. With my hands no longer clutching so desperately to the things I wrongly perceived to be in my control, God can finally work. I can see His plans slowly unfolding as I continue to let go and let God.

For instance:

Tony's job situation still worries me, but I really feel that I have nagged enough. So I pray. And this morning Bonnie told me that she has reminded Tony of his obligation to find a job if he wants to continue to see her. So, for once, I did not need to step in and begin my tirade.

I have let go of Ron somewhat, willing for us to be apart as long as we need to be. He told me yesterday that he is tired of being at his parents' house and is working hard to come home.

I prayed for a calmer, restful weekend, aware that weekend pressures are often devastating to me. And last night the kids and Ron vowed to keep me from schoolwork. We all went to dinner, a movie, then glow-bowling with the Lost Boys. What fun!

So I can literally feel God at work.

FEBRUARY 7, 2003. 11 AM.

Over the weekend, I treated myself to a nail-buffer, some hand lotion, and some beautiful fuchsia wool to begin a sweater. My little knitting club at school is growing. It is such a relaxing, stress-free time to spend with my students. A chance to catch my breath in the middle of the school day. It was Maddy's idea to start this group of knitting students and now I am provided with a much needed respite. What would I be doing, I ask myself, if I was not knitting?

Grading papers. Copying stuff. Phoning parents. All things I can do at another time. Instead, I sit and knit. "To create is to be at peace, for in creating one is joined to the Creator" (Doherty). For a few moments each day, I use my hands in an ancient art, feeling a connection to the past. And I breathe.

So while I am still learning to untangle myself from my codependency issues, I feel that I am definitely on the right track. I tend to think of Bonnie as my double, so I worry that she, too, is codependent in her relationships. Really, though, she does not try to manipulate the way that I do. Nice to know that she does not mirror me in this!

It is a daily battle, this whole codependency thing. But, with God's help, I know that I can overcome the problem. I am human, so some days will be harder than others. It would be easy to slip back into old ways. I well remember how it feels: the churning stomach, the obsessive thoughts, the need to DO something—anything, however ill-advised—to control the situation. It kept me from enjoying many moments in my life that should have been pleasurable. I was always looking ahead or behind. I was never able to stay in the moment. The challenge this week has been to stay in the moment. Sometimes, I can do it.

But other times my imagination moves ahead, to again script the lives of those around me. Or, even worse, cling to the past. What went wrong? How could I (notice my almighty power here) have changed it? Could I have prevented Ron's car accident? Known about Allen's high blood ammonia? Kept Shawn from breaking up with Bonnie? Kept Mom alive?

These are situations, Annie would say, over which I had no control. I did not cause them. I could not fix them. I just did the best I could with what I was given.

Compulsive disorders, all of them, are self-destructive. Clinging to Bonnie so tightly, rehashing the painful past, are compulsions I have. Reliving the past and blaming myself for things over which I had no control never changed anything.

Guilt is not the point. I did what I did the best that I could at the time. Maybe I did not always make the wisest choices, but I handled what I was given. Guilt just makes everything harder. Now it is time to move past it. I will no longer allow myself to feel guilty. I will not blame myself for the sometimes erratic path I trod.

I did the best that I could. And I survived.

FEBRUARY 20, 2003. 9AM.

Perhaps the most painful loss many codependents face is the loss of our dreams. –Melody Beattie

In my continuing recovery from codependency—now only a week in progress—I have come to a point where I can recognize the losses I have experienced, hopefully without anger or blame. My least favorite line for years has been, "I can't help it." I have heard Ron say it so often that I came to believe it myself. It is true that we all have situations over which we have no control. In Ron's case, he could not change his mental illness or the aftermath of the car accident. It is his attitude and his behavior that is still in his control.

But this is not about Ron. It is about me.

There are things I count as losses in my life: the dreams of a larger house, more time to write, close relationships with other couples, peace of mind, financial security, and support of my needs.

Yet, it could have been so much worse. I was handed a raw deal. No one could say otherwise. I handled it to the best of my ability.

These are the things I managed to save: our home, our family, my own sanity, my belief system, our finances, and the dream of writing, a relationship— however altered — with Ron.

Wow. Good for me. It was hard, but I did it. Often without a lot of help or support. I deserve to take a certain amount of pride in what I have done. My own accomplishments—and they are many!—are not meant to denigrate Ron. Except that he sometimes served as the catalyst for the action, they have little to do with him.

I am worth it. I am okay. I am not less worthy as a person because of my codependency or Ron's mental illness. I am right where I need to be. But, most importantly, I am healing.

FEBRUARY 21, 2003. 10:00 AM.

The roots sink deeper than the tree is tall. To us codependents, says Beattie, we are completely off balance. This is the way I have felt for the last ten years, struggling to keep myself and my kids upright while the crazy roller coaster of bipolar disorder ran through our lives. Coming home from work every day, my stomach would begin to knot up and an ache develop behind my right eye.

What has he been up to today? I would ask myself; has he burned the supper, spent the bank account, forgotten to pick Allen up at school? Is he still in the bedroom or sitting on the couch crying?

I just never knew. So coming home became nerve wracking. I began to stress about the arrival home earlier and earlier in the day. It seeped into every area of my life.

Once in a great while, like the level track on the roller coaster, we would have a calm period. The laundry would be done. The house would be neat. And I once again would allow myself to hope.

Hope floats.

It doesn't matter is that our hopes are falsely based on wishful thinking that the person will magically go away. Crushed hopes are crushed hopes , says Beattie. And mine were crushed so many times! So I stopped hoping that things would get better. I resigned myself to the situation as it was and trudged on. Not really happy, but coping. It could be worse, I told myself. The truth about the statement is this: it usually does get worse.

I actually began to look forward to the times Ron was in the hospital! This is I knew how to do, flying into crisis mode. It was a predictable routine. For a few days or a week I knew where Ron was and what he was doing. I did not come home to the unknown. It was not really a situation in my control, but it had the allusion of control.

We cannot change, continues Beattie, until we accept our codependent characteristics. We cannot change until we accept ourselves the way we are.

So here is my reality.

My husband of 27 years is clinically depressed. He may never be truly well or able to work. To my children are growing up and away. They need to live their own lives and make their own decisions. Even their own mistakes. I am codependent on Ron, my daughter, and sometimes on the man she dates. I have a need to obsess and control.

But this is also my reality:

I can change my codependency. I can learn --I am learning-- to detach from it. With work, with help, I can leave behind the anxious, driven, crazy person I became two years ago. I can get better because I want to and I am strong enough to. I'm capable of living an independent life. I am smart, well educated, and pretty. I can take care of myself. I can have interests separate from my family members.

I can both balance the checkbook and pay the bills.

I can learn to maintain healthy ties with my adult children. I do not need to controls their lives.

I can maintain healthy ties with Ron. They may be different than that of a typical marriage, but I owe explanations to no one.

I can move on.

I'm slowly learning accept it all. Codependency does not make me a bad person. It simply is what it is. Choices I have made in the past –right or wrong--are over. I did the best I could.

Now, according to Elizabeth Kulber Ross, I need to work my losses through the stages of grief.

FEBRUARY 23, 2003, 4:00 PM

It is another snowy day, with a few icy patches here and there. As I drive, it occurs to me that everyone on the road is being cautious and careful. In this winter of cold and snow, we've all learned to drive all over again. I feel it is similar to the way I have been learning to negotiate my life.

Slowly. Cautiously. Turning carefully. Not looking too far ahead. Breathing deeply. And trusting God.

Driving in the snow is not the end of the world. Only the end of the world is the end of the war.

Of late, my life journey has been treacherous. I would like green and calm pastures now and then! But God continually guides me through the snow and ice, not allowing me to plunge over the side of the mountain. Letting go is a daily struggle. It sometimes needs to be taken minute by minute.

I am convinced, says Beattie, that we do most of our codependent behaviors in the denial stage—obsessing, controlling, and repressing feelings. Many of our feelings of craziness are connected to the state. We do everything we can to put things back the way they were, the way they ought to be, even if it is not best for us. Even in is not what God wants for us.

We are all only lying to ourselves. We do not want the situation to change. It may not be ideal, but we are familiar with it. We are comfortable with it. To force change is to allow ourselves to lose the fragile control we believe we had. The control is an allusion.

In accepting-- in letting go of --my codependency on Bonnie, I have been forced to admit the illusion of control I held over both her and Shawn. I pretended that I felt good about the relationship. I would not allow myself to see the problems that always existed.

I remember this.

I would come home from class at night and find her curled up on the chair by the door. Waiting. "He said he'd be right over", she would say and glance at her watch. "That was two hours ago". She would sigh and pull a quilt around her and go back to waiting.

My stomach would cramp up. Why did he do this to her? Why did she let him? The only nights I felt peace--sort of-- was Thursdays when they went to Bible Study. She would meet him there--he never came to pick her up-- but at least she was not waiting for the phone to ring.

Lending money to Shawn was a horrible mistake, because it was manipulative on my part, a way to bind them to us. If he was indebted, he would have to stay. Loaning the car, paying for his insurance. These were the things I thought would bring him closer to Bonnie.

When he broke up with her, I was devastated, not because he was perfect for her but because he was familiar. His actions often caused pain and worry: his long list of ex-girlfriends, his perpetual lateness, and his inability to put Bonnie first, his financial problems, and his disastrous family relationships. But it was familiar. I was used to the stress, the anxiety, the unsettled feeling. Their break-up took something familiar—if not comfortable-- away. Long after Bonnie had moved on, I was still fantasizing about Shawn's return.

I'm struggling to get past it, to completely let it go. I

remind myself of my anxieties when they were dating, my own attempts of manipulation and interference. Time to move on. It would be nice if I could've done it five months ago, but grief takes time.

Goodbye, Shawn. It is not the end of the world. Only the end of the world is the end of the world.

You were just a bump in the road

ONE AT A TIME

One finger slowly pulled away

I give this care to God today.

Tomorrow I will try again

To leave it in the Master's Hand.

One finger, one care, one at a time

Till God has control, and peace is mine.

Amen.

CHAPTER THIRTY-SEVEN.

MARCH 3, 2003. 8 PM.

The only way out is through—Fritz Perls

Despite my good beginning, despite the fact that God had the situation well under control, despite the cherished calmness, I slipped back a stop or two. But at least I can recognize it and see why.

For almost three days, I ignored my journal and my forward march out of codependency. I was so busy studying for the comps on Saturday, but once they were finished I felt exhausted and edgy. I gave into the feeling instead of writing and praying. But "taking a break" from my healing process is like an alcoholic saying, "I'll just have one drink." It just can't be done.

I felt good on Thursday, felt I had really released myself of some of my obsessions, felt I was ready to move on. I began to see answers to my prayers.

Shawn told Allen he would try to pay him back the money we loaned him for the engine work after he got his income taxes done.

Tony got hired at Superfresh. Bonnie agreed it was time to return to Shawn the things he had left at our house. So the results, even if they were not exactly what I wanted, were clear.

The temptations pulling me back to the edge of the abyss today are great. How easy it would be to pick up the illusion of control again! I need to keep breathing. Take one day at a time. God, not me, is in control. Right now, we are all just where we need to be. It is not the end of the world. Only the end of the world is the end of the world.

Here I am, trying to work through the second stage of the grief process: Anger.

"We blame ourselves, God, and everyone around us for what we have lost," says Beattie. My losses have been many, but expressing anger over them has never come easy. For some reason, I always thought it would be very un-Christian! Can I face it now, when I have a better understanding of the difference between codependency and Christianity? Here goes. I am angry that:

- Ron is not a more stable, dependable man.
- I have to work so hard to support us all.
- Bonnie's romances have all been rocky.
- Mom passed away.

None of these things are fair. Other women have dependable, supportive husbands. Other people have easier lives. Other girls find the "right one." Other women still have their mothers.

The Bible gives us an example of vested anger: *O, Lord, you deceived me and I was deceived. You overpowered me and*

prevailed. I am ridiculed all day long (Jeremiah 20:7).
After ranting like this for a while, Jeremiah goes on to say: *But the Lord is with me like a mighty warrior.* When I allow myself to feel it, then stop ranting and kicking, I know that this is true. Yes, I AM angry. At Ron, at Shawn, even at God. But admitting this anger is a necessary step towards healing.

Here is the third step in the grief process: bargaining. "After we have calmed down, we attempt to strike a bargain with life, another person, even God" (Beattie). I have been there, as concerns Ron's depression and Shawn's departure. If I had been the world's best wife, the world's best potential mother-in-law, handled all the problems and never complained, everything would have been different. It was the major reason I loaned Shawn both money and the car. Isn't it amazing that God was still able to bring Bonnie out of a relationship I tried so hard to keep her in?

Here is step four: Depression. Here we are forced to see that all of our bargaining has not changed things one iota. I do not easily give up on anything, so it has taken me a while to get here! Annie calls it "reactive depression", but it is the culmination of much grief and loss. We need, says Beattie, to "humbly surrender."

The situation is what it is. We did not cause it. We cannot fix it. Our only salvation is on giving into it, at least for while. I have done my share of crying over Ron and over Shawn. There is nothing I can do. I am not really at this point with Mom's death yet, although there are moments when grief engulfs me.

Stage five: Acceptance. Finally, we are at peace. With

ourselves, with what it, with what is not. Am I at peace with it all yet? Sometimes. I have accepted Ron's illness and my inability to change it, although I still rail against it. I am getting closer to accepting Shawn's absence. I have stopped trying to manipulate him in any way.

This process of grieving is proving to be exhausting. It is depleting my energies and throwing me off balance. So important, then, to take care of myself right now and be kind to me!

I will get through this. It is not the end of the world, because only the end of the world is the end of the world. This is just Ron, struggling with his depression. This is just Bonnie, asserting her independence. This is just life moving on. It is not the end of the world.

The road ahead, out of all of this, is long. I have not yet traveled very far alone it. Each day, though, I take a few more steps. I have been able to thank God for the losses in my life, as ludicrous as that may sound. I did not want to. It was hard. And it hurt. I cried. I still do. But in thanking God for these losses, I once again acknowledged His control over my life. I put Him back in charge.

It felt peaceful. It felt right. It felt good.

I am exactly where I need to be. The steps are slow, but sure. Sometimes, I take a few steps back. I do not need to understand it all.

I just need to be.

MARCH 6, 2002. 2:30PM.

I had a good session with Annie yesterday. She says that I am at times too introspective and could drive myself crazy analyzing and rethinking everything. So I am going to try and limit my journaling to 30 minutes at a time, just writing down life as it is. Annie is clear—as in everything else—that Tony is Bonnie's choice at the moment and I need to adjust. I was hopeful that my detachment from her would mean her release of Tony. But that has not happened, not yet anyway. For now, there is nothing I can or need to do. God can change whatever needs to be changed.

Here is it, 2:45 PM and I have only just picked up my journal to write! I have felt almost good all day. What worries and concerns I have, I have been able to lay at God's feet. I can feel Him working. Continuing to release my fingers from my cares has allowed Him to work. There are no quick and easy answers, but now and then absolute peace surrounds me. All will be well. Things are as they ought to be.

I came close to this before, a year ago. But then life intervened and I was right back to obsessing, the addict who still hangs out with his addicted friends. I looked okay on the outside, but inside I was a mess.

God's will, wherever it takes me, is bound to be better than mine!

MARCH 12, 2003. 7PM.

However, I consider my life worth nothing to me; if only I may finish the race and complete the task the Lord Jesus has given me, the task of testifying to the gospel of God's grace. Acts 20:24.

In flipping through some journals last night, I came across one from June of 2000 in which I lamented Nick's break up with Bonnie, wondering at my own need to have such control over her life. I almost laughed! Two and a half years later and I am only just beginning to detach from her and let her make her own decisions and her own choices. But at least I am doing it, if only one day at a time. Breathing deeply. Living in the moment.

It occurred to me that we all make choices in our lives about how to life and who to be with. If we allow someone else to make the decision for us, then it is our choice as well. This means, as far as I can see, two things to me.

1. I did not "ruin" Bonnie's relationship with either Nick or Shawn. It was her decision not to take Nick back and not to fight for Shawn. In the end, she said neither one was worth it. So it is NOT my fault.
2. Whatever decision I make about Ron will be mine and mine alone. Our marriage does not need to conform to the standards of anyone else. It needs to be what works for us.

I got some pieces of the puzzle concerning Ron yesterday. We had a neurological evaluation done to determine if there had been brain damage from the accident. The tests revealed that there is TBI (Traumatic Brain Injury) involving organizational difficulty and the processing of new information. It means that Ron needs lots of structure to get started with a project, and doesn't always know how to follow it through.

Here, again, is hope.

I will send down showers in season. There will be showers of blessing. (Ecclesiastes 34:26)

WORDS

I thirst for words

A burning desire beyond mere need.

They are the essence of my soul

The foundation upon which I stand.

I turn them over in my head,

Backwards, forwards, upside down.

I pull them apart, twisting them out of

The origin of more clever writers

And plunge them into my own creations.

I am a destroyer and a creator

An original and a copycat.

I take my mood from words,

Form my identity from their contributions.

They are air, they are light, they are life.

Just give me words!

CHAPTER THIRTY-EIGHT.

MARCH, 20, 2003. 8AM.

Today's Stress-O-Meter? Up a bit! I'm feeling a little unsettled this morning and that's okay. After all, today is just one small piece of my life. I have learned that I do not always need to be upbeat or positive. This is progress! The past two snowy days disrupted everyone's schedule. It seems that most of us function better when we stick to a routine!

I was a little peeved at Tony last night, whose behavior bordered on obnoxious. He said he was just nervous about taking his GED test. I remember myself being short to everyone before the comps, so I will try and give him the benefit of the doubt.

I feel that Bonnie and I have lost some of our closeness. As her time and her mind are more and more occupied by other things, I am pushed aside. We had supper last night at The American Café and talked a lot. I was glad to hear that she really is quite realistic about Tony and recognizes that he may not be what she needs. There are moments when I feel okay with all of it, know that she will make her own decision and it will be wise. At least, I feel this way when I am not ranting and raving and screaming at her!

At some moments, I feel as if I have rounded a corner. I will be feeling content and peaceful and strong. At other times, I feel the mysterious corner is still miles and miles down the road. The truth is probably somewhere in between. I am not there yet, but plodding towards it.

I am continuing to thank God for my losses: Ron's disabilities, Shawn's absence, Mom's death, Bonnie's growth. I guess the last is only a loss to me.

Let go. Let God. Keep breathing. It is not the end of the world. Only the end of the world is the end of the world.

THE TWELVE STEPS.

As with other addiction recoveries, the Twelve Steps used by Alcoholics Anonymous has proven useful to those recovering from codependency. Today, I have chosen to write about the Twelve Steps and try to apply them to my own life.

STEP ONE.

I admit that I am powerless over Ron's depression and my own resulting codependency. I tried to control it. I tried to pretend it did not exist. I tried to rescue everyone. In the end, all I was able to do was to destroy my own emotional well-being to the point that functioning became impossible. My obsessions and need to control both Bonnie and Ron never solved anything. Again, Melody Beattie says it best: "We can't change things we can't control, and trying to do so will make us crazy."

STEP TWO.

My higher power—God—can restore my sanity. He alone is capable of this immense task!

STEP THREE.

I decide to turn my life and my will over to God. This is a conscious effort. Here are some more words of wisdom from Beattie: "I had spent many years trying to impose my will onto the scheme of things." Sounds all too familiar! If only people would mold themselves into what I wanted them to be, things would be okay. This desire had two problems. People seldom did as I thought they should, and if by some change they did, it never turned out the way I thought it would.

"The exciting thing in this step," continues Beattie, "is that it means there are a purpose and a plan—a great, perfectly wonderful, usually enjoyable, and worthwhile plan that takes into account our needs, wants, desires, abilities, talents, and feelings—for each of our lives." Is there any doubt that God's plans are better than mine? He is the Creator of the universe! God has a plan for each of us. It does not mean a life free from pain and challenges, but it does mean one lived in victory.

STEP FOUR.

The next step is to make a fearless and searching inventory of ourselves. This is me:

I have been strong and I have handled things I never felt

equipped to hand. When the going got really, really tough, I saved the kids, our home, and a sense of family. But I have never felt that I got enough credit from Ron for doing this. It continues to bother me.

I do not like disturbances. Bonnie, Allen, and I were able to form a tight unit. I find it really hard to let others into that circle. I have standards for myself and my kids. I abhor rudeness, but I am sometimes rude to others in the name of "their own good." I set myself up as knowing what is good for everyone. I have made myself Supreme High Ruler of my own small universe. I call the shots. I guess I am a bit of a tyrant. I like to be in control because so much of my life has been out of control. I like to keep what little power I have. I think that my education gives me an edge on wisdom, so I think that I and I alone can make the best decisions. I do not like to let go of things, even after I can no longer hold onto them.

But I do have some good qualities. I am patient and intelligent and creative. I do not give up on things or on people easily. I love and protect those around me. I have a genuine concern for others. I like to help other people and see them succeed. I am trustworthy. Well, mostly.

Four steps down. Eight to go.

MARCH 26, 2003. 11 AM.

Love God with all you have and are and love one another.

(Matthew 22:37)

It seems simple enough. So when did I allow it to become so complicated? When did I allow my emotions to so take control of me that I forgot to love God and my fellow man? When did the pressures become so much for me that I put myself in charge of the world and knocked God from His place of power in the universe? STEP FOUR.

This involves admitting the wrong that we have done, even though it had been in the name of good. Trying to control and manipulate others is wrong. God gave free will to all. I freely admit this to God and to myself. I have also made this admission to my friend Deb, who often guards my secrets as if they were her own.

I have been struggling these last two weeks to give God back His place. It is hard. I do not give up power easily, even power I only imagine I have. Still, since I have begun this process, life has taken on a calmer tone.

STEPS SIX AND SEVEN.

In these steps, we prepare ourselves to allow God to remove our defects of character. The "fearless inventory" I took earlier was hard to look at. What, me not perfect? But I am prepared to let God remove my tendency to control other people. Step Seven is joined hand in hand to Six, asking God to remove my shortcomings. In my case, codependency is both a defect and a shortcoming. There are others, all listed earlier. I am ready for God to do what He will with my life, to mold me into a more Christ-like being.

God is clearly at work in my life. Annie says I am doing well and probably do not need to see her anymore, but I want to continue for just a while longer and make sure I am strong enough to finish this work on my own. Before, I stopped the progress when the going got easier and I was not able to finish the work. I am content, right now, to rest where I am for a few brief moments. But soon I will continue to forward march!

MARCH 21, 2002. 9AM.

Here it is the last day of Spring Break and I have not done as much writing as I would have liked—either in my journal or on my novel—but I HAVE come to a more peaceful place in my life. I have more moments of contentment than anxiety. The scales seem to have finally tipped in my favor.

There are topics I still need to avoid, but I will learn to confront them in time. I have come to accept that Shawn was never right for Bonnie. It was only the circumstances of so much change that made me want to hang on.

STEPS EIGHT AND NINE.

Now it is time to list the people I have harmed in my codependency and, whenever possible, make amends to them. My daughter is at the top of the list. It is impossible to make amends to her, but she has accepted my apology whole-heartedly. Certainly there are other people I have tried to control, but it seems as if most of the damage of my codependency was done to me.

These things, however, are true:
1. God loves me.
2. Christ has already paid for my sins.
3. My eternal home in heaven is secure.
4. There will come a day when every tear will be wiped away and every heart will be made new.
5. I am never really alone.
6. I am a Child of the King!

STEP TEN.

Continue to take personal inventory and admit when we are wrong. This is hard for someone like me, who knows just how everyone should behave! But I continue to make my best effort to control no one but myself and the characters in my books. And even my characters often have minds of their own.

STEP ELEVEN.

In this step, we try to improve our conscious contact with God. I have put God back on the throne of my life. While I continue to feel sorrow over my losses, I am able to see what gains I have made from them.
1. Mom's death brought me to a closer relationship with Dad, Uncle Billy, and Aunt Eloise.

2. Shawn's departure showed me how wrong he was for Bonnie and how I tried to control her.
3. Ron's illness gave me a chance to grow and become the strong woman I am.

STEP TWELVE.

Finally. Working this step does not mean that I am done. I am certain that as I continue in my life and face challenge after challenge, I will need to work these steps again and again. They, like my computer and my cell phone, are tools to be used. This final step involves carrying the message of recovery to others. Perhaps this book, so long in coming, will become that encouragement.

MARCH 27, 2003. 9AM.

I do not doubt that God has a purpose for each of us, but I do sometimes question how He goes about it all. I am sure Joseph must have wondered what the heck was going on when his brothers sold him into slavery.

What is my purpose? I used to think it was to be a good teacher, a good wife, a good mother. But now I think there is a more all encompassing reason.

My life's purpose is to reflect God.

Perhaps the book I want to write will do this. But before I can write that book about how I conquered my codependency, I need to conquer it. I force myself to remember that I have had moments like this before, moments, of peace, but they did not last. This time, I am using the right tools.

Pray. Wait. Keep busy.

When Bonnie bounced home yesterday, she was excited to tell me two things: she had set up a bill file for herself to take care of her finances, and she had been accepted to Neumann College. So it seems as if she really is getting her life together without my help. She send me an e-mail at school yesterday that said I was the "best mommy in the world" and thanking me for giving her a chance to grow up.

This time, we both might make it.

ENOUGH

I have enough light for today.

I have enough knowledge for today.

I am letting go and letting God.

It is enough comfort for today

CHAPTER THIRTY-NINE.

MARCH 22, 2003. 7AM.

We all long to go home. It is burned deep within us, that desire to return to Heaven. We know that we do not truly belong here. The only part of eternity we can personally touch is each other.

Home. In our family, the kids say, "home is a place that, when you get there, they have to let you in." Many times during his college years, while he was yet pulling away from us and learning to live as an independent adult, Dennis would come home. Sometimes it was for the chance to talk about a decision, sometimes a chance to rest from an illness, sometimes just a space in time to regroup. He always went back. He now makes his "home" with Laura in a second-floor walk-up on 8th street. But in many ways, he says, our house will always be home. His visits are briefer these days, but just as meaningful. He calls at least once a week. Home still has its draws.

Physically, Bonnie has never left home. At almost twenty-four, she has been more tied to hearth and family than her older brother. She is struggling with her assertion of independence now. It is tough on both of us. She complains that I have not talked much to her this week and I know that it is true. I am making a conscious effort to continue to pull away and detach, trying to give her the room she needs to grow up. She complained to Tony, who told her, "You know this is hard on your mom. I think she's doing great." Why don't I like him again?

Allen is seventeen. He is still home. He probably will be for several more years. And while he is still drawn to the family, he makes the occasional bid for independence. I am learning to let him go, too.

All of them will always come home.

MARCH 31, 2003. 7PM.

Bonnie tells me that Shawn has taken Joy to his former co-workers at Sears and introduced her as his fiancée. I feel a few pinpricks of regret. A year ago, I thought she was destined to be engaged to him. But these faint pinpricks are nothing compared to the "fist slam in the stomach" that often assailed me in early fall. It is evident that Bonnie feels no regrets at all. Do the employees at Sears ever wonder what happened between the guy who worked in Vacuums and the girl who worked in Watches? Shrug. Just one of those things.

And what did happen? Another shrug. It wasn't meant to be. Bonnie can now admit that Shawn was never really right for her and they should have just "been friends" all along instead of dating. She simply shakes her head about his quick engagement to Joy and moves on. Thinking about him has always made her a little nuts.

I, too, am much better off when I do not think about him. This is sometimes a very hard act to perform, steering my mind away from topics that would lead me down the wrong path. This, too, shall pass.

Looking back to March, 2000, and thanking God for my journals! Ron was in the hospital, fighting for his life. I was worried, handling all the responsibilities and trying to support us. On top of that, there was graduate school. Allen was sleeping with weapons and seeing monsters at every turn. Bonnie was not doing well in college. Here we are, three years later, and life has changed. Ron lived. I finished grad school. Bonnie took a year off from college and now plans to go back.

This is proof to me that things I worry about now will all be resolved. My worry will contribute nothing to the solution. I wasted some time worrying today, when Bonnie's cat woke me at 4:45 and I could not go back to sleep. I remember that a few days ago, I felt well. I will feel well again.

I have enough light for today. I have enough knowledge for today. I am letting go and letting God. It is enough comfort for today.

APRIL 1, 2003. 4 PM.

In continuing the recovery process, I have been advised by

Annie to savor every stage: the beginning, the middle, the end. Nothing needs to be rushed. Each part has its own wonder.

Some things in my life are ending. I am ending graduate school. The last paper has been written, the last test taken. But I have chosen not to follow my usual pattern and rush into something else. I am savoring this time. It is a major accomplishment and I deserve my fifteen minutes of delighting in it. The world will not fall apart if I do not dust or make supper or find a doctorate program. Last Friday, I went to Borders by myself and browsed books for two hours, sipping tea and reading magazines. The world limped on without me.

I am at the beginning of something else, a job search and possible new position for next year. Neumann College has expressed some interest in hiring me. I am filling out applications and getting letters of reference, but I am not frantic about it. I have a job now. I will have one in the fall. God will lead me on when the time is right. In the meantime, I savor the peace of Westtown campus, remembering how often it has been a haven for me in the last few years. Here I found support, prayer, encouragement, and the courage to move on.

An ending. A beginning. A middle. I am in the middle of my own recovery process. I am letting go. It has been painful. It has felt awkward. I have slipped again and again. But I have kept steadily moving forward, sometimes a whole step, sometimes just an inch. Some things in my life are still painful. But they no longer consume me.

Beginning. Middle. End.

They each have a flavor.

Take time to savor.

APRIL 2, 2002. 7AM.

Ignore the doubter. Turn away from what is destructive. Let go and let God. People need to own their own power.

I told myself all these things early this morning when I awoke at 3:30 AM and could not go back to sleep. The ladies at the library board meeting last night has "expressed concern" that Bonnie was dating Tony. I told them that Bonnie needed to make her own decisions. What I should probably have done was politely decline to discuss it at all. It never, ever helps! So it nagged at me last night and interrupted my sleep. The questions swirled in my brain.

Why does she continue to date him? What does she see in him? Where is this going?

The good news is that, even as I lay awake and worried, I did not think about Shawn and what a better option he would have been. I was not tempted to wake Bonnie up and I did eventually fall asleep.

Perhaps it is only wishful thinking on my part, but the closeness she seemed to have with Tony seems to be growing distance. Is it fizzling out? In the past week—since my self-imposed silence—I have known moments of perfect peace about my daughter. All will be well.

Lord, help me hang on!

APRIL 4, 2003. 6AM.

I snuggled down onto her shoulder, the smell of her shampoo and apple body spray filling my nostrils. "I love you," I whisper and she smiles and throws her arms around me "I love you, too," she says, her eyes still closed. She hopes, I know, that I will just go away. She has two more hours of sleep before her alarm goes off.

But my heart is heavy this morning with a weight I cannot shake off. While this is certainly the wrong time and place, I being to pour out my fears to her. As always, she listens.

She cannot quite give him up yet, she says. Not yet. She knows that she is moving on with her life, making plans for her future while he continues to spin his wheel. In her heart, she knows the cotton-candy clouds she imagined are not real but were spun from the remains of my mother's ashes in December and the death of her relationship with Shawn.

"He's had eight months," she says. "A person should be able to get his life together in eight months." I agree, silently thinking how far we have come from September, when I asked Ron to leave, when she and Shawn broke up, when I lost the ability to think clearly. We have faced the world head on, this child and I. We have cried oceans of tears. And we have moved on.

It surprises me to hear that she has been listening to me for the past few months. She echoes the words I have spoken to her. "I can only do so much," she says. "People need to control their own lives."

How special and how wonderful she is, I think. She is maturing before my eyes. She is adamant now. "I told him yesterday that he has five weeks left to prove himself: job, GED, driver's license. Or I'm done."

I understand now. She really has been in control of this. I marvel at her wisdom. She cares about him, or rather the possibility of him, but she will not be his prop or support.

"I can do this," she says. "You can trust me."

And I suddenly know that I really can. Tony has been just a stepping stone, helping her over some very rough places in her life. But he is not now and never will be the foundation. She has all of me in her, I remind myself. All of my strength. All of my compassion.

I can not only trust her, I can trust God.

BEHIND THE COAL FURNACE

I sent you to live in the basement of

Nanny's house on Chester Pike behind

The coal furnace, where I was always too

Afraid to go, behind the remnants of coal

Poured through the chute into the bin.

Then I locked the door.

How, then, did you escape, floating up

Like a ghost of vapors in the rainy street,

Surprising me on Route 452?

You taunted me, laughing at my foibles,

And then you beckoned to me and I,

Knowing all long that you would do me no good,

Followed anyway driving into parking lots

And down side roads, searching and

Afraid that I would find you.

God back behind the coal furnace, you ghost of the past,

Back to the locked room where your memory

Cannot haunt me because it is till the one place

I am afraid to go.

CHAPTER FORTY.

APRIL 8, 2003. 8 AM.

It is not going to happen and she knows it. Despite some feeble attempts, Tony is still unemployed. This means no money for his GED test or his driver's license. It means no future, but I pray that it will be Bonnie, not me, that sees this. As she told me last week, eight months is long enough to give someone to get their act together.

She crept into my room last night around 1 AM. She is praying hard about this young man. God tells her to "trust and wait." She wants to give him every chance to come through. The decision, when to let go, needs to be hers.

She says she has been happier these last eight months than she has been in a long time. While some of it may be Tony, more of it is her; she had found out who she is. She is safe. I have deposited her with God. Like the other young men who have come and gone in her life, Tony is not the end of the road. God surely has someone special for her.

As always, God sends comfort when I need it most. Today's devotion is "Wait for God" using Judas Iscariot as the prime example of someone who wanted to jumpstart God. He took his own life rather than witness what his betrayal had done. If only he had waited three more days to see the Resurrection! But his pain was too great.

My pain, too, had been great. But I will just wait.

APRIL 9, 2003. 7 PM.

One the radio this morning, the announcer talked about a new album entitled, "Beautiful Lumps of Coal." Lumps of coal are the things in our lives that do not work out well, but God can still turn them into diamonds. Here are my lumps of coals:

1. Ron's ongoing illnesses
2. Our "separated" marriage
3. Mom's death

How can God make these things beautiful? I do not know, but I offer them to God to use as He sees fit. The key is forgiveness. I need to forgive Shawn instead of just ignoring the situation. I have not yet been able to do so. I keep recounting the ways he hurt Bonnie, intentionally or not. But here are two reasons I need to forgive him. First, God commands it. Second, to hold onto this grudge only hurts me, not him.

My daughter found it within her heart to forgive him long ago. They are now friends. Her advice to me is simple: pray for him. She admitted it might have been easier for her since she'd had the benefit of a final conversation with Shawn in which he almost apologized for the hurt he caused. It was enough to convince her that while his actions had been stupid and thoughtless, they were not malicious.

And so I have begun to pray for Shawn. I pray that in his life he will come to understand that neither things nor people are the keys to happiness. I forgive him. His actions may have hurt, but they did not destroy. Bonnie had grown and matured. She remembers the good times they had together without regret.

"I will keep him in perfect peace, whose heart is stayed on me" (Isaiah 26:3). I have been thinking about exactly what this means. To me, perfect peace would be no obsessions, no anxieties, no moments of panic, no feeling out of control. The verse says, "perfect peace". While I often approach a peaceful period, it is never really perfect. Something—most generally my own thoughts—always interrupts it. But if my heart is truly stayed on Jesus, there can be no wandering off into whatever worries my mind conjures up. There can be no "what if" scenarios. There can be no writing dialogue for other people in my mind. There can be no controlling what other people say and do.

Can I really fasten my mind so firmly on God that it will not wander? As I have discovered about everything in my recovery, it is not a simple trick.

"The Lord Himself goes before you and will be with you; He will never leave you nor forsake you. Do not be afraid, do not be discouraged." (Daniel 31:8). This is the image this verse gives me: I am driving my car down 452 in the pouring rain, my headlights reflecting on the water of the highway. The sun is behind a bank of dark gray clouds and the cars are going too fast.

But God goes before me. He clears the road of fallen branches, He directs me around the rain-filled potholes. Even as the heavens open up and pour down, He does not leave me. If God does this while I am driving on my way to school, won't He do this in other areas of my life? Even now, God has gone ahead of me. He is preparing the way for me, laying the groundwork for the path He will have me on. I do not see what are miles down the road. I need only know that He is there.

I can look back and see how carefully God has prepared the way.

The job here at Westtown, offered at just the right moment. Mom's fatal stroke, on a weekend I was free to be with Dad. The registration fee for Bonnie's classes at Neumann, coming anonymously in the mail before we knew we would need it.

Sometimes it is hard to see. I am still hurt and confused by much, still wondering why Ron seems so little improved. God is faithful. Bonnie is still seeing a young man I do not like. But God is faithful. I am still struggling to support my family, paycheck to paycheck. But God is faithful. I need to overcome my own illness and accept the loss of my mother, and move on. But God is faithful.

APRIL 15, 2003. 11PM.

"I came to the end of myself." These words were spoken by a man whose daughter became pregnant out of wedlock, a man convinced that such a thing would never happen in his family. He had been strong, you see. The problem with being strong is this: It takes a while to come to the end of your rope. He had been smart. The problem with being smart is this: It takes a long time to run out of your plans.

I always had a plan. I knew just how I would save the world. If Plan A did not work, there was Plan B. If Plan B did not pan out, there was Plan C. God has been urging me to let go of my plans A-z, and just to give it all to Him. To just…let..go.

This week, I "came to the end of my rope." I ran out of rope. I ran out of plans. And I gave it to God. Two important things happened. I forgave Shawn, and I deposited Bonnie with God.

Forgiving Shawn was hard. It still is. It is a daily surrender. But, in the act of real forgiveness, I released him from my plans. He was to be Bonnie's rescuer, but people have to rescue themselves. Let go. Let God. It began to go wrong between them a year ago, and I began to interfere. Old story. Long story. Time to move on. Next point.

Giving Bonnie over to God is also a daily thing. So on Monday night, on my way home from a meeting, I prayed this prayer.

Dear Lord, I give her over to you. If she remains with Tony, that will be your decision and Your will. If not, then that is up to You. I ask only that You guide her, that if be Your will, not mine.

Then, to remind myself of this prayer, I tore a deposit slip from the back of my checkbook and filled it out: To God. One daughter.

That was at 8:37 PM. I noted the time on my dashboard clock for no particular reason. I had been thinking all evening of how quickly God often works, probably because He already has everything set to go and is just waiting for us to get our sticky hands off of it. I can imagine the Almighty sitting on His throne in Heaven, checking His watch and tapping His foot. "Are you ready yet?" I was ready.

When Bonnie got home from work at 10PM, she was beaming with excitement. She had registered for classes at Neumann and realized how very much she wanted to be a teacher. We sat at the table and talked as she ate her late supper.

"The thing is," she said, "Tony says it is no big deal. About Neumann." I could hear the hurt in her voice. "Everyone is happy for me. Even my ex-boyfriend is happy for me. And all Tony can say is that I will not have time for him."

A moment passed. I did not speak. I held my breath. I prayed.

Her voice was now a whisper. "The thing is, I think I want this more than I want him." There it is. The end. She mentioned that at 3:30 she had been praying about her relationship and God had said, "Time to let go."

My eyes opened wide. God had worked even before I had come to the end of myself.

So this is her plan. She will take Tony to his job interview tomorrow, then she will tell him that he needs to develop some goals and plans of his own. She will wish him well with his life, assure him she will pray for him, but that she can no longer be with him.

"You know," she said, "you can care for someone and not be with them."

I smiled. What an adult thing to say.

DARK DAYS

*Dark days are when your mind is so fogged and clouded
With worry that getting out of bed is like climbing Mount Everest.
When your heart thumps wildly for no reason.
When you hang on tightly—too tightly—to any shred of hope.
When there is no shred of hope.
When you lie on the floor and scream and pound your fist
And you are too exhausted to scream and pound your fist.
But in your mind you are still screaming.
Dark days are when you are convinced that one person—the right
person—can solve your problems and make you happy again.
When you do everything you can to make that person act the way
you want, say what you want because that will make you happy.
Most of the time, they won't do what you want. But even if they do,
you won't be happy.
Dark days are long, lonely, dank, and dreary. They are
Spent cut off from the sunshine, pacing and raving and
Obsessing and planning how you will save the world. You do not
Sleep, you do not eat. Friends do not call you because you have*

Become a raving maniac.

In the dark days, the illusion is that you can turn it

All around. One word. One action.

But you can't. You can't turn anything around. You can't

Save anyone, you can't rescue anyone, because you are

Drowning yourself and no one can save you.

Except God.

He wants to. He is waiting to. But as long as you are

Flailing about, lost in your own ineffectual plans, trying to

Control your destiny, there is nothing He can do.

Except wait.

And love you.

The dark days seem as if they will last forever. And for

Some people they do. But when you realize, after months

Or years of such dark days, that nothing you are doing

Is working, then you are ready.

And so is God.

EPILOGUE

MAY 3, 2003. 6PM.

I knew that I had come to the end before I walked into her office. The journey had been extraordinarily hard and seemed as if it had taken an eternity. In truth, though, I had only begun back in September when the world collapsed again and I no longer had the strength to hold it up. I fell down. Long and hard.

And then I met Annie. Annie helped me to see that not only was I not crazy, I had every right to feel as overwhelmed and unbalanced as I did. My life has been full of chaotic situations and tough choices. The very fact that I had survived—that my children had survived—was a testimony to my inner strength.

Today, though, would be the last time I saw Annie. I had felt well the last month, knowing how to keep my balance, knowing how to take care of myself. I realized that I did not need to take care of other people to find fulfillment in my life. Taking care of myself was enough. I had learned to let go of my children—particularly my daughter—and let them make their own decisions. I trusted them. I trusted God. Once again, I trusted myself.

It had been a month since my last appointment with Annie and in that time the world had once again shifted and turned and now I was in a much better place than in September. I had forgiven Shawn. I had let go of Bonnie. I had sought to find new friends and do more things for me. My Master's gown hung in the closet, ready for Saturday's ceremony. Bonnie had broken up with Tony, her own choice. I was still grieving for my mother, but I was moving on. I told these things to Annie and she marveled at God's working in my life. I gave her the piece I had written, "Knowing." It made her cry.

"Well," she said, "what do you think about another appointment?"

I smiled and a tear dripped down my face. "Annie," I said softly," I don't need you anymore."

She smiled, too, also letting lose a tear. "I agree," she said. "You are well able to handle life yourself."

"Thank you for everything. For helping me."

"Nonsense. I did nothing but listen. You already had the tools you needed inside of you. You worked hard. You did this yourself." She paused. "It has been such a pleasure to meet you. You are an incredible woman. And I know that you are going to write that book." She handed me her card. "Keep in touch. Let me know how the book is going."

I nodded, thinking of all the ideas I had already jotted down. "I used to think that this would be the story of Ron's miraculous recovery, but it's not."

"It's your story," said Annie. "Please write it."

I promised her I would and stood to leave. "I don't know if this is proper or not, but I'd like to hug you."

She smiled. "I was going to hug you anyway."

And so I left Annie's office but not her life. I left as her patient by not as a fellow traveler. Her card is in my purse. I will be in touch.

Long ago, I read a book called *I Never Promised You a Rose Garden* (Greenberg, 2002). It was about a young girl's struggle with mental illness. At the end of the book, she makes a conscious decision to "hang with the world. Full weight."

I feel that way as I walk to my car. I am going to hang with the world, full weight. I am going to take care of myself. I am going to write my story and share it with other people who are also in pain. I am going to do what I can to continue to help and support my husband, but I am never again going to lose myself in the process.

But, mostly, I'm going to be okay.

KNOWING

There comes a moment when you know—you just know—that you are going to make it. You look back and see the great valley you have climbed out of and realize that while you still have a way to go—may always be climbing out—you are never going back into the valley again. Your foot may slide a time or two, but you will never allow yourself to be in those depths again and no one can make you. You have learned that you are responsible for no one but yourself. You can save no one but yourself.

You glance back at the abyss, but only for a moment. It makes you shudder to think of the crushing weight you carried, the way your feet barely shuffled as you dragged yourself along. There were times, you remember, when you were simply too weary to stand, when you clawed at the dirt and inched along the ground. When God reached down and carried you.

You turn around and look ahead, but not too far. The way looks flat and easy for a while, but you are vaguely aware that there are more mountains in the distance. That is oaky. You are strong enough now, able to take care of yourself. You have an abiding faith in God. However difficult the path may prove, He will carry you through. Some days will not go well. That, too, is okay. You will know how to nurture yourself through those days, realizing they will not last forever. You will hang onto the hope that has settled around your heart.

It all seems so right. You wonder, briefly, at your own resistance. If you had not clung on so tightly, if you had opened up your fists and let go sooner...but you did not because you could not. You did what you needed to do. You survived.

In the end, this is what matters. You made it. Some on the journey did not. Some are still in the valley. Despite your best efforts, you could only show the way. You could carry out no one but yourself. Your own burdens are heavy enough.

There is a lightness around you that wasn't there before. Your heart sometimes soars about your head and you smile for no apparent reason. Sleep is no longer elusive, but deep and healing.

You are mending. You are recovering from an illness, not of the body but of the soul. It has been a long illness. There were moments when you feared that you would not survive, that the darkness would engulf you and drown you. You struggled against it, flapping your arms wildly and kicking madly and screaming, "No! No! No!" until you were too tired to kick and scream anymore. And there you were, still in the valley, still without hope. Well, almost.

Somewhere deep inside of you, easy to ignore at first, was a small, still voice. You turned away from it, but it persisted. You did not want to listen, but it spoke to you anyway.

It said your name. Just your name. Nothing prophetic. Nothing insightful. Just your name.

And in that one word, the only word in the universe that belonged only and completely to you, there was love.

God loved you.

In the pit of despair, in the throes of agony, it became a small ray of hope. And, somehow, it was enough.

So you stand now where once you could only crawl. And you move forward. Running, sometimes. Skipping, even. Or walking. Or maybe someday crawling again when the need arises. But always moving forward.

There comes the morning when you wake up and you know that you are no longer afraid. You have formed an unbreakable partnership with God. He will never leave you nor forsake you. And while you may sometimes be tempted, you will never leave Him nor forsake Him either. You have come too far to go back.

So you turn and walk into the sunshine, bask in the warmth of God's love. You take pleasure in the clearness of your mind, the strength of your body, the wholeness of your soul.

You are well again. Truly well. You have come into the light.

And the light is healing and radiant and restoring and beautiful.

And you just know.

THE END

ABOUT THE AUTHOR

Linda Waltersdorf Cobourn has been writing since she could hold a pencil. *Crazy: A Diary* is her third book. She is currently at work on the second part of her family's story, entitled *A Crazy Life*. Dr. Cobourn is an educational specialist who works with adult college students and at-risk learners. She lives with her family in Delaware County, Pennsylvania.

Follow her blogs at:
http://writingonthebrokenroad.blogspot.com

and
http://crazyadiary.blogspot.com

and her Web Site at:
http://www.lindacobourn.com/

Cover design by John Keaton
http://www.saatchiart.com/johnkeaton

Author photo by Bonnie CobournWidger

www.ingramcontent.com/pod-product-compliance
Lightning Source LLC
Chambersburg PA
CBHW020742100426
42735CB00037B/175